A FORCED AGREEMENT

Press Acquiescence to Censorship in Brazil

ANNE-MARIE SMITH

University of Pittsburgh Press

Published by the University of Pittsburgh Press, Pittsburgh, Pa. 15261

Copyright © 1997, University of Pittsburgh Press

All rights reserved

Manufactured in the United States of America

Printed on acid-free paper

10 9 8 7 6 5 4 3 2 1

LIBRARY OF CONGRESS CATALOGING-IN-PUBLICATION DATA
Smith, Anne-Marie, 1960–
    A forced agreement : press acquiescence to censorship in Brazil / Anne-Marie Smith.
      p. cm. — (Pitt Latin American series)
    Includes bibliographical references and index.
    ISBN 0-8229-3968-1 (acid-free paper). — ISBN 0-8229-5621-7 (pbk. : acid-free paper)
      1. Freedom of the press—Brazil. 2. Censorship—Brazil. 3. Journalism—Political aspects—Brazil. 4. Brazil—Politics and government—20th century I. Title II. Series.
PN4748.B6S64   1997
323.44'5'0973—dc21

                                                      97-4624
                                                        CIP
A CIP catalog record for this book is available from the British Library.

CONTENTS

	Acknowledgments	vii
1	Everyday Forms of Quiescence	3

I THE CONTEXT OF CENSORSHIP IN BRAZIL

2	History of Press-State Relations	11
3	The Military Regime: Authoritarianism and Legitmacy	24
4	The Press: Mainstream and Alternative	39

II THE SYSTEMS OF CENSORSHIP

5	The Many Forms of Press Control	61
6	Prior Censorship	81
7	Self-Censorship	117

III "A FORCED AGREEMENT"

8	Representations and Reflections	149
9	Routine Repression, Routine Compliance	177

Notes	191
Bibliography	219
Index	225

ACKNOWLEDGMENTS

MUCH OF THE material used here could not have been located by conventional means, for example the original handwritten articles for a now defunct journal, heavily marked by the censor and later stored in soggy cardboard cartons, which at one point lay in the alley behind the home of a journalist's relative. I appreciate the cooperation of many individuals in the Brazilian press in tracking down such sources. I would also like to thank the staffs of the Biblioteca Bastos Tigre of the Associação Brasileira de Imprensa, the Centro de Imprensa Alternativa e Cultura Popular of RioArte, and the archives of the *Estado de São Paulo,* the *Folha de São Paulo,* and the *Jornal do Brasil.* Jonathan Fox, Josh Cohen, and Thomas Skidmore made many helpful comments on an earlier version of this study. I also thank William Savedoff for all of his editorial suggestions, those I rejected as well as those I accepted.

All quotations from Portuguese sources were translated by the author. All interviews cited in endnotes were conducted by the author.

A FORCED AGREEMENT

1

EVERYDAY FORMS OF QUIESCENCE

> **The federal censor prohibits the dissemination of the speech of the Majority Leader, Senator Filinto Muller, denying that censorship exists in Brazil.**
> *Federal Police orders delivered to the* Jornal do Brasil,
> *Rio de Janeiro, September 19, 1972*

REPRESSION TAKES MANY FORMS—some more direct than others. At times it is practiced in as convoluted a manner as is suggested by the order quoted above, in which Brazilian federal authorities prohibited the legally free press from publishing the news that a progovernment senator had denied that state censorship was exercised in Brazil.

Responses to repression also take many forms. At one end of the continuum, collective rebellions or full-scale revolutions occasionally threaten the state. More limited but still direct confrontations may challenge particular state practices. Further along the continuum is the more common practice of "everyday forms of resistance." These are the small acts of sabotage, petty theft, and foot-dragging that accompany overt compliance but suggest what James Scott calls a "hidden transcript" of rejection beneath a surface acceptance of a system of domination.[1]

Different forms of resistance arise from a mix of factors. These include the resources of the victims, their history, potential alliances, organizational capacities, and material wealth. Other factors are the strength of the repressive agent and the manner in which repression is exercised. The interaction of these factors and of unplanned opportunities also affects the form of resistance.

Another possible response to repression is acquiescence or assent to domination. Acquiescence also flows along a continuum, from endorsement of repression and apparent consent, to playing the rules to one's own benefit, to what might be termed *everyday forms of quiescence*. The latter is a pattern of daily acceptance of repression, compliance with the rules, and performance of expected behavior, but without necessarily according any legitimacy to the system of domination.

Acquiescence to repression is never transparent.[2] Does it represent actual consent, false consciousness, rational calculation, or perhaps paralyzed fear? What is the role of power in generating and maintaining a pattern of quiescence? How does the politics of domination play out in what appears to be a culture of quiescence? There are many ways to frame a study of acquiescence to repression. This examination of press censorship in Brazil will focus on how repression was exercised and on the impact of repressive state practices in generating press responses.

The censorship of the press in Brazil was practiced in a peculiar manner. Under the 1964–1985 military regime, and particularly in the period from 1968 to 1978, censorship of the press in Brazil took several forms, all illegal, concealed, and denied. The predominant mode of censorship, to which the vast majority of the press was subject on a daily basis for many years, consisted of news prohibitions issued secretly by the Federal Police. This practice was euphemistically known as "self-censorship."

The most distinctive attribute of this system, in addition to the multiple contradictions of being an illegal state-administered system of "self-censorship," was its routinization.

Every aspect of the censorship was highly regularized. Delivery of the orders followed a rigid pattern. Unsigned news prohibitions were brought by uniformed police officers to individual publications. These orders were never left behind, nor were photocopies permitted. Rather, their content had to be transcribed by a representative of the publication, who then also had to sign a prepared form acknowledging receipt of the prohibition. The language of the orders themselves was notably repetitious and officious and used ornate legalistic formulas. In this mundane and all-encompassing system there were no direct confrontations with authority. The system functioned smoothly, neatly, automatically.

Press compliance was virtually complete. For years press actors accepted these illicit prohibitions, signed for them, recorded them, circulated them to the correct editor, and then eliminated coverage or investigation of the prohibited news item. In the few instances where a more confrontational method of censorship was attempted, there were creative and energetic efforts on the part of the affected press actors to challenge, condemn, and reject it. But for the vast majority who were subject to the anonymous, banal, bureaucratized routines, there was ongoing daily compliance and everyday forms of quiescence.

What accounted for this quiescence? Beyond the proximate causes related to immediate resources or opportunities were two possible overall orientations of the press: support for the regime, which led the press to endorse even its own repression; or so great a fear of the regime's coercive power as to paralyze the press and prevent it from considering any rejection or resistance. Either of these would initially appear to be a reasonable account of the quiescence, but neither proves satisfactory.

Many in the press did indeed support the military regime's anticommunist, antiguerrilla, procapitalist defense of the existing order. But they also had an interest in their own professional and institutional autonomy, as well as commitments to legal and moral norms, and this prevented them from supporting the press restrictions. Indeed, even ardent supporters of the regime expressed their disgust with the censorship. They considered it an illegal farce and an immoral imposition. They tolerated and complied with the prohibitions, as did the rest of the press, but did not consider this system to be legitimate or appropriate. Their compliance with the restrictions did not grow out of their support for the regime. At no point did their support for the regime lead to an endorsement of these restrictions on their own freedom.

Fear is another reasonable explanation. This is what I expected to find when beginning my research on the press under the 1964–1985 Brazilian military regime. This regime, like other bureaucratic authoritarian regimes in Latin America, practiced state terror and generated fear within civil society. The evidence, however, does not substantiate fear as the basis for press quiescence.

Fear was indeed present among press actors, and at particular times an extremely relevant factor. But it was not a consistent or predominant experience for most. The actions and commitments of members of the press during those years (in writing for the few publications under more direct and invasive forms of state restriction, in founding alternative publications even in a repressive climate, in joining press collectives or unions, and even in beginning careers in journalism at all), as well as their reflections afterward, suggest that fear was present but not determinant or central. While the press in Brazil was often fearful, it did not suffer from a culture of fear. Fear did not leave press actors utterly silent, hopeless, isolated, or paralyzed into passivity.

The research suggests, rather, the paramount importance of the way the censorship was conducted in generating press acquiescence. With its set procedures and formulaic language repeated daily, censorship was a banal routine. Having no observable responsible agents, it seemed to function automatically. Indeed, the censorship's banality was the primary aspect experienced by the press. Censorship was perceived as a mundane and all-encompassing system that seemed to operate automatically, impersonally, and comprehensively. It was against this anonymous, routinized, all-encompassing system—and not against the raw coercive power of the regime—that the press felt powerless.

Why was this the manner in which the military regime practiced censorship? It could have been much more overt, coercive, public. Why did it go to the lengths it did to disguise and deny the censorship, and why was this practice so routinized? The answer is that the imperative factor was the regime's desire for legitimacy. Despite being an authoritarian regime that aimed at social control, it also sought political legitimacy. In that varied and sometimes contradictory pursuit, one potential basis for legitimacy was the maintenance and protection of traditional institutions and legal forms. The regime, for example, purged but did not close Congress, passed Institutional Acts that violated the Constitution but nonetheless did not discard that document, and sought many ways to manipulate but still continue to hold elections. In its treatment of the press, it claimed that freedom of the press was constitutionally protected and denied the existence of censorship, while issuing daily news prohibitions. The procedures and language of the restrictions, moreover, mimicked proper legal forms whenever possible. In part because of this pursuit of political legitimacy on the basis of correct and constitutional practice, the regime conducted its censorship in a notably bureaucratic, formalized, officious, and routinized way.

The particular form taken by the "self-censorship" was not a result of a conscious plan to design a system that would operate in this way. Rather, the routinized shape of the system was a by-product of the pursuit of legitimacy.

The regime did not achieve its goal. The press complied with the restrictions, tolerated their imposition, and felt notably powerless to act against or even evade them. Nevertheless, it considered them illegal, immoral, and temporary. While the routinization and mimicry of legality did not produce the desired result of legitimacy, it did help to generate a press reaction that was also functional for the regime: everyday forms of quiescence.

To explore this episode of quiescence, this book begins by establishing the context, exercise, and experience of censorship under the military regime. Part I presents the historical and institutional context. Chapter 2 reviews the history of press-state relations in many different periods, from the colonial to the bureaucratic authoritarian. Chapter 3 focuses on the 1964–1985 military regime itself, explaining the features that were most relevant to its relationship with the press and to censorship. Chapter 4 is an account of the press as a whole at this time, including an analysis of both the mainstream and alternative press.

Part II addresses the full range of state restrictions on the press. Chapter 5 documents the myriad forms of harassment of and restriction on the press other than censorship, from the imposition of licensing requirements and petty restrictions to the withholding of advertising and the torture of journalists. Chapter 6 looks, by way of example, at two cases of the significant but rarely applied "prior censorship" under which, for the seven or so affected organizations, all materials had to be submitted to the police before publication. These cases involved the *Estado de São Paulo*, a mainstream publication, and *Movimento*, representing the alternative press. This chapter also examines the condemnations of and challenges to prior censorship mounted by those subjected to it, which were in marked contrast to the passive compliance of publications operating under "self-censorship." Chapter 7 then documents the operation of the system known as self-censorship, including its bureaucracy, procedures, and efforts to ensure compliance, as well as the content of the news prohibitions.

In Part III, chapter 8 uses interviews and historical records to consider the perspectives of both state and press actors directly involved in the censorship. It presents voices from the mainstream and alternative press, from Congress, and from the police (the latter ranging from lower-level functionaries who conducted the censorship to the federal police chiefs who commanded them). This chapter assesses the experiences, excuses, and anxieties of the press and the justifications and rationalizations of the state.

Drawing upon all of this material, chapter 9 examines three explanations for quiescence—support, fear, and routinization. It finds no evidence that support for the regime led the press to endorse its own repression. And fear, while present, was not sufficiently predominant to produce the paralysis of a culture of fear. Rather, accounting for this particular case of quiescence in the face of domination requires attention to the particular ways that that domination was practiced. In this case, the paramount feature was routinization resulting from the regime's pursuit of legitimacy, which was not counterbalanced by any attributes of the press. Such a system left the Brazilian press practicing everyday forms of quiescence even while it never considered the censorship to be legitimate.

I

THE CONTEXT
OF CENSORSHIP
IN BRAZIL

2

HISTORY OF PRESS-STATE RELATIONS

FOR THE PRESS, as for every other social actor in Brazil, a relationship with the state is fundamental. Whether the immediate issues are financial, regulatory, legal, or political, the state and press are unavoidable interlocutors. The point of examining press-state relations in Brazil, then, is not to measure the degree of press autonomy from the state and declare the Brazilian press to therefore be "strong" or "weak" vis-à-vis the state. In the Brazilian context, where distance from the state is impossible for all social actors, the task is rather to examine the press-state relationship specifically and to explore its quality and dynamics.

In Brazil there has never been a golden age of complete press autonomy from the state, either in some long ago glorious epoch or in any recently evolved progression toward liberal freedoms. At no point has the freedom of the press been completely respected or truly substantial. It is thus not unexpected that there was no grand confrontation and demand for absolute press freedom in the most recent authoritarian period; but nonetheless, the exact nature of the accommodation or daily resistance was not predetermined. The following examination of press-state relations in colonial times, during the years of the Republic and the Estado Novo, and into the modern period will help make sense of the form that the relations took during the 1964–1985 authoritarian period.

THE STRUCTURE OF PRESS-STATE RELATIONS

The state in Brazil is extensive, interacting with society in many ways. New channels are always being created and old modes of action are rarely retired. The press for its part is unavoidably a major economic entity as well as a politically volatile actor made up of very diverse publications, which despite their common concerns have never displayed great unity. The press and the state have historically been closely entwined, influencing one another although never comparable in power.

The State in Civil Society

The state in Brazil has been thoroughly involved in almost every part of the nation's economic development, social organization, cultural practices, and political structures. Indeed, a major theme in Brazilian historiography concerns the precedence of the state over the nation and the role of the state in creating civil society.

Brazil's federal government has invested heavily in or otherwise been active in many areas of the economy, including the energy, steel, petrochemical, transportation, and banking sectors. Federal policies have led to important changes (or to stasis) in the agricultural sector, from massive price supports for coffee in the early twentieth century to the fiscal incentives of the 1970s for expanding commercial agriculture into the Amazon region. State protection of industry during the phase of import substitution industrialization was key during the 1930s to the 1950s, as was the state's promotion of exports during the 1970s and 1980s. In Brazil, as elsewhere in Latin America, the government has sponsored investment as part of a three-member partnership consisting of the state, the national bourgeoisie, and foreign capital.[1] Patterns in the nation's economy thus cannot be understood without full attention to the state as well as to various private actors.

The state has likewise been deeply involved in the organization of civil society. Governments have created institutions and structures to manage change and conflict, and have created clienteles who pursue state resources and operate under close state supervision and tutelage. The Brazilian labor movement is a classic example of the state's shaping of civil society. The government's extensive power has been exercised through labor courts, veto power over union elections, interventions in unions moving toward opposition, and collection and distribution of dues. The corporatism of the Estado Novo was the apogee of this involvement, but corporatist policies were not abandoned with the demise of that regime.[2]

In politics, the state has substantially manipulated the structure of competition. This has included outlawing certain political parties, suspending elections, canceling electoral mandates and individual political rights, and changing the laws that govern political campaigns. Those in power are always involved in defining not only the rules of the game but also who is permitted to play. This is certainly not unique to Brazil, but it is an important characteristic of its governance.

Even in the cultural realm, often assumed to be a locus of popular autonomy, the state has had a profound impact. It has been instrumental in determining when a social activity is transformed from a punishable crime into subsidized popular culture, as in the case of spiritist religions, Carnaval celebration, and the martial art of *capoeira*. The state was a key actor in the transformation of Carnaval from an illicit popular festival to an organized tourist attraction, with rules for the composition of samba lyrics, standards for judging music and dance, and time limits and content requirements for the parades. Even in their celebration of Carnaval, a supposed period of great license and freedom, Brazilians are not detached from the state.[3]

In this context of state involvement and precedence, capturing the favors of the state—whether in the form of loans, protective tariffs, exclusive recognition, legalization, or promotion—has been an important strategy for business, agriculture, labor unions, party activists, and even artists, women's groups, and cult leaders. From infrastructural investment to norms for legal strikes to samba lyrics, the state is relevant to all activities. Everyone has a stake in the state in Brazil; to operate in Brazil is to relate to the state.

Relations between state and society have not been a one-way street nor have they been static. While the state has provided important subsidies to economic activity in Brazil, it has also placed tremendous burdens upon it. The same business sectors that have clamored for state support and protection have also at other times demanded freedom from interference. Corporatist organizations created to exert control over civil society have been known to get out of control.[4] Officially sanctioned cultural messages can be reinterpreted to highlight their subversive content. Political alliances shift with opportunism or changing commitments. These are patterned but volatile relationships, subject to change through reorganization or through formulation of new identities or ideas. Likewise, the press has at times been an ally, at times an opponent of the state. The press has occasionally been a tool of the state, but it has also influenced and even toppled governments. The dynamic of press-state relations proceeds on several levels.

Multifaceted Press

The press in Brazil interacts with the state on more than one level because the press itself is a multifaceted entity. It is an economic actor as well as a sociopolitical one, and tension exists as a result of these dual but not necessarily complementary identities.

Most of the major press publications in Brazil are privately owned, profit-seeking enterprises. They are directly linked with other communication media as well as other business sectors. They aim to increase sales and advertising revenue, hold costs down and improve productivity, and expand their net worth.

Yet the press in Brazil also maintains a goal, if insufficiently realized, of being a social forum. It views itself ideally as performing an important civic role by providing information, debate, and commentary. In exercising this role, the press sees itself and is seen (at least rhetorically) as essential to responsible citizenship and democratic participation.[5] Though many members of the press express a deeply cynical view of its capacity to fulfill that mission adequately, nonetheless it has not exorcised that expectation.

Members of the press are thus recognized as both private entrepreneurs or employees as well as public servants whose activities are essential to the common good. Freedom of the press is seen not only as an end in itself, as a manifestation of freedom of expression, but also as a guarantor of many other political rights and responsibilities. As both a business enterprise and a political forum, the press interacts with the state on multiple fronts. In tracing press-state relations, it is necessary to look at these multiple fronts and to be aware of the tension that their multiplicity creates.

State-Press Interaction

In the economic realm, the press has sought substantial loans for its business ventures as well as permission to import equipment and newsprint. Any newspaper owner pursuing a concession in another medium, such as for a radio or television station, must also appeal to the state.[6] Further, because the state itself is a major economic actor, it maintains a substantial advertising budget that is often crucial to the economic viability of newspapers. These are among the sources of the press's economic dependence upon the state.

The press does have other economic resources. These include press owners, investors, and advertisers. While defending its own business interests, generally shared by either the national bourgeoisie who are its owners or the international corporations who are among its advertisers, the press has at times mounted important opposition to state economic policies, such as the nationalization of petroleum resources in the 1950s and the attempts at "basic reforms" by President Goulart in 1963–1964.

In the political realm, the state has also been notoriously involved with the press. This has included direct censorship, refusal to disclose information, onerous press laws, harassment or courting of the press, creation of propaganda departments, bribing of editorial writers, and planting of misinformation. The state has frequently sought to use the press as a means to influence or control society.

The press has also managed at times to influence or pressure governments. Its attacks on President Vargas in the 1950s were instrumental in the collapse of his administration and his suicide, and the press was also very important in delegitimizing President Goulart in the period preceding the

1964 coup. As a political actor itself, the press may be available for alliances with opposition or subordinate factions within the state. If the press has sometimes been the tool of the state, it has also been a partner in alliances against the state.

Whether measured in terms of financial ties, political machinations, direct regulations, or more subtle manipulations, the state and press in Brazil are deeply, though asymmetrically, intertwined. This has been the case throughout the history of the press in Brazil. The practices and institutions that shaped press-state relations in the 1964–1985 period had been established over many decades. The historical overview in the next section reveals some precursors to the rationalizations and debates of the 1964–1985 period.

THE EARLY PERIOD

State censorship in Brazil began with the first exercise of the press.[7] In 1808 the Portuguese royal court fled Napoleon's armies and transferred itself to Rio de Janeiro, bringing both the first printing press in the colony and the first set of press regulations. Nothing could be printed without prior examination by the royal censors, and no statements against the government or against religion or good morals were allowed. The censorship orders that have been preserved from the early nineteenth century eerily parallel prohibitions of the late twentieth century. In ordering the confiscation of the *Correio Brasiliense* in 1809, for example, the royal court pointed to that newspaper's criticisms of the government as well as its "political venom and falsehood which may deceive simple and ignorant people."[8] Protection of the vulnerable—particularly those who are vulnerable because of their simplicity—occurs again and again in Brazilian history as a justification for state coercion of a subgroup. The rhetoric emphasizes a relationship of benevolence and protection, precisely at the moment of coercion. At issue is whether the state is coercing the press as a genuine attempt to protect the simple, or coercing the simple by denying them information and a forum for their views. Rather than educating the simple or debating the press, the state destroys or disciplines the critic.

With independence in 1822 the situation of the press—like that of the slaves, the elite, and the agricultural economy—seems to have changed very little. That same year the Council of State passed measures to protect the government from "incendiary and subversive doctrines and disorganizing and abhorrent principles"—language again echoed by the 1964–1985 regime in its justification of censorship.

State pressure aside, the press in this period was by no means necessarily a good citizen or public servant. The nineteenth century was the heyday of the *pasquins,* satirical lampoons in broadside or pamphlet form. Much press activity consisted of political diatribes or personal invectives. The journalist Alberto Dines characterizes this period as "full of abuses on both sides. . . . If political debate went on at a low level, journalism crept right along beside it."[9] The press did play an important role in major political changes, such as the abolition of slavery and the gaining of independence from Portugal, but there never was a golden era of press freedom or lofty press institutions.

After the turn of the twentieth century, the artisanal *pasquim* press was succeeded by an incipient industrial press. This accompanied other changes in Brazil's society and economy: urbanization and industrialization, the emergence of a national bourgeoisie, and the formation of a working class.[10] Major newspapers with conventional modern formats were established in the larger cities. They were privately owned, required large capital investments, made use of modern technology, and became emblematic of modernity.[11] This is not to say that they necessarily revolutionized their content or quality, but there was movement toward international standards of what constituted news and appropriate coverage.

During this period the state continued to exercise censorship. At the same time that the press was free to develop technically and professionally, it was also highly restricted. While the *Jornal do Brasil* was modernizing and beginning to purchase the services of United Press International for its international news coverage, the circulation of the *Correio da Manhã* was halted by the government from August 1924 to May 1925. The limited victory that the newspaper eventually won through the judicial system affirmed only its freedom to circulate, not its freedom to publish, for the court upheld prior censorship by the government.[12]

From the Empire to the time of the independent Republic, from the earliest *pasquims* to the establishment of an industrial press, there was no period when the state was not attempting to monitor and shape the press to some degree. Neither, however, do those efforts appear to have been naturalized. Some part of the press continued to criticize government positions (even if not entirely constructively) and to challenge government restrictions. Although the *Correio da Manhã* won only a limited victory in the 1925 court case, it succeeded in getting government censorship discussed in the courts. While these are not the dominant themes to be found in press histories of the early twentieth century, there clearly is in the Brazilian press a long-standing precedent of some resentment of and resistance to state efforts at control.

THE ESTADO NOVO

The relationship between press and state shifted notably with the demise of the Old Republic in 1930 and the installation of Getulio Vargas's dictatorship, the Estado Novo of 1937–1945. Repression became more institutionalized, systematic, and coercive, while at the same time state support for the press became more extensive, pervasive, sophisticated, and subtle. Although 1945 brought the end of the overtly dictatorial Estado Novo, important pieces of legislation and institutional relationships of the 1937–1945 era survived into the period of electoral populism that followed. Patterns of corporatism or control do not pass away with an administration; political culture endures. The Estado Novo was a watershed in state-society relations in Brazil.

With the revolution of 1930, state intervention in the press became direct and intensive. Many newspaper operations were physically destroyed and those that remained were placed under careful surveillance. The new government created the Official Department of Propaganda in 1932, which was responsible for the exercise of censorship. In what became a familiar formula, the Constitution of 1934 guaranteed freedom of the press with, however, prohibitions against anything inciting war, violence, or subversion of the social and political order—restrictions that could be and were given broad interpretation. Censorship at this time was exercised unevenly, for some periodicals were permitted to print material prohibited to others. In another foreshadowing of the post-1964 experience, some articles condemned by the censors did reach at least a limited public, being read to the Constituent Assembly by representatives making use of their parliamentary immunity.[13] After the revolution of 1930 the state was thus using force against the press, developing a censorship bureaucracy, manipulating an ambiguous formal constitution, and practicing censorship selectively—all precursors to the practices of the 1964–1985 military regime.

With Vargas's coup of November 1937 and the establishment of the fascist-leaning Estado Novo, press freedom in Brazil entered one of its darkest periods. Indeed, civic and political freedoms as a whole entered their darkest period. Under the dictatorship, police torture became routine, the secret police were very active, civil rights (including freedom of association) were severely restricted, and supposed opponents of the regime faced imprisonment, abuse, or exile.

In this environment of repression and substantial use of police force, the Official Department of Propaganda evolved into the Department of Press and Propaganda (DIP), the "fundamental piece of the entire censorship system."[14] Each day, the DIP issued orders to the editorial boards of every newspaper, prohibiting "any news against the regime, or any [news the DIP] thought was against the regime."[15] According to the memoirs of the journalist Edmar Morel, his newspaper's director would simply post each day's prohibitions on the office bulletin board, an action indicative of how pervasive and unmediated this exercise was. In addition, proofs were reviewed by government officials. Morel remarks, "There had already been censorship in Brazil before, and from long before. . . . But DIP was different: it institutionalized censorship and lying."[16]

In addition to restricting news, the DIP also planted it. A 1939 government decree identified the press as having the task of "clarifying public opinion regarding plans for material reconstruction and national rebuilding."[17] Apparently no one could be clearer about the role of the government than the government itself, hence the DIP also inserted, and the press duly printed, materials lauding Vargas, such praise ostensibly being one ingredient of national reconstruction. General Otavio Costa, head of the propaganda arm in President Medici's government (1969–1974), refers to this period as having a "carbon copy press" that simply printed what it was fed by the DIP regarding national events and government policies and decisions.[18]

The Estado Novo also used a variety of other means to influence the press. One important tool at its disposal, from the same 1939 decree, was its power of registration. Journalistic businesses could be established and individual journalists formally exercise their profession only if they obtained proper registration from the DIP. It was thus possible to control the emergence of periodicals. And in fact, beginning in 1940 the DIP refused registration to 420 newspapers and 346 magazines. A similar means of control was the license for importing newsprint, another activity within the DIP's domain. Some sixty-one newspapers and magazines eventually suspended publication simply for lack of access to paper.[19] The press was not outlawed, but press outlets existed and functioned only by permission of the state.

When these various forms of pressure did not work, there was force. The *Estado de São Paulo*, for example, was simply taken over by the DIP for five years. The independent line of the newspaper irritated the government, and under orders of the minister of war it was invaded by police on March 23, 1940. Alleging that the *Estado de São Paulo* was fomenting armed struggle and had a hidden cache of weapons, the police searched its premises but found nothing. Two days later another search discovered arms hidden in the attic—wrapped in the previous day's *Diário Oficial*. The *Estado de São Paulo* was then removed from the control of the Mesquita family and placed in the hands of the DIP, which published the newspaper until 1945, when it was restored to the Mesquita family.[20] This traumatic episode in the newspaper's history later influenced the choices made by the newspaper's owners and employees in dealing with the 1964–1985 military regime. During its centenary celebration in 1975, the newspaper refused to acknowledge the DIP years as belonging to its past.

Favors and bribes were also available as means of state influence. They were extended to individual journalists, to entire newspapers, and to journalists' organizations. According to stories of the period, the DIP bribed everyone bribable, and to an unprecedented degree. It paid regular salaries to a great number of journalists.[21] For newspapers faithful to Vargas, there was a monthly "contribution" whose size varied with the influence and circulation of the newspaper. In the opinion of historian Antonio Costella, "The few exceptions in this sea of corruption, the few press people who avoided the comfortable steamroller of bribery, leave us an image which approaches the boundaries of heroism. After all, it was difficult to be honest." And according to a frequently cited appraisal, "Newspapers enriched themselves and journalists were corrupted whenever it was possible to become enriched and corrupted."[22]

Journalists began to be formally professionalized and organized in 1938; however, their unions were no freer than any others in the Estado Novo.[23] Their professional organization, the Associação Brasileira da Imprensa (Brazilian Press Association) (ABI), had a slow start. Founded in 1908 in a period of anarcho-syndicalist labor organizing, the association was originally designed to be a mutual aid society offering pensions, medical aid, self-improvement courses, and a vision of a future in which the Brazilian press would be collectively owned. Its first meetings drew fewer people than there were positions to fill. Municipal laws in 1921 and 1922 gave the organization land in Rio de Janeiro for its headquarters, but it lacked the resources to do anything with the property.

During the Estado Novo period, however, its fortunes changed. The Estado Novo gave the ABI the funds to construct its first headquarters, and Vargas was proclaimed honorary president in 1931. He was feted there in 1934 and 1936, and came to inspect a new headquarters building in 1942. In 1944 and 1952 he was again part of ABI ceremonies. Press historian Nelson Werneck Sodre points to the irony that the "ABI had its patrimony enriched and became a powerful entity precisely in a dictatorial phase."[24]

Some of the government's manipulation of the press does seem to have been accepted, with the press posting censorship orders and taking bribes. Intellectuals, including editors and journalists, found themselves in an ambiguous relationship with a state that lauded their role in forming and expressing the national consciousness and gave them resources for this task, while also manipulating and coercing them.[25] Thus there was a mixture of sufferance, accommodation, and opportunism. But there was also some resistance to state repression and censorship. Resistance appears to have been sporadic and symbolic, rather than organized and effective. That may indicate more the surplus power of the state rather than the press's lack of will. In terms of historiography and self-understanding, it is interesting that certain anecdotes relating to press challenges to censorship have been immortalized, even though the period is generally characterized as an era of spinelessness.

The publisher of *O Globo*, Roberto Marinho, became infuriated with incompetent, unqualified censors. He publicly assaulted one in the offices of *O Globo*, following which the newspaper's publication was suspended for twenty-four hours and an order for Marinho's imprisonment announced, although later suspended. In the memoirs of a journalist who witnessed the scene, the event was memorialized because of Marinho's prestige and because it was so out of character for the generally accommodating publisher.[26] At a personal level, even without any orchestration with other newspapers, there was some outrage toward the censors among owners and publishers.

Carlos Castello Branco, the distinguished author of a regular column of political observation and commentary that ran for decades in the *Jornal do Brasil*, recalled trying to outwit Estado Novo censorship by quoting speeches from Roosevelt and Churchill on the front page, speeches that emphasized the words *democracy* and *liberty*. By quoting such speeches, he aimed to create an antifascist spirit, although, as journalist and press observer Alberto Dines noted, this "could be perceived only by the informed."[27]

From the period of the Estado Novo there is ample evidence of collaboration, corruption, and co-optation. There is also more than ample evidence of coercion. With respect to the press's own political culture, this period is interpreted by historians as one of submission and acceptance, in which few journalists even tried to avoid the "comfortable steamroller of bribery." The exceptions manifested themselves as symbolic gestures or outbursts of sporadic fury by individuals, not organized collective resistance or defense. The very institutions to which the press might have appealed (such as the ABI) were themselves receiving too many favors. Thus the Estado Novo period figures in press history as a time when efforts at state control were met by press weakness. And while there are some parallels with the repression practiced by the 1964–1985 military regime, the press does not seem to have emerged from the Estado Novo period with new tools or insights for meeting that repression.

ELECTORAL POPULISM, 1945–1964

Vargas was deposed in 1945 and a new constitution was written in 1946. Although there was a change of regime followed by elections, many important corporatist features of the Estado Novo remained intact. The DIP was dismantled, but much of the former press law remained, including prohibitions against publishing anything that challenged the social and political order. Thus press law continued to be open to interpretation, and much depended on who was in power. Newspapers continued to be confiscated and suspended on occasion.

Another legacy of the Estado Novo was simply that the press had a history of being manipulated, whether by force or by favors. Indeed, favors became the focus of press-state relations in the post-1945 period, always with ambiguity regarding the degree of favor and obligation as opposed to right and freedom.

When Vargas was elected president in 1951, the mainstream press was largely hostile toward him. He responded by helping Samuel Wainer establish the pro-Vargas *Ultima Hora,* a newspaper chain with affiliates throughout the country. The assistance was in the form of a loan approved by the government-owned Bank of Brazil. Although the loan was repaid, it became symbolic of graft in the Vargas administration. Vargas's opponents, and especially the rest of the press, seized upon it and explored it in detail. In June 1953 a congressional tribunal began an investigation of Wainer's dealings with the Bank of Brazil, only one of several scandals plaguing the Vargas administration, all of which contributed to Vargas's belief he was "standing in a sea of mud," and to his eventual suicide.[28]

The *Ultima Hora* episode illustrates the ambivalent relationship between press and state in this period—the financial dependence of the press upon the state and, at the same time, the press's political factionalism. In 1953, as Sodre recounts, "The entire press concentrated itself in demonstrating the obvious: that this newspaper was made possible only by the concession of large loans from official credit institutions," like many industries of the time. Sodre documents the government loans, often larger than those received by *Ultima Hora,* which were made to all the major newspapers of the period. He concludes that "What is curious, then, is not that there was an accusation in chorus, but the fact that the members of the chorus were susceptible to the same accusation."[29]

All of the mainstream press seems to have leaned heavily upon the government for loans, as indeed did many other businesses. But this did not necessarily make the press subservient to the executive. In this case the press maintained its alliance with factions opposed to Vargas and contributed substantially to the president's downfall.

Although Vargas's relations with the press were the stormiest of those in the 1946–1964 period, other presidents also clashed with the press. Juscelino Kubitschek had the *Tribuna da Imprensa* confiscated in 1956 and revoked a television concession to the *Jornal do Brasil* following its publication of an embarrassing photograph of him.[30] The resignation of Janio Quadros on

August 25, 1961, was another opportunity for censorship, as were the disputes over João Goulart's assuming the presidency.[31]

At no point, then, was the press sacrosanct, in this period of electoral populism any more than during the overt dictatorship of the Estado Novo. Whenever there was a major political dispute or crisis, the press was involved as either actor or pawn. This was certainly true of the prelude to the military coup of 1964.

THE MILITARY COUP OF 1964

The press was one catalyst of the coup of March 31, 1964. Certain publications were privy to the conspiracy, and others contributed wittingly or not to public rejection of Goulart.[32] Like much of the middle and upper class, the Catholic Church, and such organizations as the Brazilian Bar Association, the mainstream press was opposed to Goulart's mass mobilizations and his proposed "basic reforms" such as land redistribution and unionization of the military. The press campaign against him included front-page editorials calling for his ouster. Some of the most famous of these were published in the *Correio da Manhã*, later harassed and closed by the military regime.

The language of the *Correio da Manhã*'s editorials captures the debates of this period and offers a portrait of the elitism and classic liberalism of the mainstream press at the time. This Rio de Janeiro daily was a prestigious newspaper, already boasting a long tradition. Its front-page editorials entitled "Enough!" and "Out!" have come to symbolize the rejection by the bourgeois press of any form of democracy that included substantive socioeconomic reform. The editorials also reveal, however, some genuine commitment to the principles of constitutional rule, distance from the military, and willingness to take risks in order to express criticisms.[33]

The editorials of the *Correio da Manhã* just prior to the coup demanded Goulart's removal, but they did so on the newspaper's terms, articulating a concern for constitutional rule, which they argued he was threatening. The newspaper was not at the very forefront of agitation for a coup, nor was it subsequently the mere tool of the coup leaders. Indeed, the *Correio da Manhã* lost no time in condemning the violence and excesses of the coup itself and of the regime it brought to power. Its editorials just after the coup, including one ironically titled "Enough and Out!" swiftly equated chaos and abuse of power under Goulart with chaos and abuse of power under the military regime. Over the next several months, the *Correio da Manhã* was the newspaper reporting most audaciously on mass arrests, torture, and political repression. In so doing it aroused the ire of the military regime. By 1969 it had been closed down. This followed several confiscations of the publication, police occupations of its offices, arrests of its principal editors and publishers, a mysterious bombing of its headquarters, and financial pressure brought by the state.[34]

THE LEGACY OF PRESS-STATE RELATIONS

The press and state in Brazil have unavoidably had a closely entwined relationship. Their interaction has taken different shapes at different times. For the purposes of examining press-state relations under the 1964–1985 military regime, three points regarding this history are particularly significant.

First is the issue of institutional memory and momentum. Experience showed that the state interfered in the press; this was how things worked. Thus it was not unprecedented, nor even very surprising, when the new military government began encroaching upon press freedom. From the colonial period through the Estado Novo and the populist years just prior to the coup, the press could expect from the state some interference and attempts at control.

Second, history could not be among the best resources of the press in mobilizing or articulating resistance to state restrictions. The fact that there had never been a glorious era of secure state respect for the freedom of the press meant that such a claim would have to be created and defended. Freedom of the press could not be argued for by referring to a recognized and shared heritage.

Finally, although the 1964 coup was experienced initially as a complete break with the past, historians are beginning to appreciate that there were important continuities with previous regimes.[35] While there were many new aspects to the relationship of press and state in the 1964–1985 period, there was also substantial continuation of patterns inherited from the past. This legacy was a starting point, and was among the factors in setting the parameters of the press-state relationship during the years of the military regime.

These were the patterns and practices, then, that formed the legacy of press-state relations in Brazil. What became of that relationship in the 1964–1985 period had to do not only with these precedents, but with the identities, choices, and capacities of the state and the press. The next two chapters provide accounts of those two actors during the years of the military regime.

3

THE MILITARY REGIME: AUTHORITARIANISM AND LEGITIMACY

THE MILITARY REGIME that seized power in Brazil in 1964 formulated its own ideology of national security and constructed new legal procedures and institutional foundations for its actions. It also sought to exercise control through repression, with a plethora of security agencies conducting surveillance, interrogation, and torture. The regime changed or ignored laws, even those of its own making, as it saw fit. But despite all this power, the regime was not omnipotent. It was limited by internal divisions, with different factions competing for dominance. The regime was also constrained by a notably ambivalent yet continuous search for legitimacy. The at times contradictory attempts to validate its system of domination and justify its occupation of the state put some limits on what it could do.

SECURITY AND DEVELOPMENT:
THE TRAJECTORY OF THE REGIME

The twin goals of the 1964–1985 regime were security and development. The regime changed over its two decades, adapting in unforeseen ways to new circumstances as it sought to institutionalize itself and meet challenges. But it remained authoritarian and maintained the goals of security—meaning control and absence of conflict—and development—meaning economic growth at any cost.

Historians have labeled the regime *bureaucratic authoritarian*.[1] Proceeding from a National Security Doctrine, it accorded absolute importance to the fight against subversion. Rather than battling external forces, the military looked for subversion from within the nation. The threat of internal warfare transformed the citizenry into a potential enemy, and new measures, from psychological warfare to counterterrorism, became relevant. Political disputes were displaced into technocratic debate and military arenas, thereby engendering or exacerbating divisions within the military. Opposition was considered treason or insubordination, and was punished as such.

In the political realm, existing parties were outlawed, the executive taken over by the military and made predominant, and Congress purged. Many elected representatives lost their seats and political rights. Two parties, the progovernment Aliança de Renovação Nacional (Alliance for National Renovation, ARENA) and the opposition Movimento Democrático Brasileiro (Brazilian Democratic Movement, MDB), were created, and in a further effort to control elections a series of electoral laws (providing for such things as indirect elections, disqualification of certain types of candidates, and restrictions on campaigning) were passed at each critical juncture. There were major changes in the forms of choosing government at all levels, in the organizational structure of the political system, and in the regulation of political behavior.

Autonomous civil society became suspect. Labor activists, rural organizers, students, and church workers were among the people treated most harshly by the regime. Many popular organizations, including labor unions and national student confederations, were disrupted or banned. Activists from outlawed political organizations were particularly persecuted.[2] The growth, creativity, and autonomy of organizations within civil society, despite the harsh conditions they faced, was one of the integral aspects of the eventual demise of the military regime.[3]

In the 1964–1985 period, the state increased its already heavy involvement in the economy by expanding state enterprises as well as by such measures as wage indexation, tax incentives, direct subsidies, and manipulation of price indexes. The aim was to spur private growth and investment (including foreign investment). The regime maintained an orientation toward growth rather than welfare, a posture epitomized by finance minister Delfim Neto's famous dictum that before the pie can be divided, it must be increased. While Brazil did achieve astounding growth rates during the "miracle" years of the early 1970s, this was accompanied by growing indebtedness and increasing inequality. During the military regime the Brazilian economy had grown to eighth largest in the world in terms of gross domestic product, but it also exhibited one of the world's most unequal distributions of income.

The regime's greatest turning point came in December 1968, with the so-called coup within a coup. Up to then people had continued to think that the military had only temporarily taken power to "restore order," and would shortly be returning control of the nation to civilians. After 1968, however, rather than relaxing its control, the military strengthened its hold and moved in a much more abusive, repressive, and authoritarian direction.

Throughout 1968, pressure was building from every direction for the military to step aside and restore the government to civilians and power to civil society. The political class had formed the Frente Ampla (Broad Front), which included prestigious politicians and former adversaries such as Carlos Lacerda, Juscelino Kubitschek, and João Goulart. The Frente was beginning to absorb what little momentum there was in the formally recognized but largely moribund MDB. Students were mobilizing and demonstrating. A march of one hundred thousand students in the streets of Rio de Janeiro was attacked by the police, resulting in one student's death. Workers were organizing and striking in the important industrial regions of Minas Gerais and São Paulo.

The crackdown that followed these events was a victory for the military hard-liners. Although the hard-liners had been a part of the regime from the beginning, after 1968 they took control of all major positions within the government and held them through the Medici presidency of 1969–1974. In this period torture and repression reached their apex.

Subsequently, a variety of factors contributed to a very gradual and controlled *abertura* or political opening. Parts of the military became concerned about the growth and autonomy of the intelligence apparatus. Civil society created new strategies and allies for its protests and demands. After economic growth slowed in the mid-1970s, and especially with the economic crisis of the early 1980s, the business class became less enamored of the military state as well. Although it took two further administrations and much careful maneuvering—from manipulating electoral rules to declaring a general amnesty for political exiles and police torturers alike—the military eventually exited in 1985. There was no dramatic rupture or definitive overthrow of the regime. Its controlled and gradual withdrawal thus left a rather ambiguous legacy.

For the purposes of examining press-state relations and censorship under the military regime, four issues are particularly relevant. The transformation of the formal legal system and the actual exercise of repression, regardless of legal niceties, are two of these key issues. These formed the context for the exercise and experience of censorship. Press control, as it was conducted in Brazil under the military regime, had both quasi-legal and directly coercive components. These were the twin faces presented to the press: an officious one of specific and codified restrictions and a de facto one of direct repression. And yet these two were not entirely distinct, but rather part of a continuum, because the formal procedures were often not actually legal and because the extralegal repression was openly conducted by "constituted authorities."

Two other relevant issues are the regime's internal divisions and its search for legitimacy, which shaped the choices made and options exercised by the regime at each juncture. The regime's internal divisions and the search for legitimacy could weaken the press's position, as when press actors were caught like pawns in struggles between military factions. These features could also benefit the press, as when the state refrained from acting against the press if such actions would jeopardize a claim to political legitimacy. Internal divisions and the search for legitimacy help to account for some peculiar aspects of the censorship itself, such as its secrecy, its uneven application, and the manner of its implementation.

THE TRANSFORMATION OF THE LEGAL APPARATUS

Before the 1964 coup, many Brazilians lived outside the rule of law. In the rural Northeast, traditional landholders exercised tremendous political as well as economic and cultural power in the absence of formal state institutions. Throughout Brazil common prisoners and local vagrants were subject to police brutality and torture. There was, however, a formal legal structure. The mainstream press operated largely within that formal world. It was familiar with the rule of law, the formal rules of the game, and the means of playing that game. The press was comfortable with and competent at using the legal system. This changed drastically after 1964.

The military regime transformed Brazil's legal system by means of executive decrees. The most notorious were the Institutional Acts, supplemented by myriad Complementary Acts, Instructions, National Security Laws, and even Secret Decrees (under which one could be tried for something one had no way of knowing was illegal). Through these instruments, every aspect of the Brazilian judicial system was altered, including the criminal code and the rules for place of trial (military versus civilian courts). Habeas corpus was eliminated, as were, in some cases, the right of appeal and restrictions on length of sentence. The immunity of judges from interference by the executive was also curtailed, for judges could now be arbitrarily removed from office by the regime. The effect, in one contemporary's observation, was to break the back or "devertebrate" the judiciary.[4]

The most important Institutional Acts were known as AI-1, AI-2, and AI-5. These were directed at controlling the national population as well as actors within the state and the military itself. Each Institutional Act was implemented as a reaction to a particular crisis and was shaped by the challenges the regime faced from its opponents. The first two acts were explicitly limited in duration; AI-5 was established indefinitely.

The history of the regime can be discerned in the timing, scope, and justificatory language of those acts. The first, implemented at the time of the coup, was unnumbered, as though it would be unique. It called for punishment of those who acted against the security of the country, the regime, and the probity of public administration; the right to punish was said to be "in the interest of peace and national honor." There was no equivocation about the right to exercise such power: "the victorious Revolution is legitimated by itself . . . let it be entirely clear that the Revolution does not seek to legitimate itself via the Congress. Rather it is the Congress which receives its legitimation from the Institutional Act."[5]

The second Institutional Act followed the 1965 elections, in which the opposition won the governorships of several important states, including Minas Gerais, São Paulo, and Guanabara (later Rio de Janeiro), despite considerable machinations on the part of the regime, extending to disqualification of several candidates. After Congress rejected a version of the proposed act on October 13 and was put into recess by the regime as a result, President Castello Branco issued the act by decree on the 27th. AI-2 made the executive predominant and dissolved existing political parties. Its stated rationale, more elastic than that of AI-1, covered any actions deemed incompatible "with the objectives of the Revolution." The regime was acting not in the name of the people or the nation, but "in the interest of preserving and consolidating the Revolution."

The fifth and most devastating Institutional Act came at the end of 1968, although it had been prepared much earlier. During the course of that year, tensions between state and society escalated. Student street demonstrations in Rio de Janeiro were met with police violence, resulting in the death of student Edson Luis in March. The Frente Ampla, which was creating a new locus for opposition within the political class, was declared illegal in April. Strikes organized by industrial unions in Osasco were met with stiff repression in July. A clandestine gathering of a national students' organization in Ibiuna was invaded in October and its participants imprisoned. This trajectory of violence was brought to a culmination in the aftermath of a September speech by an opposition congressional representative who metaphorically challenged the virility of military officers. When Congress refused to remove him from office in December (prior emergency powers granting this capacity to the president having expired), it was put into recess and AI-5 was implemented.[6]

The effect of the three Institutional Acts (AI-5 being a much harsher version of the first two) amounted to a transformation of Brazil's legal and institutional system.[7] Maria Alves describes the powers given to the executive branch by the acts as follows:

the power to close the federal Congress and state and municipal assemblies; the right to cancel the electoral mandates of members of the legislative or executive branches at federal, state, and municipal levels; the right to suspend political rights of citizens for ten years . . . the right to dismiss, remove from public office, transfer, or retire employees of the federal, state, and municipal bureaucracies; the right to fire, dismiss, or transfer judges, and the removal of all guarantees to the judiciary with regard to job tenure, nontransferability, and the maintenance of salary levels; the power to declare a state of siege without any of the impediments that had been written into the 1967 Constitution; the right to confiscate private property for state use as punishment for subversion or corruption; the suspension of *habeas corpus* in all cases of political crimes against national security; trial of political crimes by military courts with no other judicial recourse; the right to legislate by decree and issue any other institutional or complementary act; and finally, the prohibition of any consideration by the judiciary of appeals from those charged under any provision of AI-5. All stipulations of the act were to remain in force until the president signed a decree specifically revoking it.[8]

Although this list seems comprehensive, AI-5 was not the final Institutional Act, for several others were passed in response to further changes in the country's political situation. AI-13 stipulated exile and banishment for political crimes, AI-14 created the death penalty for crimes against national security, and AI-17 permitted the removal of members of the military who acted "against the unity of the armed forces."[9] Decree Law 477 of 1969 summarily punished professors, students, and school administrators who participated in actions deemed to be against public order (nearly one thousand students were expelled from their places of learning in its first year). And the National Security Law, first passed in 1967, covered not only citizens who jeopardized "security" (a nebulously defined concept) but also any citizen who witnessed but did not denounce such a crime, and provided for even greater penalties if the crime were committed via the press (as in printing an insult to the honor of the military, the government, or visiting dignitaries, or publishing the remarks of someone whose political rights had been denied).[10]

One study finds that 4,841 people were sanctioned under AI-5 from 1964 to 1974; their punishments included cancellation of electoral mandates, suspension of political rights, and dismissal from various public sector posts. Another study estimates that some seven thousand Brazilians lost either their political rights or their employment through application of AI-5 provisions.[11] The myriad Institutional Acts and other Decree Laws had a profound impact on many lives, and not only on those to whom the sanctions were directly applied. The transformed legal system also influenced the risks Brazilians were willing to take and the commitments Brazilians would maintain and act upon.

THE GROWTH AND INSTITUTIONALIZATION OF THE REPRESSIVE APPARATUS

If the 1964–1985 military regime broke the metaphorical bones of the judicial system, it also broke the real bones of many individuals who were deemed subversive. Agencies of surveillance and repression multiplied, often acting with considerable autonomy and impunity. Indeed, the institutionalization of the repressive apparatus and the significant autonomy it enjoyed have been suggested as distinguishing features of Brazil's authoritarian regime in comparison with similar Southern Cone regimes during this period.[12]

The repressive apparatus comprised numerous organizations whose main functions included surveillance, apprehension, interrogation, and counterterrorist action. There were many overlapping duties and channels of command. Some entities that ostensibly were only for surveillance also engaged in direct action; some that were technically under the command of the police were actually controlled by the military. Some were officially funded yet clandestine. Others were under army command yet operated with private funds. The intricate web of the repressive apparatus, centralized yet also dispersed, can thus be hard to trace.

The National Information Service (Serviço Nacional de Informações, SNI) had offices in every government ministry, state enterprise, and university. Each branch of the armed forces also had its own surveillance wing—CIEx for the army, CENIMAR for the navy, and CISA for the air force. Of these, CIEx had by far the worst reputation for its involvement in repression. There was also a network of counterinsurgency units and antiguerrilla agencies whose command structures, funding, and operations were complex. Operação Bandeirantes (Operation Bandeirantes, OBAN), based in São Paulo, was semiofficially under the military but was funded by local and multinational industrialists. Its staff included members of the army, navy, and air force as well as state, federal, and military police.

Each military region also had an Internal Operations Unit (Destacamento de Operações Interna, DOI). Like OBAN, the DOI were staffed by operatives from all the armed forces as well as the military police. Funding for the DOI came from a variety of official and unofficial sources. DOI operatives wore no uniforms. Although formally under the command of regional general staffs, the DOI had a parallel chain of command through CIEx to the minister of the army. The Nunca Mais project's exhaustive study of torture in Brazil remarks that the DOI, "Strengthened by their legal underpinning and their army commanders, and provided with a regularly budgeted income . . . were the most important organs of political repression. They were also responsible for the greatest number of human rights violations."[13] The repressive apparatus also included the country's many police forces (military, federal, state, and municipal), as well as offices of public security and public order. Although bureaucratically elaborate, parallel chains of command permitted some of these units to act clandestinely, making it difficult to control or trace responsibility. Beyond this official apparatus of surveillance, security, and repression were the many death squads, paramilitary groups of off-duty police, and private security forces operating not only with impunity but often with assistance from or the participation of officials.

As the repressive bureaucracy grew, methods of torture multiplied and became institutionalized. The use of torture in this period has been thoroughly and carefully documented.[14] Ingenuity was applied toward causing excruciating pain, using medical professionals to keep victims alive to prolong the torture, and dehumanizing victims so that the effects of the torture would haunt them long after the torture had ceased. While efforts at documentation have been very careful, it is obvious that much brutality went unrecorded; many episodes of beatings in the street and mistreatment in prisons went unregistered in the files.[15]

All of this repression was openly if only vaguely known, or at least suspected. Considerable effort, however, was expended by the regime to conceal it. Deaths under torture were attributed to suicides, traffic accidents, or escape attempts. Corpses were buried in hidden graves or under false names. Attempts to clarify this history continue, but the perpetrators are none too forthcoming.[16] Their proclamations of ignorance are so self-serving as to lose all credibility. Given the plethora of repressive groups that existed, including some that acted without active state support, it is unlikely that anyone will be able to provide a truly comprehensive account of the repression.

Repressive practices and authoritarian decrees were mutually reinforcing. Direct coercion was the counterpart to the contortions of the legal system represented by AI-5 and the National Security Law, with their denial of *habeas corpus* and the right of appeal. Such laws gave the security forces great autonomy and scope for their actions and permitted them to operate with impunity. Because of their power, the security forces could in turn prevent challenges to AI-5 and the other semilegal foundations of their actions. The particular form of the curtailment of press freedom—as of other freedoms during this period—resulted from the interaction of these two features of the regime.

Two other circumstances were also relevant to the trajectory of the regime and to press-state relations in particular. These were the internal divisions between "hard-liners" and "moderates" within the regime, and the shifting but continual pursuit of political legitimacy. These are the subjects of the remainder of this chapter.

INTERNAL DIVISIONS

The basic division within the military is usually construed as being between hard-liners identified with President Medici (1969–1974) and the more moderate wing identified with President Castello Branco (1964–1967) or President Geisel (1974–1979). These two labels are often understood to refer to positions on such matters as the degree of repression deemed necessary or the appropriate amount of consultation with civilians.

The hard-liner/moderate dichotomy, however, emerges more from contrasting the two groups rather than from their own coherent political positions. For example, the first president of the military regime, Castello Branco, is often characterized as a genuine constitutionalist intent upon saving the political system from Goulart's demagoguery. Nevertheless, he was responsible for leading a military coup; for passing a self-legitimating Institutional Act that claimed primacy over a representative Congress; and for presiding over a period of initially harsh repression, especially in the Northeast. His successor, President Costa e Silva (1967–1969), is characterized as representing a shift to greater authoritarianism, although some evidently believed he would be the one to restore democracy. His authoritarianism, however, pales in comparison with Medici's, whose administration was the most repressive of all. And while Geisel's subsequent presidency was an important and delicate victory for the moderates, his administration nonetheless continued political censorship and was responsible for some of the boldest casuistry in interpreting electoral rules. Geisel's key aide, Golbery, was an architect of both the *abertura* (political opening) and the SNI. The legacy of each administration or major actor is mixed, and the so-called moderates have gained a reputation for restraint or openness perhaps largely in contrast to the hard-liners, more than by committed action of their own.

Whether the disputes are best construed as hard-liner versus moderate, or as opportunistic power struggles and factionalism, there clearly was considerable divisiveness within the military. Marcus Figueiredo carefully documents how the Institutional Acts were used to punish members of the regime and the military itself. He concludes that members of the military—including the civil and military police as well as the three branches of the armed forces—were disproportionately targeted by state repression during all three eras of punishment that he identifies.[17] Figueiredo's analysis challenges the image of a tightly unified military pursuing its goals through a bureaucratic authoritarian regime.

Further evidence for the existence of disputes within the armed forces is the fact of the *abertura*. Many analysts conclude that one of the most significant motives for the *abertura* was fear among the more moderate figures within the military that the repressive forces were getting out of control, and that the autonomy of those forces threatened the "integrity" of the military as an institution.[18] If people within the military could commit terrorist acts without the approval of their superiors, the reasoning went, then there was also the potential for the agents of repression to turn against their superiors.

The divisions within the military (however characterized) meant that the regime could not simply evolve along a predetermined bureaucratic authoritarian course. Thus the course of the regime was continually affected not only by opposition from civil society but also by internal power struggles.

The military regime's internal power struggles had a substantial impact upon the press. As will be discussed in later chapters, while the executive branch under President Geisel was lifting its controls on the press, the Ministry of Justice (under Armando Falcão, an ally of the hard-liners) was strengthening and extending its control. At another point, when President Geisel and his chief of military cabinet, General Hugo Abreu, were in disagreement, the press never knew whether orders emanating from Abreu's office represented Abreu's own interests or the decisions of the executive. At times the press's decisions were guided by assumptions about the divisions within the regime and the fortunes of the different factions. Invited to join a collective lawsuit against prior censorship, the censored *Estado de São Paulo* declined on the grounds that its allies within the military government were about to gain power and would surely lift the censorship (which they did not in fact do for some time).

Individual lives were also affected. The death under torture of journalist Vladimir Herzog is believed not to have been the result of animosity aimed primarily at Herzog himself. Rather, Herzog became a pawn in the power struggle between different military factions. To offer another example, jobs were lost and journalists were imprisoned as disputes within the regime were played out against the staff of the *Folha de São Paulo*.

When there was already a pattern of concealing the extralegal actions of the military, the fallout of these internal divisions further obscured the transparency of any state action. About any decision or action one could reasonably ask, was it directed at me, or directed at the competing military faction? Is this coming from those really holding power, or from a subgroup trying to score points against those in power?

This made it more difficult for the press, or any other potential opponent of the regime, to assess a situation, formulate a strategy, or anticipate a reaction. The press was confronted not only by the tremendous changes in formal legal rules and the growth of repressive capacity, but by the further unknowns that resulted from the divisions within the regime. In any given situation of government repression, much of what one faced might be the unintended consequences of these struggles, or even the result of a direct contravention of those supposedly in power.

POLITICAL LEGITIMACY

A final significant feature of the Brazilian military regime was its pursuit of political legitimacy. Despite being authoritarian, the regime also sought to legitimate its occupation of the state—sometimes on contradictory grounds.

The regime made diverse and sometimes conflicting claims to legitimacy. Some claims appealed to important continuities with traditional forms of governance in Brazil and tried to benefit from whatever residues of legitimacy could be extracted from the past or from hallowed institutions. Other claims emphasized specific accomplishments (such as security or economic growth), locating the validity and the glory of the regime in its capabilities and achievements. In addition, there were some limited efforts at establishing populism as a basis for legitimacy. And finally, there was the perennial assertion that the legitimacy of the regime followed from its mission of saving democracy.

Different claims were made at different times and were directed toward different constituencies. None of these efforts to establish the legitimacy of the regime succeeded entirely, but neither did they fail completely. Even as partial successes may have strengthened the regime, the attempt to assert the validity of its domination placed important constraints on its scope of action, and the press was affected by the outcomes of these sometimes contradictory appeals for legitimacy.

Traditional Institutions

The military regime carefully maintained key traditional institutions of formal Brazilian politics. It never actually eliminated the federal Congress, although it did repeatedly purge Congress, encircle it with troops, and put it into recess while the executive branch implemented by decree what the representatives had refused to legislate (such as AI-2 and AI-5). Congress was reduced to a registry of laws and became primarily a body for ratifying what was proposed by the military-controlled executive. Similarly, the Constitution was not abandoned, but was instead amended, rewritten, and overridden, incorporating contradictions so as to encompass both constitutional and institutional authority.[19] The regime continued the practice of elections, but often postponed them and made them indirect, placed restrictions upon campaigns, and permitted the existence of only certain parties and candidates. The regime adhered to fixed terms for the presidents and duly replaced them at the end of their terms, but the presidents were always members of the military, as were many in the Cabinet. This story has its parallel in press censorship. The mainstream press was almost never formally censored; the censorship was instead a gentleman's agreement—or so claimed the "constituted authorities."

The continuity of traditional forms, to the extent that it was intentional and not just the result of inertia, was directed toward the elite and the middle class. Their political culture would include a concern for the rule of law and an expectation that it would be upheld. For these Brazilians, whose support was key to the stability and success of the regime and toward whom many of its policies were directed, the continuation of certain traditional institutions would be reassuring.[20]

The outcome of these maneuvers was of course paradoxical. Having retained the Congress and the Constitution as bases for legitimacy because of their historical and formal integrity, the military regime so robbed them of power and autonomy that it rendered them incapable of conferring legitimacy. As Lúcia Klein observes, by imposing limitations on the functioning of political institutions, the revolutionary legal order contributed to restricting the legitimating capacity of those institutions, making necessary the intensive recourse to new instruments of legitimation.[21]

Security and Economic Growth

Claims of legitimacy also rested upon the accomplishments of the regime in such areas as security and economic growth. Protection from allegedly ubiquitous communists, terrorists, and subversives was touted as a paramount achievement of the regime, and the particular province of the armed forces. While there was some urban terrorist activity in Brazil in 1968–1969, the "terrorist threat" continued to be used as a justification for police and military action long afterwards, precisely because it could justify the military's occupation of civilian government.

When the economy began to expand after 1968, and until it began to falter in the mid-1970s, economic growth was another important basis for claims to legitimacy. The military regime, it was argued, could lead Brazil to miraculous economic feats through the application of technocratic proficiency and administrative efficiency.[22] One by-product of the prevalence of this discourse, Klein points out, was that the ARENA party adopted technocratic language, trying to present itself as a locus of technical expertise rather than of political debate. The technical language was supposed to be depoliticizing, but ironically, technical jargon became instead the new political idiom.[23]

A credible press, the regime believed, would be an important tool in ensuring the success of this effort to establish legitimacy. Someone had to proclaim the regime's accomplishments. Official public relations departments worked hard to distribute information on the building of new highways, bridges, and hydroelectric dams, and the press could be an important ally of the regime in making this information public (though at the same time a source of danger if it were to challenge or criticize the social costs of these accomplishments).

Basing claims of legitimacy upon economic and other accomplishments could also be a double-edged sword. If the regime failed to reach its goals, its hold on the state would be questioned. And once goals were reached, the military would lose one basis for justifying its continuation in power. Thus McDonough argues that the success as well as the failure of development programs could undermine the rationale for the military's occupation of the state. Stepan points out that the business sector's disapproval of immense state expansion into the economy in 1967–1973 began to be voiced only in 1975, precisely when the state ran out of largesse to distribute.[24]

Populism

Certain members of the regime also made appeals to populism. Presidents were portrayed as "regular guys" by the propaganda offices. Costa e Silva attempted to cultivate the image of "Seu Artur," a friendly uncle, and Medici was shown avidly listening to soccer games on a common transistor radio. The regime readily exploited Brazil's 1970 World Cup soccer victory as a great boon to national pride, which it sought to extend to the government as well.[25] The Special Advisory Council on Public Relations and other offices produced slogans and cartoons touting Brazil's enormous power, prestige, and potential. These were meant to foster patriotism and enhance the *ufanismo* or boastful celebration of the nation's grand manifest destiny.

These appeals to populism, however, were quite limited. The regime never chose to take the next step toward mass mobilization through establishment of a populist party.[26] In rejecting such a strategy, it nonetheless did not eschew popular regard. If the regime could not be populist, at least it could avoid the charge of callous antipopulism, and this it tried to do in part by suppressing those publications most inclined to cover the wretched living and working conditions of the majority.

Democracy

A further appeal to legitimacy was the perennial claim that democracy was being protected. The regime argued that the purpose of the 1964 coup had been to save democracy before it could be destroyed by President João Goulart. The authoritarian measures of the next two decades were necessary to accomplish this mission, and were, indeed, directed at "perfecting" democracy. "Perfecting democracy" became almost a code phrase, and was used in justifying each authoritarian step. The old democratic system, the argument went, had been faulty. There had been corruption among the political class and abuse by the likes of Goulart. The military regime was thus not at all opposed to democracy, but rather was working to perfect it before returning power to the citizenry.

This was not necessarily self-serving nonsense. The assertions about democracy are often quoted to demonstrate the regime's hypocrisy. The hard-liners, of course, may have been manipulating the language for their own purposes,[27] but there is evidence that some parts of the military had genuine regard for democratic norms.[28] As Figueiredo shows, members of the military were punished disproportionately under the Institutional Acts —some presumably for opposition to authoritarianism.[29] AI-17 was directed specifically at protecting the unity of the armed forces, again to facilitate the hard-liners in punishing or expelling their opponents. On the other hand, nothing was more unpalatable to many of the military hard-liners than the notion of an open democracy. These disputes were ideological and conceptual, as well as about who had power. That appeals to democracy occurred at all is another indication of the internal diversity of the military.

The regime's efforts to seek legitimacy, on the basis of democracy, would provide the press with an opportunity to assert its freedom, in that a free press can be identified as a pillar of democratic systems. But while an open democracy would require a free press, perhaps a "perfected" democracy would require a "perfected" press likewise shaped under the tutelage of the military.

The pursuit of legitimacy with respect to any of these myriad claims could be a double-edged sword. The success of any legitimation claim could strengthen and stabilize the regime, yet also set tacit standards by which it could be judged on its heritage, probity, accomplishments, appeal, concerns, or commitments.

Whether the regime ever succeeded in gaining legitimacy, it certainly never quit trying. It never ceased its attempts at self-justification. This desire for legitimacy placed important constraints upon the regime's range of action. It hardly ever practiced its repression nakedly, but cloaked its seizures of power behind the semilegal formulas of Institutional Acts and Decree Laws. It practiced torture in clandestine prisons and denied their existence, claiming that prisoners died in traffic accidents or "while trying to escape." In dealing with the press, the regime fabricated procedures that obscured the act of censorship. It lied about the existence of press restrictions and censored news of press censorship.

The regime's pursuit of legitimacy then had two general effects on the press. First, whether needing a free press as credible reporter, useful publicist, or genuine democratic participant, the regime's pursuit of legitimacy often made the press a more sensitive actor, a more politically valuable entity than it would have been had the authoritarian regime simply disdained legitimacy. Second, the pursuit of legitimacy affected the way the regime sought to control the press, that is, by intervening on a massive scale, but always behind the scenes.

In summary, several of the essential features of the military regime were particularly salient in its relationship with the press. First, by devertebrating the legal system, the regime made it difficult—for the press as much as for any other actor in civil society—to mount legal challenges. The changing legal setting also made it difficult even to be sure of what counted as legal, for legal activities now included things that were unconstitutional but justified by an Institutional Act. Second, through direct and generalized repression, the regime required the press to reassess the dangers of direct challenge. Repression changed the calculus of risk. Third, internal divisions made the regime difficult to read or predict. One could be made a pawn in a larger struggle, but just whose pawn might not be clear. Finally, the pursuit of legitimacy placed important constraints upon the regime, even at times when there was no opposition to counterbalance the regime. This made the press a more sensitive entity and affected the way it was restricted. The next chapter will provide a portrait of the press, to complete the context for an analysis of the full array of restrictions imposed by the regime upon it.

4

THE PRESS: MAINSTREAM AND ALTERNATIVE

THE BRAZILIAN PRESS under the 1964–1985 regime was quite diverse but can be divided into two general categories: mainstream *(imprensa grande)* and alternative *(imprensa alternativa)*. The two kinds of publications had different goals, styles, readerships, organizational structures, and methods of financing. While this division into mainstream and alternative was fundamental, it was also informal and inexact, with a substantial overlap of experiences and actors, as well as some shared professional organizations. The structures and resources characteristic of each category shaped how state-imposed restrictions were experienced and what responses emerged.

There is no politically neutral language for the division between mainstream and alternative. The term *mainstream* implies representative or majority, though it may merely be the dominant or most commercially successful. Alternative implies critical, though it may simply be deviant or idiosyncratic. As with the term responsible press, attention must be given to how and by whom these labels are used.

No publication ever had to register as either mainstream or alternative, and there are cases where the distinction is not helpful. The *Tribuna da Imprensa,* for example, had a traditional format and a long history of being a conventional daily newspaper, but also a reputation for such scandal-mongering and stretching of the truth that it hardly fit into mainstream notions of probity and verity. On the other hand, the famous satirical newspaper *Pasquim,* for many the classic example of the alternative press, was so egregiously sexist and persistently racist that one has to ask, alternative to what?

Moreover, the crime tabloids, with their gory photographs and sensational headlines, may have been covering more of the actual daily news of Brazilian society than the major reputable organs.[1]

The distinction between the categories is also blurred because many journalists were working for both types of publications simultaneously. Press umbrella organizations and associations also included publications from both categories, and all publications were formally subject to the same laws. Hence, while the division between mainstream and alternative was one of the primary defining characteristics of the press scene in Brazil, that division was not precise, and there was substantial shared experience.

THE MAINSTREAM PRESS

The mainstream press was made up of the traditional dailies of the major cities. Those with national reputations and the largest circulations were in São Paulo and Rio de Janeiro: the *Estado de São Paulo*, the *Folha de São Paulo*,[2] *O Globo*, and the *Jornal do Brasil*, as well as the *Correio da Manhã* before its demise in 1969. The major cities also had other daily papers such as the *Tribuna da Imprensa* and *O Dia*. Every state capital and medium-sized city also had its own newspaper, although these were of more variable quality. Some of the more prominent were the *Estado do Parana*, the *Diário de Pernambuco*, the *Estado da Minas*, and the *Correio Brasiliense*.

Circulation and Readership

One of the striking features of the Brazilian press has been its small readership. Brazil stands out as having one of the worst income-distribution profiles, one of the highest levels of business profitability, and one of the lowest levels of newspaper readership, which in Brazil has been low not only in comparison with industrialized nations but with other developing and Latin American countries as well. In 1972, for example, the Brazilian press issued 37 newspapers per 1,000 inhabitants, compared with Argentina's 154 newspapers per 1,000 inhabitants.[3] This consistently low level of readership may be due to several factors. First, reading a daily newspaper has not been part of mass culture in Brazil. Another factor is high rates of illiteracy. Brazil's 1974 illiteracy rate of 36 percent was considerably worse than Argentina's 7 percent.[4] Poverty has been another factor limiting readership. A newspaper becomes a luxury when the minimum wage is insufficient for satisfying minimum needs.

In recent decades there has also been increasing competition from television and radio,[5] which are indisputably the principal means of disseminating information and entertainment in Brazil. Newspapers are a means of elite communication,[6] although there are also crime tabloids and scandal sheets. And there have been some late night talk shows of comparatively high quality that are used by different groups within the political elite to communicate with one another.[7] But essentially, television and radio are the mass media, while the mainstream newspapers are read by the more educated and affluent.

The relatively small readership is perhaps evidence of a failure to expand circulation and reach a larger audience, or on the other hand of a deliberate strategy. M. F. Nascimento Brito, owner of the *Jornal do Brasil,* asserted in a 1976 interview that "We have a genuine tendency to be a newspaper which influences the ruling classes—political, economic, cultural. Our aim is circulation not among the masses, but among the prestigious." He presented this as a "technical option" rather than elitism, in that it means producing a specific kind of newspaper.[8] While Brito's remarks may have been self-serving, they also offer some truth. Given the tremendous social and economic cleavages in Brazil—with respect to purchasing power and education, among other things—it may indeed be hard to produce a newspaper that can reach the majority and the elite simultaneously. Newspapers have their own niches. Circulation has been relatively small—in comparison to newspaper readership in countries at a similar stage of development, or to television viewership in Brazil—but it has been constant, and influential beyond its numbers.

The disproportionate importance of newspapers relative to their circulation arises from several factors. It is the elite who are communicating with each other via newspapers. Data, analyses, criticisms, accusations, judgments, and rumors are delivered to the elite by this medium, and newspapers therefore have the power to affect elite debates. Newspapers are also read by those who produce the mass media. Television news is shaped by newspaper coverage and selection of stories, thereby also extending the influence of newspapers beyond their immediate readers.[9] Furthermore, the major newspapers are cultural artifacts in themselves, distinct and identifiable icons even among those who do not read them regularly. Newspapers are an elite media in Brazil and always have been, but they produce repercussions well beyond their immediate readership.

Content and Quality

The appearance and format of Brazil's mainstream dailies from before the 1964 coup through to the present would be entirely familiar to a U.S. reader; indeed, both U.S. and Brazilian newspapers follow the same international models. International news and national news, including political news, are placed in a front section. City news and police reports are at the back. Separate pages, or sometimes special sections, are devoted to economics (business news, commodity prices, other financial information), sports, culture or entertainment, and occasionally education, medicine, and science. The newspapers are visually sophisticated, using the most modern printing technology and graphics.[10]

The style of reporting is likewise entirely recognizable. The dominant pattern is the lead and "the five w's" (referred to in Brazilian journalism texts by their English abbreviation, as though to imply a truly technical formula). The goal of discovering the who, what, when, where, and why is accompanied by a commitment to objective neutrality, and material is presented in the short, direct paragraphs of international journalistic prose.

Alongside this paradigm is a body of criticism of its results: that newspapers reduce social trends to isolated facts, obscuring the social-structural sources and interrelatedness of social trends, and place excessive emphasis upon individual holders of formal power. Journalism texts include instruction on the five w's approach, but also include a critique of this ubiquitous style.

The major newspapers at the time of the 1964 coup produced competent news coverage, but they were conventional and rarely critical of the existing order. International news coverage, always on the front page, was almost entirely purchased from international agencies.[11] Coverage of national politics concerned mainly the activities of political parties, often focusing on their ceremonial affairs. There were daily accounts of the honors accorded to or committee positions filled by party members. By contrast, little was available on such issues as public health, working conditions, living standards, housing, and education. While some newspapers had dependable columns analyzing political events (such as Carlos Castello Branco's in the *Jornal do Brasil*), others, including the *Folha de São Paulo*, lacked even an editorial page. Presentation of local news was rarely undertaken in a critical fashion, despite the difficult urban and social problems of the time. One finds instead traffic reports and surveys of potholes. Cultural news dealt with visiting ballet troupes, chamber music performances, Hollywood stars, and the like, and much less, for example, with Brazilian popular music or contemporary film.

Mainstream newspapers were providing general reporting but little independent investigation. After reviewing several years' worth of the major mainstream newspapers of the period, one is left with a feeling of surprise that these uncritical and uncombative publications would be viewed by the military regime as threats, and deemed worthy of censorship.

Political Identity and Mission

The major mainstream newspapers were classically liberal in their style and content, as well as in their self-defined political identity in support of the status quo. This was reflected not only in the editorial line followed on many issues but also explicitly asserted by representatives of each of the four newspapers with a national circulation, the *Folha de São Paulo*, the *Jornal do Brasil*, the *Estado de São Paulo*, and *O Globo*.

The *Folha de São Paulo* did not have the prominence in the 1960s that it later acquired, but it was significant enough to be monitored and pressured by the military regime. Boris Casoy was its editor-in-chief during some of its most difficult confrontations with the government. In Casoy's estimation, "The newspaper, like myself, has always been in favor of market capitalism, liberalism, the bourgeoisie." Thus it would generally support protection of human rights—"human rights is a universal issue, it has no ideology"—but it did not support any type of agrarian reform or substantial change in the market system.[12]

The *Jornal do Brasil* was similarly characterized by its owner, Brito, in a 1976 interview as "a newspaper which defends private initiative, is of liberal tendency and conservative inclination; . . . it is a newspaper which believes in the force of ideas and not the ideas of force. . . . Lastly, we do not believe in socialism without dictatorship or in capitalism without democracy."[13] An example of not challenging the status quo was the *Jornal do Brasil*'s approach to the return of political exiles in 1979. Walter Fontoura was editor of the *Jornal do Brasil* when the government passed the Amnesty Law permitting the return of individuals who had been charged with crimes against national security and exiled from the country. As Fontoura readily acknowledged, many of these charges may have been fabricated or based upon statements obtained under torture. Thus, at the time of the return, there was some debate among *Jornal do Brasil* journalists about how to handle the story. The section covering the story was to include a photograph of each returning exile and a list of the charges against that individual. Some of the newspaper's journalists wanted to list the charges in the subjunctive tense, to underscore the contention that these charges were mere claims, perhaps entirely unfounded, and not to be reported as fact. Fontoura, however, insisted that an accusation is an accusation, a thing in itself, with its own objective existence: "For me, it didn't matter if the accusation was obtained at the cost of torture. The accusation still existed. Now, if it was true that the accusation was gotten under torture—well, that was for the accused to prove, to come defend." In the end, the indicative tense was used to identify the charges.[14]

The *Estado de Sao Paulo* was a traditional bastion of the mainstream conservative press. Before the 1964 coup people joked that the União Democratica Nacional, one of the major political parties, had in the *Estado de São Paulo* its own major newspaper, to which the retort was: no, the *Estado de São Paulo* had in the UDN its own political party.

Although it later faced prior censorship from the military regime, the *Estado de São Paulo* was an early supporter of the coup against President Goulart. The newspaper also maintained a consistently conservative approach in its handling of international news. Following the 1968 left-wing military coup in Peru, news from Peru and Castro's Cuba appeared on the same page as Eastern European news. This was, in effect, a "behind the Iron Curtain" page, while news from all other Latin American nations was grouped together elsewhere.

The newspaper most famously supportive of the military government was *O Globo,* part of the vast media empire controlled by business magnate Roberto Marinho. In 1976 Evandro Carlos de Andrade, the newspaper's editor-in-chief, defined *O Globo*'s objectives in this way: "It aspires to the continual perfection of the democratic regime in Brazil, but at the same time it is aware of the difficulties of this project. It tries to be a newspaper which makes criticisms, but whose spirit is not destructive. *O Globo* would not have disseminated, for example, the Pentagon Papers."[15]

Internal Organization

The internal organization of these publications was vertical, and their hierarchies clear. The owners were the final, if distant, authority. Editors-in-chief wielded actual power and responsibility in the day-to-day running of the newspapers. The top level of the editorial staff participated in many important decisions. When disputes occurred they were resolved by deferring to the person one rung up the ladder of authority. The reporters were at the bottom of this hierarchy, with little autonomy or even input, and well aware of their powerlessness. While the vertical organizational structure determined that many decisions were made hierarchically, this did not mean that there were not conflicts between or within any level. The editors in particular seem to have been caught between conflicting commitments and allegiances.

The number of owners was small. Whatever their commitment to the press, they were for the most part businesspeople. All the owners of larger mainstream newspapers were also involved in other business ventures. Like their other businesses, the newspapers had to be viable enterprises. The press is a business in Brazil, and it is the owners who are most connected to the business side.

Some owners were also involved in determining the content of their publications. This ranged from having the final say on the general editorial line to participating in some aspects of daily editorial decisions. Some newspapers were much more closely identified with their owners than others. *O Globo* was seen as Roberto Marinho's mouthpiece by the newspaper's staff as well as the public. The *Estado de São Paulo* was identified with generations of the Mesquita family, many of whom were involved in various aspects of the media.

But whether distant financial figures, or daily presences in the newsroom, in the vertically organized press the owners had the final say. Roberto Civita was a scion of another well-known publishing family, which owned Editora Abril (publisher of the major newsweekly *Veja*). Fifty-one percent of the now defunct news magazine *Realidade* was owned by Civita, who was closely involved in its production. Whenever a discussion with the magazine's staff became difficult, he would invoke his 51 percent to end the argument. He became known for his joke that *Realidade* was an editorial cooperative—with the difference that he had control of 51 percent of the votes.[16]

The next level in the vertical organization of the press was the editorial staff. This was the top echelon of the professional staff, yet it also had an internal hierarchy. Below the editor-in-chief and managing editor were the editors for international news, domestic politics, economics, urban affairs, sports, and so on. Their responsibilities encompassed daily decisions on content, coverage, emphasis, and tone.

These were the press actors with the strongest press identity. While the owners were also businesspeople who owned numerous and diverse enterprises, and the reporters were employees who often held other jobs, the editors were usually involved exclusively with the press. They might move from publication to publication, or from newspapers to television and back again, but they stayed within the press.[17] This was their profession and identity.

That identity, however, was not without its complications. On the one hand, editors had a strong interest in protecting their professional and institutional autonomy against any controlling power, whether owners or the state. They were motivated to some degree by wanting to get the news and to inform and further public debate, and they wanted to maintain the freedom to accomplish those tasks. On the other hand, they were employed by the owners, whom they needed to placate at the risk of losing their jobs. They also needed to avoid attracting the animosity of the state, which would jeopardize both the immense advertising revenues gained from diverse state sources as well as the benefits of having the state as a major news source. From inside tips and inclusion in press conferences, to simply obtaining official credentials for their journalists, editors could not afford to anger the state.

The top editors were part of an insiders' group. They exercised substantial power within their publications and had access to news many others did not have, yet they remained employed at the pleasure of the owners, and could function effectively, given the relations between press and state in

Brazil, only if they did not antagonize the state. This left them in a somewhat ambiguous position, feeling the pull of having to maintain their professional integrity and institutional autonomy, yet also needing, for both material and news resources, to stand with the owners and the state.

The base of this vertical organization was occupied by the reporters. They might enjoy their work, but they had no control over the final product, and they knew it. Because they were very poorly paid, most journalists held more than one job.[18] As the job market for trained journalists was inadequate, this often meant shifting into public relations for businesses or the government—often the same enterprises or offices one was simultaneously covering as a journalist.[19] There was also little job security for journalists. Few stayed with one newspaper for long. Even their physical workplaces were not necessarily safe, for their newspapers often barred representatives of journalists' unions from their premises, and the state planted police informers.[20]

There was clearly a gulf between the editorial staff and the reportorial staff. It took on different forms in different publications, but nowhere was there a sense of press solidarity. Journalists were more likely to portray themselves as "employees" against the editorial "management" and the owners, rather than as participants in a shared press identity.[21] That this was generally acknowledged as simply the way things were does not mean that it was not resented. Rather, us-against-them was precisely the sort of language deployed when disputes arose. Fed up with Civita's demands for rewrites, the riposte of the journalists at *Realidade* was, "Okay then, 51 percent, *you* do it."[22]

Finances

As businesses, the mainstream newspapers did not fare too badly in the 1964–1985 period. A 1976 article entitled "Our Newspapers and Their Businesses," published in the magazine *Visão*, reviewed data on finances, the importation of new equipment, and the construction of new headquarters. The *Visão* article concluded that the press as a business was doing relatively well in Brazil. It noted profit rates of 15 percent and stable demand from advertisers despite competition from television and radio.[23]

Because readership was so low, the revenue of the mainstream newspapers came more from advertising than from sales to readers (the international pattern was 50 percent from advertising and 50 percent from sales). In 1975 the Porto Alegre newspaper the *Correio do Povo* (described as "the oldest and most powerful paper in the south of the country") earned 68 percent of its income from advertising, 30 percent from sales. As its publishers readily admitted, "Without advertising the newspaper wouldn't survive." The *Estado do Parana* received 55 percent of its income from commercial advertisements, 15 percent from classified advertisements, and 30 percent from sales. The *Estado de São Paulo* reported that 79 percent of its income in 1974 was advertising related. In 1975 the figure was 78.8 percent, with approximately 17 percent of total revenue from sales.[24]

This revenue structure placed the newspapers at the mercy of their large advertisers, though press commentator Sérgio Caparelli offered an important qualifier with respect to private corporate advertisers: "One often hears advertisers described as a force of pressure on the contents of the major newspapers. This is not always the case, except on minor issues. On what really matters, the ideology of the owners of the traditional newspapers is very close or identical to the values, interests, and behavior of the dominant economic groups. The truth is that one as much as the other belongs to the same dominant class which uses the press as well as advertising to reproduce the conditions of its hegemonic situation."[25]

Of greater concern in the case of Brazil was the tremendous role of state advertising in generating newspaper revenue, estimated to account for 15 percent to 30 percent of the revenue of many major newspapers. Federal, state, and municipal governments bought newspaper space for all manner of public announcements, including the legally required publication of laws, decrees, regulations, and requests for bids on government projects. Sometimes government announcements were thinly veiled vehicles for electoral campaigning, in which the accomplishments of an administration were broadcast just prior to an election. In addition, because the state owned so many businesses, it also produced conventional advertising aimed at consumers. Government advertising, an enormous source of newspaper revenue, was thus available for the regime's tactical use. Newspaper advertising revenue was therefore vulnerable to state displeasure.[26]

Private advertising was also linked to the state, in that so many private businesses depended upon the state for business, services, or favors. A private company with a loan pending at a state-controlled bank might be instructed to reconsider where it was spending its advertising budget. Companies with state contracts were also vulnerable to such pressure. Even without direct instruction, a similarity of perspective might lead private advertisers to be amenable to the state's indication of disapproval toward one or another newspaper.[27] Although mainstream publications as a whole were financially viable, they were nonetheless quite vulnerable, given their dependence upon advertising over sales and upon state-generated revenue (either from government sources or from private sources readily influenced or pressured by the state).

The mainstream press, then, had a readership that was low in numbers but high in power and influence. The quality of the mainstream press was adequately professional, if conventional. Its project was clearly in support of the status quo, although this did not necessarily mean that it behaved cravenly toward the state. Its internal organization was strongly vertical and hierarchical, although the editors in particular were in a somewhat anomalous position, given their potentially conflicting commitments. And the mainstream press was financially stable, yet readily susceptible to pressure. It was established, conventional, and dominant, but not invulnerable or independent, and some of its most important actors were responding to multiple claims on their professional integrity.

THE ALTERNATIVE PRESS

The most comprehensive list of alternative publications in Brazil under the military regime, published in 1982, includes over eight hundred entries.[28] Politics, culture, humor, fiction, racial issues, feminism, gay rights, and community affairs were some of the subjects covered by the alternative press. Some alternative publications were ephemeral or appeared irregularly, while others were very professional and lasted for many years. Few had regular staffs or resources; many contributors moved from one publication to another. Among the better known and more successful alternative publications were *Pasquim, Opinião, Movimento, Coojornal, Versus, Em Tempo, Crítica, Repórter, EX, Brasil Mulher, Nós Mulheres,* and *Lampião*.

As a whole, these publications constituted a stable trend throughout the 1970s.[29] Individually, many came and went quite rapidly. The most durable was *Pasquim*, which started in 1968 and is still publishing. Much more typical were the innumerable publications that lasted but one issue. The alternative press was part of the cultural experimentation of the period, available to any who wanted to make the attempt. It was much more feasible than trying to launch anything in the mainstream press, and required little more than access to a mimeograph machine or rented time on the press equipment of a mainstream publication, and the donated labor of friends (who often were journalists).

These were small-fry publications (as is indicated by their nickname *nanico*, meaning midget), yet they suffered state harassment in myriad ways. Just as the uncontroversial content and coverage provided by the mainstream newspapers make it surprising that those publications were censored, so too does the small scale of many of the alternative publications make it odd that they were targets of the state's energetic animosity.

Circulation and Readership

The circulation of alternative publications varied enormously. Many were marketed in just one city and sold directly by their producers. Others had national circulations and a professional distribution system. One of the most successful was *Pasquim,* which had a national circulation that exceeded one hundred thousand. *Opinião*'s circulation was over fifty thousand, and *Movimento*'s over thirty thousand.[30] These figures may be a little lower than actual readership, for many people recall a copy of some favorite alternative publication being passed around to many readers when there were difficulties in purchasing an issue, either because the issue had sold out or because one did not want to be seen making the purchase.[31] Because of possible police scrutiny of mailing lists, subscribing could be risky. On several occasions the police tried to obtain copies of the list of *Movimento*'s subscribers. Purchasing alternative publications from a newsstand also had its risks, as newsstands were threatened and bombed for carrying certain alternative publications.

Whatever the actual numbers, the circulation of the alternative press was fairly restricted. Many have reproached the alternative press for this, saying that it merely served an alternative elite. Caparelli is one exponent of this critique:

> the alternative press was not a mass media. The style, carefully selected phrases, topics, contents, all together, made it the press of intellectuals, reaching only the vanguard of social movements. . . . it informed those who already had access to other sources of information and said what this privileged minority often already knew. The greater impasse is the lack of an alternative for the majority of the population, since those marginalized by the social, political, and economic system do not have at their disposal the alternative of this press: they have neither the economic capacity for its consumption nor the means to comprehend its contents, in most cases presented in a language accessible to an extremely small number of Brazilians.[32]

While this is an accurate assessment, it may nonetheless be unfair. The implication is that the alternative publications were less authentic because they were not read by the masses, or that they could make no contribution at all unless they were an absolute popular success. In the Brazilian context, this was an unrealistic standard, for the alternative press, like the mainstream press, was read by only the educated and affluent.[33] Whereas the mainstream press reached the conservative elite, the alternative press reached the oppositional elite. Neither was read by the majority. But the alternative press, one can argue, was significant beyond its numbers. It was essential in forming a political opposition, in offering a forum for debates, and in providing alternative sources of information.

And what were the costs of being popular? Luis Alberto Bettancourt became editor of *Repórter* after its first few issues and changed the publication's character dramatically. He offers the following assessment:

Repórter aimed to be popular, a rupture with the opposition press up to that time. The alternative press was more an alternative for the journalist than for the reader. It covered specific themes—torture, repression, denunciations. If you didn't already have these values and perspectives, you were not going to read this, you couldn't be seduced to. The alternative press was flat, a journalism of essays; . . . *Repórter* was intended to be an alternative for the reader, with price and topics to reach everyone. And we sold well, had the most sales of any opposition press for three years. . . . I prefer to call the alternative press the opposition press, because alternative implies marginal or minority, and I always speak for the majority. I am not the spokesperson of minorities—not Indians, not women, etc.[34]

Bettancourt worked at the same time for both *Repórter* and *O Globo* and asserts that he exercised the same journalistic standards for both. *Repórter,* however, is the best example of a sensationalist tabloid within the general rubric of the alternative press. Carefully prepared exposés of police brutality or police-sponsored terrorism in the first few issues gave way to gory or pornographic photo-essays in later issues. An issue promising coverage of overloaded, unsafe trains in Rio de Janeiro was in fact a photo-essay on a train accident, with the cover showing a close-up of a severed head and a headline urging the reader to see inside for pictures of the dismembered corpse. One of its final issues, for the 1981 Carnaval, consisted solely of lewd photographs. This may have been a best-seller, but in what sense was it an expression of political opposition? The question of content and quality merits further consideration before dismissing other alternative publications as irrelevantly elitist because of their small circulation.

Content and Quality

The alternative press is much harder to characterize than the mainstream press because of its great diversity. The mainstream was striving for conformity and its models of success were uncontested. The alternative press, on the other hand, was heterogeneous and actively sought new models. Its categories and criteria were broad and ill-defined because they were in the process of being defined. The results were extremely mixed—from superb journalism to absolute trash, from considered analysis to total foolishness.

At their best (and I have in mind *Opinião* and *Movimento,* but not only these), the alternative publications were simply superb. One looks in vain for their equal now. They provided investigative research on socially relevant topics, lengthy analysis of the issues, and good writing. There were exposés on corruption, conflicts of interest, and public health hazards, and features on topics not covered elsewhere, including the living and working conditions of the bulk of the population, reproductive health issues, corporate investments and practices, environmental hazards, and the destruction of the Amazon rainforest. Articles on the economy added explanations and critiques to the press releases from the economic ministries. Articles on politics addressed social conditions and identified internal party factions in addition to covering congressional debates and foreign news. *Movimento* experimented with "Cena Brasileira," a series describing the daily lives of people usually neglected by mainstream press coverage. This was a first of its kind, and has since been much copied. Foreign coverage came from sources that were otherwise unavailable, including translations from such publications as *Le Monde* and the *New York Review of Books*. Cultural articles covered Brazilian popular music, *cinema novo*, and contemporary Brazilian fiction and theater. Considerable space was also devoted to political cartoons and the use of parody, satire, irony, and sarcasm. A ludic approach was the hallmark of much of the alternative press, not only of the lampoons.

The writing was characterized by a conception of journalism different from that found in the mainstream press. Concern for the five w's was replaced by journalists' self-conscious relationship to their material and readers. There was more interpretation of the news and evaluation of the quality of the data, and a diversification of sources away from official channels.

There was also an effort to reveal and demystify the process of journalism itself. For example, the preliminary issue of *Repórter* reproduced on its second page one of the journal's proof-sheets (see fig. 1). A proof-sheet would have been a familiar sight to anyone active in journalism, but quite unfamiliar to others. On the proof-sheet were scribbled corrections and handwritten annotations concerning the size of the typeface, headline, and margins. The text itself contained a brief description of the journal's founders. Entitled "The Generation of Fear," it began: "We are a generation of journalists formed by AI-5, by paranoia."[35] The page was an exercise in self-revelation, of the identity of the journalists involved as well as of the process of producing *Repórter*.

The quality of the alternative press, however, was quite variable. Some publications were of very high quality, while others could be quite poor. Along the continuum of quality, considered analysis deteriorated into pop Marxism and sweeping generalizations unconstrained by the data. Careful journalism was replaced by the desire to do away with the journalist as filter or mediator. There was an elevation of the raw or *cru*, typified by transcriptions from open microphones. Investigation was sometimes displaced by sensationalism. Willingness to examine society became an apolitical fascination with trends and behavior. Politically challenging humor was replaced by graphically sexist and racist humor. Liberty was license, and wound up being exploitive.

Although there was a wide range of quality in the alternative press, the

[A GERAÇÃO DO MEDO]

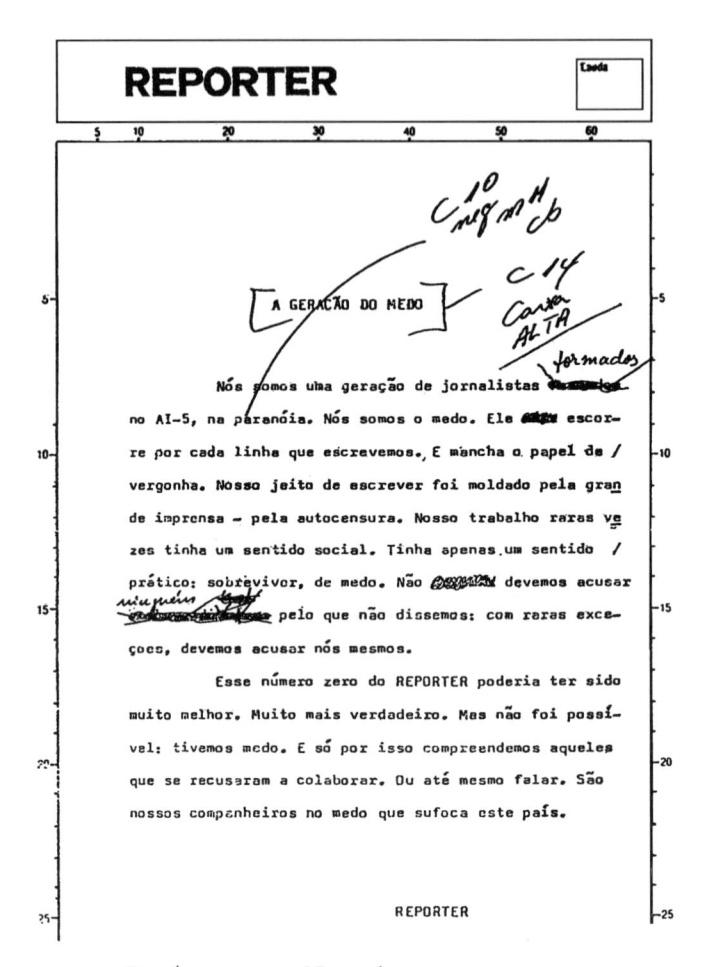

Nós somos uma geração de jornalistas formados no AI-5, na paranóia. Nós somos o medo. Ele escorre por cada linha que escrevemos. E mancha o papel da vergonha. Nosso jeito de escrever foi moldado pela grande imprensa – pela autocensura. Nosso trabalho raras vezes tinha um sentido social. Tinha apenas um sentido prático: sobreviver, de medo. Não devemos acusar pelo que não dissemos: com raras exceções, devemos acusar nós mesmos.

Esse número zero do REPORTER poderia ter sido muito melhor. Muito mais verdadeiro. Mas não foi possível: tivemos medo. E só por isso compreendemos aqueles que se recusaram a colaborar. Ou até mesmo falar. São nossos companheiros no medo que sufoca este país.

REPORTER

FIG. 1. REPÓRTER, no. 0, November 1977

genre as a whole can be credited for its experimentalism. It broadened the options available to the press in Brazil, in a period when journalism was restricted to the traditional elite mainstream dailies.

Political Identity and Mission

These were essentially opposition publications, but "opposition" was a very broad category. When the regime was at its most repressive, all press actors could claim a similar identity of opposition. As the journalist Carlos Alberto Sardemburg remarked, because there was just one river, all the boats floated in the same direction.[36] Some publications openly attacked the regime and its powerholders and decisions; others were against the entire status quo, from the underlying economic model and social organization to behavioral trends and literary tastes.

The projects of the alternative papers varied considerably, but having a further project beyond conventional reporting was what they had in common. Many of the publications articulated their project in their initial—sometimes their only—issue. The *Almanaque Biotônico Vitalidade* (Rio de Janeiro, 1976) was "against inertia, against the law of gravity, against againstness." *Cenoura* (Recife, 1979) presented itself as a magazine that "conceives of the text and its creation as expressions of pleasure. The pleasure of the text. The pleasure of the pre-text. Of pretext. The pleasure of intelligence. The pleasure of politics." *Cordão* (Santa Catarina, 1976) declared that its aim was not long-term survival but the promotion of "literature as an instrument of happiness and of social and human betterment ... a challenge to all to participate." *Laconicus* (Rio Grande do Sul, 1973) described itself as "a journal which, if it offers no help to improve the situation, at least serves as an opening for all those youths who suddenly discover themselves lost in the middle of an arena complete with wolves dressed in sheep's clothing."[37] In their preliminary issue, published in July 1975, the journalists who began *Movimento* explained that they were "a bit tired of journalism in the mainstream press; believe[d] that the task of the journalist is not merely to describe the world, but to help to transform it; and that the major journalistic businesses have almost all accustomed themselves to a situation of creeping censorship which has been suffocating the Brazilian press for some time."[38]

The alternative press meant to address all these challenges. There was, throughout the alternative press, a mixture and at times a confusion of motives and standards. The value of the alternative press was sometimes said to lie in its mere existence as a force bucking the tide of the mainstream press and opposing those elements of the political culture fostered by the regime. At other times the alternative press held itself up to a standard of actual social effectiveness, demanding results in increased public awareness or social change. And sometimes the alternative press seemed to consider itself worthwhile simply for providing a highly gratifying personal and professional outlet for its participants.

Internal Organization

Very few people actually held full-time jobs with the alternative press. Many journalists contributed articles, but almost none of the publications had the resources for a sizable paid staff. For the most part, work on alternative publications was accomplished in conjunction with other jobs. The editorial councils of the publications could be quite large, however, with decision making ostensibly shared by many people. As the alternative press sought to redefine news and recreate journalism in a manner distinct from the patterns set by the mainstream press, it also pursued experiments in internal organization to escape the rigid hierarchies of the privately owned dailies.

Although the establishment of cooperatives and work collectives was the goal, these did not always work successfully. Experiments in nonhierarchical structure did not necessarily do away with power games. *Movimento* was started by some of the staff who left *Opinião* following a dispute over the owner's alleged excessive control of that publication. Yet *Movimento*'s staff meetings, in which everyone would participate in decisions, were also remembered by more than one participant as "a game of marked cards."[39] Key players would have prepared their allies ahead of time, and open debate could be quite limited. Eventually *Em Tempo* was begun following a staff rupture at *Movimento* over these issues.

Remuneration, for those who were paid, was quite low. Journalists who worked exclusively for the alternative press earned much less than their colleagues at mainstream publications. The majority held several jobs. Resources were also scarce for other aspects of the production and distribution of alternative publications, and this affected the journalists' work experience. For example, *Opinião*'s correspondent in Brasília had a desk and telephone in a corner of the office of another business; this had been arranged by agreement between *Opinião*'s owner and a business associate.[40]

With minimal resources and low pay, in addition to the political risk, anyone who worked for the alternative press was quite aware that he or she was making sacrifices and taking part in a mission. The sense of being a member of a team, in contrast to the identity of employee in the mainstream press, is well remembered by many of the participants in the alternative press. And while the actual staffs were small, the number of contributors was much larger. Such participation had returns of its own. As was noted in a 1975 issue of *Unidade*, the newspaper of the São Paulo journalists' union, "The professional, in the majority of cases still earning a living from a traditional newspaper, seeks in the small press some intellectual compensation, escape from rigid commercial patterns, the struggle for the plain liberty of the press, the defense of national culture, and even a journalism closer to people, free of business impositions and the patterning of news determined by national and international news services."[41]

Finances

The alternative press was well aware of the contradictions of capitalism, of the pitfalls of becoming dependent upon advertisers for revenue (particularly upon advertising revenue from a state that they opposed), and of the negative experience of hierarchy and editorial control by owners. Several alternative publications therefore set out to diversify both ownership and revenue, creating cooperatives such as *Coojornal* of Rio Grande do Sul, or selling shares to participating journalists, as did *Movimento*. In contrast to mainstream dependence upon commercial and state advertising, revenue for many of the publications came almost entirely from sales. *Versus* earned 90 percent of its revenue from sales, *Movimento* 91 percent, *Pasquim* 75 percent, *Coojornal* 75 percent, and *De Fato* 70 percent.[42] The remaining revenue in many cases was not from advertisements, but from fund-raisers such as concerts or shows.

Although most of the revenue of the alternative press came from sales, this did not free it from state financial pressure. When the state prevented sales, for instance through confiscation of an issue, it could cause enough financial damage to close a publication. Without a product to sell, many alternative publications, already marginal operations, were quickly eliminated. This became a major threat, particularly to the smaller journals.[43] Lawyers for *Repórter* even condemned its frequent confiscations, which often occurred without any formal authorization, as "a drastic violence against private property, which is one of the principal pillars of our system."[44]

The alternative press, then, was highly diverse. It included much writing of high quality, but also considerable nonsense. Its experiments were notable and challenging, whether in journalistic style and coverage or in internal organization and revenue structure. As a whole, the alternative publications constituted a significant trend in the Brazilian press, but only infrequently did any one of them get beyond being a single-issue "midget."

PROFESSIONAL ORGANIZATIONS

A final aspect to characterizing the period's press, whether mainstream or alternative, is to identify the various professional organizations to which its practitioners belonged. These ranged from local unions for journalists to international organizations primarily for the owners of the mainstream press. Though helpful in voicing press concerns, none of these associations could begin to be powerful enough to protect the press when confronted by the military regime.

The InterAmerican Press Association

For publishers and owners of the mainstream press, the key group was the InterAmerican Press Association (IAPA). Its members were (and are) major newspapers throughout the hemisphere. IAPA, which gave considerable attention to the press in Latin America, held regular meetings at which press issues were discussed, offered awards to its members for various accomplishments, and monitored attacks upon press freedom. While the organization lacked any substantial political power, it could cause embarrassment by expressing international solidarity for the press in nations where journalistic freedom was not secure.

IAPA members in Brazil were almost entirely from the mainstream press, and there was little contact with the alternative press. The chairmanship changed hands on a regular basis and was held for a time under the military regime by Ruy Mesquita of the *Estado de São Paulo*. While IAPA itself might have lacked the power to be an effective lobbyist, the organization was used as an international forum. Mesquita undoubtedly gained international attention for some of the press restrictions in Brazil through his frequent speeches at IAPA meetings. IAPA was one of the international audiences that the military regime was aware of in avoiding closure of certain newspapers.[45] Thus IAPA appears to have been an international forum for the press and something of a deterrent to more aggressive state action against some newspapers, but this protection existed primarily for the traditional daily newspapers, which best fit the international mold.

The Brazilian Press Association

The Brazilian Press Association (Associação Brasileira da Imprensa, ABI) was the leading professional organization. Its members included journalists and editors from all over the country. From its headquarters in Rio de Janeiro, the ABI sponsored many seminars and courses for its members. It was concerned with the press as a profession and as an institution, including improving journalistic standards, making training available, and defending freedom of the press.

By the late 1970s the ABI was among the leading professional organizations in Brazilian civil society, together with such groups as the National Conference of Brazilian Bishops (Conferência Nacional dos Bispos do Brasil, CNBB) and the Brazilian Bar Association (Ordem dos Advogados do Brasil, OAB), which could express dissent toward the regime without being susceptible to a blanket accusation of subversion. Despite a sometimes less than independent past, the ABI had an unassailable reputation. A regime seeking middle-class legitimacy could not very well attack it. The representatives of freedom of the press, like the representatives of Catholicism and of the rule of law, would have to be attacked carefully, by attacking them as false representatives while avoiding attacking what they represented.

The ABI was perhaps the most formal channel regularly open to anyone in the press with a grievance against the regime's restrictions on press freedom. In these cases it was a repository for collective memory, a place to lodge a complaint, and an organization that would in turn lodge a complaint with the regime. It often appears, however, to have been most effective in its alliances with other major groups in civil society, and less effective in the nitty-gritty work of defending particular journalists or publications. As a leading professional organization, the ABI became the conduit for press alliances with other groups in civil society. By the time of the *abertura*, the trio of the ABI, the CNBB, and the OAB could be counted upon to voice a protest against the human rights violations and other forms of repression practiced by the authoritarian state, and to host forums on such issues as political amnesty.

Unions

Journalists' unions were found all over the country but were everywhere weak. Like other unions throughout Brazil, they were subject to an onerous burden of state regulation and had not developed an independent voice or forum. They were often exclusively concerned with issues relating to pay and regulation of work.

The unions gradually became a target of journalists' activism, and in the mid- to late 1970s progressive slates won election in São Paulo, Brasília, and Rio de Janeiro. After these electoral victories, the unions became more important as bases for debate, solidarity, and activism. They never had extensive power or prestige, but following the elections they could be a useful forum for journalists. When Audalio Dantas won the leadership of the São Paulo union just before the murder of Vladimir Herzog in October 1975, he was able to make the union a locus for the outrage and protest over that death. The union's newspaper, *Unidade*, began at that time to direct less attention to salary issues and more to the role of the press in society and the restrictions imposed by the regime.

The unions, however, were not equal in strength or in their inclination to protect journalists from the state. In March 1976, within five months of Herzog's murder, two journalists from Rio de Janeiro were secretly detained by the military authorities. The ABI made an effort to locate them and issued a statement pointing out the lies in the official account of their whereabouts. The journalists' union in São Paulo offered its solidarity, but the union in Rio de Janeiro did not even issue a statement, on the grounds that this would be have been "inopportune." The president of the journalists' union in Rio de Janeiro limited himself to stating that "although no love is lost between me and [the two detained journalists], I am in contact with civil and military authorities for the swiftest liberation possible of these two union members."[46]

These were the different associations available to press actors. IAPA was primarily for owners and those who followed the international press. It did not address the Brazilian public, but it was of concern to the regime. The ABI was open to a wider membership and was recognized as speaking for the Brazilian press as a whole. It was most effective in standing with other leading organizations in civil society. Unions were just emerging at this time into a new, more independent stage. All of these organizations were available for attempts at publicizing abuses of the press, but none were very effective in getting the regime to stop its harassment or restrictions. None could get the regime to respect the language of press freedom in its own constitution.

The press in Brazil at the time of the military regime was diverse and can be divided into the two categories, mainstream and alternative. Although this was not a strict or complete division, the two kinds of press were characterized by differences in goals, readership, content, internal organization, and financing. The mainstream press was successful by conventional international standards; the alternative press constituted an important opportunity for experimentation. Neither type, however, would have seemed to most people such a threat to the military regime as to warrant the expenditure of the energy required for severe or systematic harassment or restrictions, yet both were subjected to such actions, which will now be examined.

II

THE SYSTEMS
OF CENSORSHIP

5

THE MANY FORMS OF PRESS CONTROL

THE 1964–1985 MILITARY REGIME in Brazil developed and used many devices other than direct censorship in its attempts to control the press. With a variety of methods for restricting the press at its disposal, the regime could select and tailor its tactics to any particular target while also minimizing its own bureaucratic and political costs. Although never formally denying freedom of the press, the regime could effectively obstruct the ability of the press to practice that freedom. The press was vulnerable on many fronts—not only financially and professionally but also in terms of the personal safety of its members.

Measures to restrict and discipline the press were used at all levels of the regime. On the one hand, antagonism to the press seems to have been so widespread in the regime that harassment was the general orientation. On the other hand, there is also evidence of the construction of covert strategies to control the press yet escape detection. Decisions were made at the highest level to undertake such practices.

PERVASIVE ANIMOSITY

Animosity toward the press was pervasive throughout the regime. There was no need for a single centralized decision to shun, obstruct, or harass the press, precisely because that was the predisposition of most officials. A policy of dispersed harassment of the press probably would not have succeeded had it needed to be hierarchically enforced. Officials' statements about the press from the period, as well as recent remarks made by former officials, range from disdain to paranoia, whether expressed by civilian or military members of the government, in the executive or legislative branches, at the state or federal level, or in the armed forces.

Congressional Representative José Bonifácio, leader of the progovernment ARENA party in the House of Representatives, observed in 1976 that "Almost all the journalists [who cover the House of Representatives] are cryptocommunists, especially those with mustaches."[1] In 1977 Bonifácio insisted that "The Brazilian newspapers aren't communist. The communists are the reporters who put the communist line into the newspapers. And this problem is unsolvable because the directors of the newspapers do not pay attention to what the newspapers are saying."[2] That divisive observation, pitting journalists against the press establishments they worked for, was heard in many other quarters.

General Antonio Bandeira, chief of the Federal Police Department (which was responsible for censorship), dismissed the entire media in 1974 in the following terms: "All the communications media are committed to the propaganda campaign and to psychosocial actions in an insidious and unscrupulous manner, distorting events and compromising individuals as it suits them, through publications and broadcasts, messages and images, with the deliberate objective of destroying the sacred values of the community and of undermining the confidence of the people in the government and in the current political regime."[3] Such a broad condemnation, which admitted no distinctions between various press entities, fit in well with national security ideology.

The press became an easy scapegoat for various ills in national politics, the economy, foreign relations, and other areas. Congressional Representative Minoro Myamoto asserted in 1979 that "Journalists do nothing more than foment rumors so as to create a climate of tension. The political crisis which the nation is experiencing was created in the editorial offices of the principal newspapers of the country . . . [They are also guilty] of provoking inflation."[4] Konder Reis, military-appointed governor of the state of Santa Catarina, charged that the "infiltrated" press presented a "caricature" of Brazil to the outside world, "as though we are a nation dominated by a totalitarian regime and the enemy of liberty."[5]

The rancor of the period has not dissipated with time. In 1990 General Meira Mattos declared, "I don't like the press. I don't talk to the press. They're incapable of reproducing what you say. The goal of the press is sensationalism, not truth. Official decrees should be sufficient [for informing the public]. Anything that needs to be divulged should be announced, and that's that."[6] Jarbas Passarinho, a former colonel and senator and a Cabinet minister in the military regime, vividly recalls his distrust of the press: "Just look at the name, *Pasquim* [lampoon]. The name *signifies* bad intentions. Their goal was to demoralize."[7]

The individuals cited here occupied a broad range of civilian and military positions of authority within the regime. They were also relatively high in the regime's hierarchies, and as such were more likely to have left behind a record of their statements and opinions. The historical record is often weighted in favor of such spokespersons, but it includes other evidence as well.

Among the many cases from the period that exhibit the general animosity toward members of the press is the following story from Belo Horizonte. On an April evening in 1974, the journalist Rogerio Alberto Cavalcanti witnessed police beating a drunken man in the street. While passing by, Cavalcanti commented to his companions that the man was getting a "real bruising." The police heard the remark and demanded to see his documents. When they realized he was a journalist, their response was, "Oh, you're a journalist, are you? Then come and get a different coverage." He was surrounded by six officers, who began beating him. One officer was injured when Cavalcanti dodged a blow and the officer's fist hit a wall. The police immediately took Cavalcanti into custody, charging him with assaulting the officer.[8]

Because animosity toward the press was so widespread within the regime, it required no central direction or coordination. And in addition to this general animus toward journalists, there was also a focused, elaborate, and sophisticated effort to obstruct the press. One of the starkest examples was the strategy carefully outlined in a document prepared by the army's intelligence branch, CIEx, in September 1978. This document proposed such tactics as exhaustive financial audits designed to cripple the press without the regime ever having to admit its intentions.[9] The CIEx document asserted that the beauty of audits—especially of small, informal publications not likely to have kept careful books or to be in full compliance with financial rules and regulations—was precisely that no one could say that the state was attacking freedom of expression. Furthermore, the document stated, audits were much quicker than judicial means when attempting to silence or punish annoying publications:

With an aim to obstruct the disgraceful activity of the contentious alternative press, we offer practical suggestions which will produce satisfactory results if adopted. It would be a pure fantasy to consider a course of action which did not take into account as an important factor the current political juncture of the country, which in this area presupposes ample liberty of the press. No effort is made to analyze the merit of this position, but rather to take it as a given fact which has been exploited with total irresponsibility by the communists, especially in the alternative press, where they exercise almost absolute control.

Another factor which should be remembered is that economic sanctions have a more rapid, direct, and positive effect upon any publication than do judicial actions which, due to the characteristics of our legislation, are apt to be excessively prolonged.

Given these concerns, the following suggestions, which do not restrict the liberty of thought directly, are valid.[10]

There followed a list of measures to control the press. In addition to audits to be conducted by the security forces, immediate measures included obligatory full disclosure of the sources of a publication's funds, and prohibiting anyone facing charges under the National Security Law from participating in the business or editorial affairs of their publication. The document also recommended that the law be amended so that a publication's registration could be canceled whenever there was proof of indebtedness to the national treasury (as in the case of unpaid taxes): "Once its registration is canceled, a publication becomes clandestine, and therefore subject to confiscation." The document observed that "the great majority of newspapers would not be able to withstand a demand of this nature, in that many of them, or almost all, are in debt to the National Treasury, which always rolls these debts over for social reasons. The proposal is useful and objective, because it reaches all the newspapers and periodicals via economic sanctions, without clearly configuring restrictions on the liberty of thought of the press." The proposed medium- and long-term measures for controlling the press were also quite comprehensive, and targeted, among other things, the job market, journalism schools, and press laws.

There was nothing subtle in the document about concerns over secrecy and legitimacy, or about the regime's antagonism toward the press. The intent was clear: to attack the press, but to do so in an indirect manner, so as to be swift, effective, and devastating, and yet covert. Troublesome publications were to be destroyed without the regime ever having to declare restrictions upon freedom of the press, for with the *abertura* in full swing, freedom of the press had to be accepted as a given, as unfortunate as that was in CIEx's eyes. CIEx knew just what it was doing. Its goal was press restriction, its strategy financial harassment. This strategy was adopted to hide the regime's intentions and cover its weak spot of legitimacy.

Many of the document's suggestions were already in use by the time it was prepared in 1978. Except for a few innovations, CIEx was merely systematizing the regime's tactics. The alternative journal *Repórter*, as well as being closed down several times and prosecuted under the National Security Law, was subject in June 1978 to an inquiry by the Federal Revenues Office, which wanted to know the source of the journal's funding, the identity of its shareholders, and whether any debts were owed to the national treasury. That same month auditors from the Ministry of Labor also began to appear weekly, "just to see whether everything was in order."[11]

The alternative journal *Versus* underwent several audits involving a number of official agencies. In 1978 one of the journal's major shareholders was summoned to the National Intelligence Service—not to the Federal Revenues Office, as should have been the case—to clarify the state of its finances. A detailed financial investigation was begun, which involved agents from the Federal Police, the Ministry of Labor, and the Federal Revenues Office. The investigation extended to reviewing the financial records of shareholders' relatives.

Complying with official audits consumed both time and resources, particularly for smaller publications. When the auditors included not only tax authorities but agents of the intelligence and security forces as well, audits were also frightening. The cases indicate no independent financial reasons to justify the selection of these publications for audits. These measures were purely punitive.

The use of selective and exhaustive audits amounted to political persecution disguised as routine fiscal review. This was another case of the regime's appropriation and misuse of conventional procedures to forward its goals of restriction and repression. As was indicated by the CIEx document, which merely codified existing practice, the intent was to hamper the press not only forcefully but secretly, thus obscuring the regime's purposes. The dual objectives of protecting the legitimacy of the regime while destroying freedom of the press were well served by this strategy.

BUSINESS PRESSURES

The CIEx document is notable for its explicit self-consciousness. Many long-standing practices of the regime toward the press parallel the strategies outlined in that document. Given the large role of the Brazilian state in businesses of all kinds, including the press, there were many opportunities for the state to interfere in press finances: by withholding advertising, denying loans from state banks, refusing licenses to import equipment or newsprint, or seizing print runs. All of these were well-established means of bringing effective pressure on the press without overtly restricting formal press freedom.

Blocking advertising revenue could be accomplished in several ways. If a publication was directly dependent upon state advertisements, these could simply be suspended. If a publication had managed to minimize its use of state advertising, then the regime could pressure the publication's private advertisers to cancel their advertisements. Virtually any business was susceptible to such measures. With such tactics, the regime could reach both mainstream and alternative publications.

The Mainstream Press: "Always Attentive to Conversations with the General"

The percentage of advertising in mainstream newspapers that originated from state sources was very large. Federal, state, and municipal governments, and state companies, spent sizable amounts on advertising. State-sponsored advertisements encompassed, among other things, announcements of vaccination programs, changes in interest rates at public banks, solicitations of bids for construction work, the sale of goods, celebratory proclamations related to state-funded projects, and promotional messages from incumbents just before election time. In addition, official decrees had to be published in both the *Diário Oficial* and in a major national newspaper. All of this was paid advertising; governments were very large customers of the press.

Waldir de Góes, former managing director of the *Jornal do Brasil*, noted that state advertising amounted to 15 percent of that newspaper's total revenue in 1978. Niomar Sodre Bittencourt of the *Correio da Manhã* asserted that the state accounted for 36 percent of the Brazilian newspaper advertising market. This figure is corroborated by estimates that official publicity represented approximately 30 percent of the accounts of advertising agencies.[12] Given that Brazilian newspapers were particularly dependent upon advertising for their revenues, the state's disproportionate weight as a customer provided a clear opportunity for abuse.[13]

At times the withdrawal of advertising appears to have been an isolated punitive jab, often the result of a spat between an official and a local newspaper. An official would feel crossed, as in the case of an exposé of corruption or mismanagement, and would cut all government advertising. Such cases were quite common and occurred in several states and many of the smaller cities around the country.[14]

Applying pressure by withdrawing advertising was never the only instrument at the disposal of the regime, and was often used in conjunction with other methods. In 1969 withdrawal of advertising was only one of the injuries suffered by Rio de Janeiro's traditional daily, the *Correio da Manhã*. The others included bombings, confiscations, and imprisonments.[15]

In other cases advertising pressure replaced instruments that had become less attractive to the regime. The experience of the *Jornal do Brasil* was a very compelling case in point. From 1969 to 1973 it accepted prohibitions from the Federal Police under the process known as "self-censorship" (to be discussed in chapter 7), and also received ample state advertising. When Geisel assumed the presidency in 1974 and asserted a commitment to *abertura*, the prohibitions were substantially reduced (from 106 in 1973 and 117 in 1974 to 8 in 1975)—but not the inclination to control the press. There would simply be other means, such as the audits recommended in the CIEx document, or the selective use of state advertising funds. This was the situation in which the *Jornal do Brasil* found itself in 1977–1978.

As Góes recalls, at that time the *Jornal do Brasil* was publishing material on secret nuclear accords between the U.S. and Brazil.[16] In its editorials, the newspaper favored cooperation with the United States, but challenged the secrecy of government agreements as being counter to the *abertura* that was supposedly being pursued. Its editorials also questioned the practice of directing large sums from the federal budget to secret nuclear activities in a supposed era of openness.

None of this pleased the government. In this period the press was monitored not only by President Geisel's own press advisor and by the Ministry of Justice, but also by the Military Cabinet, headed by the hard-line General Hugo Abreu. Each day General Abreu would read the *Jornal do Brasil*, marking with a red pencil whatever he disliked. These criticisms were transmitted to Góes who, as the newspaper's director, was responsible for handling relations with the government.

Throughout 1977 the government complained but the *Jornal do Brasil* persevered. At that time the newspaper had, Góes noted, a particular commitment to protecting its editorial integrity. The year 1977 was thus a rather tense period in relations between the government and the *Jornal do Brasil*. There was a climate of confrontation: "They insisted, and we resisted. Such that, in 1978, they decided to apply a more dramatic therapy."

Meetings took place between the newspaper's owner, M.F. de Nascimento Brito, and various federal representatives, particularly Mario Henrique Simonsen, minister of the treasury. As relations became more tense, Geisel decided that Abreu would be the sole interlocutor. Nascimento Brito tried without success to have this authority transferred to the chief of the Civilian Cabinet, General Golbery, the government's political coordinator. Geisel, however, was "absolutely inflexible" on this point.[17] Some meetings took place between Nascimento Brito and Abreu, but the routine negotiations were left to Góes.

Negotiations between Góes and Abreu swiftly arrived at an impasse. This happened, Góes noted, because "the government representative was a military officer, a parachutist, without much political sophistication." Abreu then obtained from Geisel an order to impose a boycott of state advertising upon the newspaper. This, to Góes, amounted to an "economic blockade." Any entity connected with the government, including state companies, was prohibited from purchasing advertising space in the pages of the *Jornal do Brasil*. Abreu sent two hundred telexes containing the order to ministries, offices, and state companies.[18]

At the time, the newspaper's profit rate was 5 percent, and state advertising accounted for 15 percent of its revenue. The blockade instantly created a deficit of 10 percent. It was, Góes said, an "act of war." And as by far the weaker combatant in this war, the *Jornal do Brasil* did what, in Góes's view, it had to do—it caved in. Góes met with Abreu, "And from there we proceeded into, shall we say, an attitude—negotiations are negotiations—and we began to pull things out, to avoid, to remove, more at the level of language, I would say. We softened the language." After forty days of negotiations and softening on the part of the *Jornal do Brasil*, the blockade was relaxed, and two hundred new telexes went out.

Abreu, however, had found that he "liked the work." Although Abreu had brought an end to the blockade, he continued to monitor the *Jornal do Brasil* closely. Denial of advertising had been demonstrated as an effective means for keeping the newspaper fairly tractable, and so it remained available as a threat. The *Jornal do Brasil* found itself under "a sort of Sword of Damocles," recalled Góes, "so we were always attentive to conversations with the general."

The final months of 1978, when all this was occurring, were also a time of heightened tensions over the presidential succession, which was to be decided by the military. On this matter, Abreu strongly disagreed with Geisel and Geisel's allies in the military. Hence, the *Jornal do Brasil* was in a difficult position. It never knew whether Abreu's complaints and demands reflected the concerns of the Geisel government or of Abreu's faction. This dilemma remained unresolved until Abreu left the government and Geisel stepped down.[19]

The Alternative Press

The withdrawal of state advertising was not as great a threat to the alternative press as it was to the mainstream press, simply because the former received less state advertising.[20] But if the regime did not have its own advertisements to withhold, it could certainly pressure private companies to withhold theirs. This happened with considerable frequency, particularly during the Geisel administration, when the regime moved away from the direct coercion typical of the Medici years and diversified its means of repression into more dispersed and elaborate forms of pressure.

The alternative weekly *Opinião*, which published lengthy analytical articles on politics, economics, foreign affairs, and culture, suffered a full range of attacks, from prior censorship to the bombing of its headquarters, the detention of its owner and editors, the confiscation of several issues, and state pressure on its advertisers.

When it began weekly publication in 1972, *Opinião* was well aware of the risks created by dependence upon advertising, whether public or private. It therefore aimed to sustain itself by sales, and limited income from large advertisers to no more than 20 percent of its revenues, in order to prevent particular advertisers from gaining significant influence over its editorial decisions.[21]

Among those advertising in the weekly were several book publishers. José Olympio Editora had a regular advertising contract with *Opinião* until the publishing company sought a loan from the national bank, BNDES. At that point the publishing company abruptly but apologetically canceled its advertising contract, even offering to continue the payments specified there. Advertising in *Opinião* was "not seen well" at the state-controlled bank and would jeopardize the publishing company's chance for a loan.

The state research institute, Fundação Getúlio Vargas, also advertised its many publications in *Opinião* until the director decided, "We cannot advertise in a journal that criticizes the CIA." *Opinião* sought to collect payment for the advertisements that had been printed in earlier issues, but did not succeed. Petrobrás was another advertiser that breached its contract with *Opinião*, after three years of advertising in the journal. *Opinião* maintained well-defined nationalist positions and had always supported the state monopoly on oil. When the regime began to reconsider that monopoly, and to look at the possibility of foreign risk contracts, Petrobrás abruptly canceled its advertisements.[22]

Those who advertised in other publications also suffered blatant government pressure. In 1977 the alternative paper *Coojornal* published an article on the regime's cancellation of the political rights of certain individuals, which included a list of those individuals. Agents of the Federal Police then visited companies that were advertising in *Coojornal*, threatening them with "difficulties" if they continued to do so.[23]

Other business relationships were also susceptible to state pressure. In the case of Bahia's alternative monthly, the *Boca de Inferno*, local printers were pressured into refusing to print the journal, which eventually had to seek printers in São Paulo.[24] The company that sold newsprint to *Versus* suspended the supply after being informed by the Federal Revenues Office that the publication's permit had been canceled, which was false. The company that printed the journal was told that it in turn would be subject to an exhaustive audit if it continued to do so, and so suspended that service.[25]

There were no publications, mainstream or alternative, that could not be subject to business pressure from the state. Those receiving sizable state advertising could find themselves cut off from this major source of revenue. Cooperatives and alternative publications that pointedly avoided financial dependence upon the state found that pressure was applied indirectly, by the regime withholding loans from or making threats against their private advertisers. All businesses that had a relationship with the press were potential targets for state pressure.

Confiscations

Another way to harm the press was simply to confiscate newspapers before their distribution. The police would arrive at a newspaper's headquarters or distribution center and seize the entire print run. This occurred throughout the country and with sufficient frequency that the chief of the Federal Police during this period, General Moacyr Coelho, recalled, "Oh, we got tired of confiscating them."[26] All types of publications were subject to such seizures. Major mainstream newspapers (the *Correio da Manhã*, the *Tribuna da Imprensa*, and the *Estado de São Paulo*) were subject to confiscations, as were small alternative journals (*Repórter, Em Tempo*, and *Resistência*). City newspapers as well as newspapers of national circulation, dailies as well as weeklies, fell prey to confiscation. For some newspapers confiscation was a one-time affair; for others it became almost routine. The *Tribuna da Imprensa* had its print run confiscated by the Federal Police eight times in 1977 alone.[27]

Confiscation could represent a serious financial loss to any publication. If a newspaper went out of circulation for a day it lost all the materials, time, and effort that had gone into that edition, saw its advertisements interrupted, and lost sales revenue. Cash flow was so tight at many publications that the confiscation of a single issue would have a substantial impact. Luis Alberto Bittencourt, the director of *Repórter*, asserted that this form of pressure did more to destroy the alternative press, which often operated on a slim profit margin and depended upon newsstand sales for its survival, than any other tactic of the regime. *Repórter* itself suffered fifteen confiscations from 1977 to 1982.[28]

But it was not only the alternative press that experienced confiscations. Walter Fontoura, editor of the mainstream *Jornal do Brasil* in the 1970s, asserted that mainstream newspapers were "forced" to submit to government commands. He then qualified this statement: "Well, not forced. It wound up being because no one knew what might happen if you didn't comply. There were confiscations."[29] Confiscation was seen as an extreme form of pressure that all sought to avoid.

Confiscation was also a measure that could originate in local concerns. As with other measures employed by the federal authorities, this tactic was also used by local powerholders seeking retribution against local papers.[30] Critical stories on and exposés of local political doings could bring swift confiscation.

Dealing with the business side of the press thus presented the regime with many avenues for bringing pressure: audits, withdrawal of state advertising, pressure on private advertisers and printers, and confiscation. All of these could substantially hamper press freedom, without the need for publicly declaring the legal curtailment of that freedom.

CONTROL OF THE NEWS

News as a Controlled Substance

The press was also susceptible to state attempts to control the news itself. At every level of the regime, and throughout the course of its many changes, news was simply hard to get from the authorities. This fact reveals the existence of a contemptuous attitude toward the news itself and toward the populace, apart from the regime's views of the press itself.

In general, news was treated as a controlled substance, not as a public good or a product of the public sphere. News properly belonged to the state, and was shared at the regime's discretion. As such, it was to be controlled by the regime for the good of society, but without society's participation or knowledge. This, in microcosm, was the attitude of the regime toward governance in general.

News, furthermore, was seen as complete in itself, as not requiring elaboration, interpretation, or debate. As General Meira Mattos asserted, announcement should be sufficient. This attitude paralleled the regime's technocratic approach to the formation of public policy. Policy choice was to be a technical and professional process, not a public or political collective activity. In theory, dialogue and participation were irrelevant to governance as well as to news; even the commitment to making government acts public was negligible.

The effort at control concerned news on both the inner workings of the state and other matters. Topics deemed sensitive included not just kidnappings, strikes, and disputes over presidential succession or within the Cabinet, but also agricultural and petroleum production figures, petty crime, public health, international trade agreements, inflation, and train accidents. Some topics were censored on the grounds that they were strategically sensitive. In the eyes of the regime, which sought to provide security against internal subversion, every aspect of national life was potentially of strategic importance. Any negative news was seen as ammunition for the enemy, or evidence of subversion. Accounts of subversive acts could serve as a "recipe" for those considering similar acts.

Apart from a specific strategic concern, the effort to control the news was also an outcome of the regime's low opinion of the populace. The people's interpretive powers were generally disparaged or scorned. State elites saw the "masses" as uncultured, simpleminded, and ignorant, and therefore vulnerable and in need of protection.[31] This was further justification for restricting the availability of news.

Distrust of the press was also a standard rationale for limiting the news. The press could not be an ally in educating the people, because it itself was distrusted. Colonel Moacyr Coelho, who for many years headed the Federal Police Department, defended the censorship not only of news of terrorist acts, but also of much seemingly innocuous material, and even public health information. To Coelho, the content of what was censored did not matter, because anything at all could be distorted by an untrustworthy press.[32] That position justified the prohibition of any news item, entirely at the regime's discretion.

Thus the regime's predisposition toward controlling the news was the outcome of an attitude toward news itself, toward the populace, and toward the press. There were numerous strategies for asserting this control.

Packaging the News

Although the press often had no direct access to immediate news sources within the government, it was given prepared releases and statements whenever the government was ready to divulge information. Interestingly, these were known as "o *press release*," the use of English suggesting a specific technical apparatus, foreign implement, or precision instrument (the careful timing implied by "release"), rather than simply an "announcement." It was a technical term with connotations of professionalism and management rather than general public knowledge and access to the news.

Press releases were used for any kind of news, from policy decisions to production figures to official appointments. While press releases were not in themselves tools for asserting control over or a monopoly on the news, the way they were deployed reveals an effort in that direction. Press releases would be read aloud by a designated official (or even played from a tape recorder). Often, no questions were accepted and no requests for corroboration or verification were permitted.[33] A press release was not a starting point, an initial provision of information as a basis for questions, but rather a definitive statement, a non-negotiable, technically correct, and complete source of data—or at least that was the way press releases were presented. This was consistent with the notion, widespread in the regime, that there was one news, and its announcement was sufficient.

Press advisors and press briefing rooms were also used to manage the news. Reporters were often strictly limited in their government contacts to press advisors.[34] In 1978, for example, an order prohibited even those journalists approved to cover the Ministry of Justice from directing any questions to ministry employees without prior authorization.[35] And of course, one of the best tactics for preventing revelations to the press was simply to keep the press advisor uninformed. While not unique to authoritarian governments, such use of press advisors was certainly consistent with the regime's attempts to limit access to the news.

Press briefing rooms were set up for credentialed journalists by various government offices, and were equipped with typewriters, telephones, and refreshments. Indeed, the only things lacking were news (other than the official press releases) and access to government officials. The press briefing room of the Army Ministry, for example, happened to be located, at least until the time of the Geisel administration, five miles from the ministry building itself.[36]

All of these instruments—press release, press advisor, press briefing room—were employed at every level of the regime's bureaucracy, military as well as civilian, state as well as federal. These means of packaging the news made it possible for the regime to shape the news and channel press access to it without resorting to overt refusals.

Withholding the News

On many occasions the regime refused to divulge news. Geisel's minister of justice, Armando Falcão, became famous for his unvarying response to any journalist's question: "No comment." His was an "entirely personal style of disinformation," in the opinion of journalist and researcher Paulo Marconi.[37] Among the examples Marconi records is an interview with Falcão which consisted of nine questions and nine evasions, followed by this exchange:

Q: Minister, then upon what topics are you able to respond, that we may ask those questions?

A: Oh, I think you're intelligent enough to dispense with my answers.

Q: The problem isn't intelligence, Minister, it's information.

A: But you only ask me questions about topics on which I'm not competent to respond.

Q: Very well, Minister, then let us speak of matters of the Ministry. How is the reformulation of censorship proceeding?

A: Today I'm not going to say anything about censorship.

Q: What about the studies toward the reformulation of the National Security Law?

A: The National Security Law, by its very nature, is a reserved topic, and therefore I will not speak about it.

Q: And the Luftalla case?

A: It hasn't yet arrived in my hands. . . . See how I responded to your questions. I responded to everything you asked me.[38]

74 A FORCED AGREEMENT

"No comment" became Falcão's trademark, and he once suggested to journalists that he simplify their task by making a recording of it for them.

A general unwillingness at the federal level to provide information to journalists was paralleled by a similar unwillingness at the state level. One journalist noted that no newspaper even maintained a reporter at the governor's office in São Paulo. "It's not that all the journalists feel an invincible antipathy toward the sad figure of the governor of São Paulo. It's just that there is nothing to do there."[39] A fundamental antagonism toward the press and a tendency to hoard and hide information seems to have characterized the regime at all levels.

An attitude that viewed the news as a controlled substance, the people as vulnerable, and the press as untrustworthy inclined the government toward trying to control the news. Some of its efforts—the use of press releases, press advisors, and press briefing rooms—might have seemed at first to be tools designed to facilitate access to the news. The way they were deployed, however—as tools for the dissemination of definitive information, no questions or investigations permitted—reveals the regime's intention of limiting and managing access to the news. Another practice was the consistent refusal to respond to the press, used by ministers and other officials even in matters that were their direct responsibility. The regime could thus make use of a variety of measures to limit the availability, content, and verification of the news. Although none of this amounted to a violation of press freedom, it certainly obstructed the ability of the press to practice that freedom.

PRESSURE ON INDIVIDUALS

Another area in which the regime could exert some control over the press was by moving against individual journalists' exercise of their profession. Like all measures employed by the regime, such pressure could be used selectively and tailored to particular targets. Owners, editors, and prominent journalists might be subject to legal proceedings. Journalists might be denied professional credentials and thus their capacity to work. And any individual, at whatever level, might suffer physical aggression, from petty harassment to torture.

Legal Proceedings

One way of pressuring the press was the use of legal proceedings against individuals, under either the press law or the National Security Law. In Brazil, the individual editor or journalist and not the newspaper bears final responsibility for press crimes. Indictments targeted both journalists and their editors, for the latter were held legally responsible unless they were willing to name the journalists involved. There was thus pressure upon editors to identify and deliver to the police journalists who had written offending articles.

The list of indicted journalists is lengthy and includes both the prominent and the unknown, from mainstream as well as alternative papers. *Movimento* journalists Antonio Carlos Ferreira and Raimundo Rodrigues Pereira were indicted under the National Security Law even before the journal began publication, on the basis of material in a preliminary circular announcing the weekly's launch.[40] Here indictments were used to intimidate opposition journalists. But indictments were also used against reporters in the conventional press. One case involved Lorenço Diaféria, who wrote human interest columns for the *Folha de São Paulo* and was charged with insulting the military (see chapter 8).

Being charged, even repeatedly, was a common occurrence. Luis Alberto Bittencourt, who wrote for *O Globo* and was also editor of *Repórter*, had twenty-two indictments brought against him, three under the National Security Law and nineteen under the press law.[41] These indictments, which were issued by military prosecutors, would sometimes take years to move through the system, only to be found inappropriate for a military trial. They would then be transferred to the civil court system, and the process would begin all over again.

The government exercised considerable discretion in resolving some of these cases. Three legal proceedings were initiated against Carlos Chagas, a nationally known journalist for the *Estado de São Paulo* and former press secretary for President Costa e Silva. All three proceedings were eventually dropped, the first perhaps because it was found to be useless as a form of intimidation, the second because a judge decided it was baseless, and the third because Geisel decided it was a product of military infighting.[42] It is arguable that Chagas's professional prominence and official appointment, quite apart from his individual temerity, protected him to a degree from ill treatment. Chagas's perspective, however, is that if anything his standing made him more of a target.[43] Assistance or protection could be hard to come by. In one case, Chagas was able to provide important assistance to journalist Jaime Sautchuk, who was charged with him. Sautchuk was abandoned by his own newspaper after being indicted, and Chagas extended to him the legal assistance he received from the *Estado de São Paulo*, with the result that Sautchuk was included in the dismissal of Chagas's case.[44]

Hazy legal proceedings were also threatened but never formalized against a very different group of journalists, the entire staff of *Pasquim*, who were kept in prison for sixty days in early 1970. They were then let go without charge, and the inquiry was eventually dropped.[45] Like the *Pasquim* case, many cases against journalists never resulted in a judicial determination, but they nonetheless caused considerable anxiety among members of the press.

The mere threat of legal proceedings was a useful weapon for the state. Because of the breadth of the definition of national security and the discretion of the authorities to protect it, journalists and editors were frequently subject to inquiries and indictments. How they fared in these proceedings depended upon many factors, including their own connections, their institution's support and resources, and factional infighting in the military. The outcomes of legal proceedings could rarely be foretold, but the consistency of their application against individual journalists and editors made them a prime feature of the professional landscape of the period.

Denial of Credentials

Another means of limiting or controlling the activity of individuals in the press was through the denial or cancellation of credentials. Any journalist covering a government office, at any level, in any branch, had to be officially screened and given proper credentials. This included not only all the journalists working in Brasília, but also those covering state enterprises, local governments, and public universities. Not just any journalist could be rebuffed by Justice Minister Falcão's "no comment." For the privilege, one had to submit oneself to review by the security authorities.

The process began with a newspaper's request for credentials for a journalist who would be covering official agencies. Security and intelligence agencies, particularly the SNI's Division of Security and Intelligence, reviewed these applications and held veto power over the issuance of new credentials.[46] Journalists had no opportunity to present their case or to challenge or even review files created by the state.[47]

Requests for credentials were frequently rejected. Explanations were rare, and once credentials were granted, they could be and often were revoked. The evidence here is primarily anecdotal, but refusals were frequent enough that the procedure is recalled by editors and journalists as a real obstacle, not just a pro forma bureaucratic exercise.[48] From 1975 to 1979 twenty journalists at the *Estado de São Paulo*'s Brasília bureau reportedly had their requests for credentials denied; the credentials of another twenty-five were canceled.[49] Carlos Chagas, head of the *Estado de São Paulo*'s Brasília bureau for many years, noted that whenever reporters did some effective investigative work, they lost their credentials: "It's backwards. The bad ones stay on, the good ones lose their jobs."[50]

The regime's dissimulation occurred on several levels. The necessary official approval of a journalist was referred to as "credentials," a term suggesting professional criteria, a review of professional competence and preparation. Clearly, however, with the involvement of the SNI and other intelligence agencies, what these journalists were being granted was "clearance"—that is, credentials based upon a security review. And this review was warped, because any actual danger to security often seems to have been determined on political or ideological rather than security grounds. The final casuistry was to disguise revocations as instances of personal animosity. Antonio Carlos Pereira, a journalist at the *Estado de São Paulo*'s Brasília bureau from 1964 to 1974, observed that when credentials were canceled, this was often presented as the result of bad feeling on the part of a military officer toward a particular journalist: "It was never presented as a political thing. But of course it was also obvious. Publicly masked yet also obvious, both."[51] The process often seems to have been arbitrary, but even the type of arbitrariness—professional, political, or personal—was hidden.

The granting and denial of credentials was thus another avenue for pressuring the press, by acting not against institutions but against individuals. As with other means available to the regime, those in power could choose to hide or disguise their actions. The regime could also use credential granting as an instrument of intimidation, as one step in a larger process of gaining compliance without having to exercise greater coercion.

Other Forms of Maltreatment

In addition to legal proceedings and credential granting as weapons against individual journalists, the regime employed other forms of maltreatment, ranging from petty harassment to harsh threats to severe physical aggression. Owners, editors, journalists, newsvendors, and other workers were subject to such treatment. Both faces of the regime, that which favored the legal casuistry of unconstitutional Institutional Acts, and that which resulted in the proliferation of such repressive agencies as OBAN and the DOI, were at times directed against the press.

Bombs were planted in the headquarters, bureau offices, and newsstands of both mainstream and alternative publications around the country. None of these incidents were successfully investigated by officials, much less brought to trial. Among the many establishments that were bombed were the *Tribuna da Imprensa*, the *Correio da Manhã*, the *Estado de São Paulo*, *Movimento*, the *Hora do Povo*, the *Voz da Unidade*, *Coojornal*, the *Tribunal da Luta Operária*, *Em Tempo*, *Opinião*, and the headquarters of the ABI.[52]

Individual journalists could also face abusive treatment. Many publications issued by journalists' groups include stories of reporters and photographers being beaten by the police, having notebooks seized, and tape recorders or cameras smashed.[53] Sometimes these incidents were designed to prevent journalists on the scene from covering the events they had witnessed. At other times they seem to have arisen from a general animosity toward the press. Such stories come from all over the country and are often presented as though they were so commonplace as to be unremarkable.

In 1973 Fernando Gasparian, owner of *Opinião*, and two of the newspaper's editors, Raimundo Rodrigues Pereira and Tarik de Souza, were briefly held incommunicado. Gasparian's wife and Representative Francisco Pinto (who had been present when they were detained) were told that the newsmen were not being held.[54] A few weeks later Gasparian was detained again, this time by an "apoplectic" police inspector who took care to inform him that "I'm not afraid of the cardinal [Paulo Evaristo Arns, of São Paulo], I'm not afraid of *Le Monde*, and I'm not afraid of any congressman [meaning Representative Francisco Pinto]. If you keep it up, I'm going to shoot you in the face."[55]

Gasparian was by no means singled out for this kind of treatment. Oliveiros Ferreira, editor of the *Estado de São Paulo*, was also held incommunicado for a time.[56] Evandro Carlos de Andrade, editor of *O Globo*, had to be convinced in 1971 to respond to a summons to give a deposition (by the same police inspector who later threatened to shoot Gasparian). He was sure he would be imprisoned, and went only because accompanied by the newspaper's director, Rogerio Marinho. Andrade subsequently surmised, "It was all just a show, of no importance at all, just to scare me."[57]

The regime had many ways to scare people, to get across an intimidating message. In 1967 Helio Fernandes, owner of the *Tribuna de Imprensa*, angered the regime by publishing an ugly obituary of former President Castello Branco. He was then imprisoned, ostensibly for his own safety from popular fury, on Fernando de Noronha, an island citadel far off the northeast coast—indeed, far from anywhere. The message was clearly that he could be banished, locked up, and the key thrown away, all at the discretion of the justice minister.

Many journalists felt scared; many felt watched. Ricardo Kotscho, a journalist then with the *Estado de São Paulo*, recalled walking along the street with his wife, a university student. They realized that they were being followed by an unmarked car. Neither had any reason to suspect that they were targets—any more than other journalists or university students, two categories of people against whom the regime harbored antagonism. Kotscho and his wife parted, to allow at least one of them to escape. The car followed Kotscho, although he was not apprehended.

Some, however, were apprehended. Carlos Garcia, head of the Recife bureau of the *Estado de São Paulo*, was imprisoned in Recife on March 11, 1974, three days before Geisel's inauguration. He was apprehended presumably because he had sent a report to São Paulo that the office of the leader of the MDB in the State Assembly of Pernambuco, Jarbas Vasconcelos, had been invaded by "unknown persons." After telegrams from the Mesquitas to the Ministry of Justice, Garcia was released, but not before being subjected to beatings and electrical shocks by hooded torturers.[58]

The best-known case of torture is that of the São Paulo journalist Vladimir Herzog. In October 1975 Herzog learned that Second Army security forces were looking for him. Sure of his innocence of any wrongdoing, and mistakenly thinking that that would protect him, he reported to the DOI, where, within hours, he was tortured to death. Officials claimed Herzog had confessed to being a communist and then committed suicide. As part of the cover-up, they provided a sickening photo of the dead Herzog, whom they claimed had hanged himself, but the pipe that held the cord was only chest high, and Herzog supposedly hanged himself while on his knees. The uproar that followed the death under torture of this politically uninvolved professional culminated in a public ecumenical funeral service attended by Cardinal Arns and ten thousand others who defied police cordons around the cathedral. The event was a turning point in civil society's expression and solidarity, as well as in relations between President Geisel and the security forces he sought to control.[59]

Opinião's owner, Gasparian, sought to open a dialogue with CIEx in the aftermath of the Herzog case. Fearing that Brazil was on the brink of a far more terrifying confrontation between state and society, he arranged (through the police censor responsible for *Opinião*) for a meeting with three CIEx officials at their headquarters in Brasília. The exchange immediately became a challenge: "So why do you think we were the ones who killed Herzog?" Gasparian recalls thinking, "Oof! I didn't want things to heat up so. This was no game." They discussed Herzog, nationalism, patriotism, and foreign intervention. Nothing resulted from the meeting. But when Gasparian departed, trembling, he left behind his identity cards (which had duly been deposited at the main desk upon his arrival) in his haste to leave.[60]

Herzog had had no reason for thinking he would not walk out of the DOI building just as he had walked in. And Gasparian had no reason for thinking that all he would lose in visiting CIEx were his identity cards. Terror is arbitrary.

With these cases in mind, it is very important to review some figures. The Nunca Mais project, which examined virtually all Supreme Military Court proceedings from 1969 to 1974, provides the most exhaustive documentation of human rights violations in Brazil under the military regime. Of all those who were processed for some alleged violation of national security, fully two-thirds were members of outlawed political organizations. These activists were the major targets of the repression. Other targets included students, labor activists, the military itself, political figures, the church, and journalists. Of the 707 cases in the Nunca Mais archive, only fifteen involved journalists.[61]

This statistic substantiates the claim that the press was not a major target of state terror. Being a member of the press did not present the degree of risk faced by members of other groups, particularly people belonging to clandestine organizations. Nonetheless, terror and aggression were available to the regime as it pursued control of the press.

The regime had at its disposal a wide array of measures for obstructing freedom of the press. Each was tailored to a different vulnerability of the press. On the business side, there were audits, the withholding of state advertising, pressure on private advertisers and printers, and confiscations. Access to news could be strictly limited by the carefully deployed vehicle of "o *press release*," with no further investigation, clarification, or corroboration permitted beyond the oft-repeated official "no comment." Professional freedom and personal safety were also at risk, whether through legal proceedings, denial of credentials, or other forms of maltreatment.

There were many ways to harass, intimidate, obstruct, and endanger the press without the regime, which sought both legitimacy and authoritarian control, having to forsake a formal commitment to freedom of the press. Just as the regime maintained the Constitution but countered it with its own Institutional Acts, continued to hold elections but altered electoral laws, restricted candidacies and canceled mandates, so too it proclaimed press freedom but engaged in carefully planned audits, advertising boycotts, denials of news access, and at times gross mistreatment of individuals.

It was in this climate of official animosity toward the press that Representative Bonifácio could recognize communist journalists by their mustaches, that journalist Cavalcanti could merit a "real bruising" from the police purely because he was a journalist, that CIEx could argue for a strategy of audits as a means of destroying publications without being accused of restricting press freedom, that General Abreu found he "liked the work" of keeping an eye on the *Jornal do Brasil,* and that Gasparian was threatened and Herzog murdered.

With only fifteen of 707 cases in the Nunca Mais involving journalists, it is clear that the press was not a major target of state terror in Brazil. But considering all of the devices used against the press, as well as the argument made in the CIEx document, it is equally clear that there was ample intent to pressure, coerce, and control the press, so long as this could be done without publicly denying freedom of the press. When censorship was practiced, it was undertaken with the same concern. The next two chapters document not only the operation but also the careful concealment of the most elaborate forms of press control—prior censorship and self-censorship.

6

PRIOR CENSORSHIP

TWO KINDS OF CENSORSHIP were practiced by the regime against the press in Brazil. One was known as prior censorship, the other as self-censorship. Both labels were misnomers. Prior censorship, directed against only a handful of publications, required that everything a newspaper prepared be reviewed by the police before publication. Self-censorship consisted of news prohibitions distributed by the Federal Police to publications prior to their investigation and reporting of, and even knowledge of, many news events. Thus prior censorship did not intervene as early in the process as self-censorship, and self-censorship was certainly not self-imposed.

The two forms of state censorship had certain features in common. Both were illegal and hidden from public view as much as possible. Both were conducted according to a standardized set of procedures duplicated throughout the country. A major difference in the two forms, however, was that self-censorship flowed from anonymous unsigned orders, whereas prior censorship had an immediate, identifiable agent in the figure of the Federal Police censor.

Perhaps partly as a consequence, prior censorship also generated much more reaction and much more resistance from the affected press, including both daily acts of sabotage and grand schemes of formal challenge. The press reactions to prior censorship were ineffective in stopping the censorship, which ended only when the regime saw fit. But the reactions were more elaborate, creative, and energetic than anything encountered in self-censorship.

In examining prior censorship it is possible to lose sight of the fact that this form of state censorship was illegal, secret, and rare. The entire process was unconstitutional. Brazil had long-standing laws permitting "moral censorship" of entertainment, particularly of movies and television. In 1970 Justice Minister Buzaid announced executive Decree Law 1077, permitting moral censorship of books and entertainment-related magazines, but not political censorship of news or information. According to the pivotal Institutional Act of 1968, AI-5, freedom of the press (as well as other rights guaranteed by the Constitution) could be suspended in the event of a state of siege, but no state of siege was declared during the period of prior censorship, and it was this issue that legal challenges to prior censorship eventually addressed. Political censorship of the press was illegal according to the regime's own formal rules.

Not surprisingly, then, given the regime's often contradictory but nonetheless recurrent concern for legitimacy, efforts were made to keep the censorship fairly secret. Being placed under prior censorship entailed no public official action. There was no notification by a judge, nor were there public regulations regarding the procedures and limits of the censorship. Newspapers were simply advised by the Federal Police to submit all materials. Publications could not announce that they were being censored, and indeed, censorship itself was one of the most censored topics. There was no parallel to the imprimatur carried on the masthead of every newspaper in Spain under Franco or in Portugal under Salazar, which stated that the contents of the newspaper had been reviewed and approved by the authorities. The Brazilian regime's consternation and anger over the lawsuits brought by censored publications came in part from having to admit the existence of censorship.

This was one aspect of the peculiar duality resulting from the regime's repressive character and concomitant desire for legitimacy. The regime needed prior censorship to be a relatively *public* secret (that is, public at least within the press) in order to effectively fend off potential challenges from other publications; on the other hand, for the sake of legitimacy based upon an appeal to traditional institutions and formal rights, the regime needed to conceal this illegal violation of a constitutionally protected freedom.

A key observation about prior censorship is that it affected a very small number of publications throughout Brazil, probably fewer than ten. The seven publications most frequently listed as having been subject to prior censorship are (with their dates of censorship) *Pasquim*, November 1970 to 1975; the *Estado de São Paulo*, September 1972 to January 1975; *O São Paulo*, June 1973 to June 1978; *Opinião*, January 1973 to April 1977; *Veja*, 1974 to June 1976; *Movimento*, April 1975 to June 1978; and the *Tribuna da Imprensa*, occasionally from 1968 to June 1978. In actuality there may have been several more, perhaps among the shorter-lived or less well-known regional papers.[1] Establishing the exact number is less important than recognizing that the proportion of publications under prior censorship was minuscule relative to the total of more than one thousand publications produced throughout the country.[2]

These seven publications were very broadly representative of journalism in Brazil: a mainstream daily with a long and prestigious history, two new opposition political weeklies, a diocesan newspaper, a mainstream glossy newsweekly, an iconoclastic alternative publication, and a city daily. There does not seem to have been a pattern of the regime targeting one or another type of publication. Prior censorship was conducted against alternative as well as mainstream publications. It was applied to those of national as well as local and parish circulation. It hit humor as well as news analysis. Each case was unique.[3]

The range of targets suggests that the targeting would have been difficult to predict—and arbitrariness can be harder to fight than a determined policy. The variety of publications subject to prior censorship meant that a common identity among them would not arise automatically but would have to be constructed. Just being subject to prior censorship would not be enough. The potential for solidarity existed, but remained just that: potential.

Furthermore, the limited number of publications placed under prior censorship does not indicate a limited willingness on the part of the regime to impose this kind of stringent control. Many other publications were threatened with prior censorship or actually ordered to submit to it, and chose to shut down rather than continue under strict government oversight, publishing only approved material and with no sure way of publicizing, or even alerting their readers to, this condition.[4] These included *Politica, Extra, Em Tempo,* and *Argumento.*

While few in number, the cases of prior censorship were nonetheless very important symbolically to the press. They were relevant reference points for all involved, providing worst-case scenarios of elaborate state intervention.

Prior censorship came to an end at each publication much as it had begun, abruptly with a simple notification, and also individually rather than as a result of a single centralized decision. There were some attempts by the press to negotiate with the authorities or lodge formal complaints, which for the most part were squelched or ignored by the regime (to be discussed later). The demise of prior censorship was not the result of a successful press campaign, but fit into the larger pattern of the regime's *abertura*, and may have served the purposes of a state trying to present itself as seriously pursuing a gradual transition toward democracy.[5]

The *Estado de São Paulo* was freed from prior censorship in early 1975. This was a long-anticipated "gift" from Geisel, presented in time for the newspaper's one hundredth anniversary. *Veja*'s release came in mid-1976. *Opinião* never saw the end, because it closed in protest while still under prior censorship in April 1977. Its final editorial (no. 230, April 1, 1977), gave the history of the publication's censorship and stated the newspaper's commitment to resume publication only when completely freed from all such restrictions. This issue was never submitted to the censor and was immediately confiscated. *Movimento, O São Paulo,* and the *Tribuna da Imprensa* were the last to be freed from prior censorship, in June 1978. For each, notification came abruptly with a telephone call that provided no explanations or assurances.

Pasquim, freed from years of prior censorship in 1975, had a characteristic experience. One of its principal collaborators, Millôr Fernandes, noted that the demise of prior censorship was as mysterious as its beginning. The publication was simply alerted that "superior orders" had declared the end of the censorship. The threat of its resumption lingered, however, as the cessation was communicated along with the phrase, "now the responsibility is yours."[6]

THE PROCESS OF PRIOR CENSORSHIP

Prior censorship might have been illegal, it might have been concealed, it might have been denied, but it was also quite standardized, with assigned personnel, established procedures, material accoutrements, and set schedules and locations.

Prior censorship was conducted by the Federal Police in Brasília. The Federal Police were under the civilian Ministry of Justice but were headed by a military officer and had close ties to the armed forces and security agencies. Orders and general policy direction with respect to the censorship came through the Ministry of Justice, with further information provided by the security agencies.

The implementation of prior censorship was entirely in the hands of the Federal Police. A Special Advisor was appointed for this task, a post held for most of the period of censorship by Helio Romão, a former police officer. Romão began with three assistants in Brasília and a few staff members in São Paulo and Rio de Janeiro. Staff numbers expanded as necessary to meet demand.

The Federal Police insisted that all censors were carefully trained. At the beginning of prior censorship, at least in the cases of the *Estado de São Paulo* and *Opinião*, it appears that staff were brought in from the moral censorship offices that reviewed public entertainment. Later, as prior censorship became routine, censors must have been hired just to handle the daily volume of work generated by the *Estado de São Paulo,* for example. Its editor, Oliveiros Ferreira, raged at their incompetence, recalling moonlighting bus drivers and drunken functionaries. Regarding *O São Paulo,* Cardinal Arns expressed particular ire at being censored by a third-year medical student: "It's the limit, isn't it? Not even the pope censors me."[7]

Censorship has so far been discussed here as an exercise in repression within press-state relations. It was also, however, just a day-to-day job. The censors of *Opinião* and *Movimento* worked in the Federal Police offices in Brasília, and those of the *Estado de São Paulo* passed through the same doors as the journalists they censored. They arrived each day equipped with the tools of their trade: a set of orders provided by the Federal Police, red pens or black markers, and a collection of stamps bearing such labels as "vetoed," "with cuts," and "liberated." Some manufacturer was producing a regular supply of those stamps, and the censors were employing them daily, in an illegal but nonetheless standardized activity.

The censors reviewed everything: articles, headlines, editorials, advertisements, obituaries, captions, cartoons, announcements. It must have become quite routine, given the speed with which they went through a considerable amount of material. As they worked, they marked up the material, whether it was the typeset proofs of the *Estado de São Paulo* or the typed or handwritten articles produced for *Movimento* and *Opinião.* They might put a red slash through the mention of a stolen sum, brackets around a phrase or a name, a box around an offending paragraph, or an X through an entire editorial. As they moved from article to article, week after week, they might take a black marker and blot out short passages, paragraphs, whole pages, or an entire article. Then they would often stamp their work. The label "vetoed" might be stamped on page after page of a twenty-page article. "Liberated with cuts" might appear on an article slashed through with black lines. They would often add the date and occasionally their initials to their stamps.

It seems a rather tedious job; the smallness of some of the prohibitions implies that the censors were at times carefully combing the texts for certain names or sums. And it was an enormous volume of material—both what was read and what was prohibited. The culling may have been tedious, except that considerations of national security rather than points of grammar or spelling were the arbiters in cases of doubt.

After the cuts were made, the pages were returned to their owners. The publications then used what was left—sometimes only half of what had been submitted, in the cases of *Opinião* and *Movimento*—to produce an issue. They could use only what had been approved. They also had the option of not including something that had been liberated, such as choosing not to run an article that had been eviscerated by partial cuts. But they could not add or substitute text. And once mounted as an issue, the material would be reviewed again by the police to ensure compliance.[8]

One very important factor in any publication's daily experience of prior censorship was the location of the censors, whether at the publication's offices, the local office of the Federal Police or, in the worst case, the Federal Police headquarters in Brasília. The administrative and production costs related to compliance, not to mention the loss of the prohibited material itself, could be enormous, and were borne entirely by the censored newspapers. If material had to be transported to the police, these costs included both the time lost as well as the expense of delivering the material.

The case of *Opinião* illustrates this burden. This weekly aimed to appear on the newsstands on Fridays, but prior censorship required that *Opinião* fly all of its material from its headquarters in Rio de Janeiro to Brasília on the preceding Monday night, to be at the offices of the Federal Police first thing Tuesday morning. The material remained in Brasília being censored until Wednesday night, when it would be flown back to Rio de Janeiro. In order to learn of the cuts beforehand and accelerate the process somewhat, *Opinião*'s staff would carefully label the parts of every submission, keeping a copy in Rio de Janeiro. Then *Opinião*'s Brasília employee would telephone the results to Rio de Janeiro in order to gain a day. What was left would be typeset on Thursday and printed that night. Only then would the issue appear on newsstands, on Friday. Not only were the costs of reproduction, transportation, communication, and extra staffing borne exclusively by *Opinião*, but this weekly publication lost at least two days of every week, and thus its timeliness. As an alternative publication that wanted to be relatively independent from commercial advertisers, its survival required strong newsstand sales, for which timeliness was essential.[9]

These were the schedules, personnel, and procedures that constituted prior censorship, which the affected press confronted with every issue. Despite being illegal and secret, and used against only a few publications, the censorship practices discussed here were well established and resulted in a rich documentary record of censored materials.

THE DOCUMENTARY EVIDENCE

The documentary evidence of prior censorship raises two important points. First, censorship necessarily shifts journalism from a communicative to a strategic action. If journalism only occasionally approximates the norms of communication, the imposition of censorship certainly shifts this practice into the realm of strategy, second guessing, and contention. Statements that would seem to carry no hidden import were a newspaper publishing freely, may take on new meaning when considered from the perspective of having been under censorship.

A second point is that in prior censorship, the censors could cut only what was submitted to them. The documentary evidence that remains is never the outcome of the actions of just the Federal Police censor, although that figure would appear to be in the position of greater power. Rather, the record is the result of the asymmetrical interaction between the censor and the newspaper.

The record is a partial portrait, in typed copy, red pencil, and black marker, of each publication and of the regime. That portrait was drawn not for accuracy or beauty, but strategically, by different actors working at cross-purposes, drawing against each other. The record cannot be read easily, and not too much should be read into it. Nonetheless it provides a revealing portrait of the military regime and the publications subjected to prior censorship by that regime.

The *Estado de São Paulo* and *Movimento* provide contrasting examples of prior censorship. One was a prestigious mainstream daily, the other an oppositional, journalist-owned alternative weekly. They operated with different standards and goals and followed different projects. Their political outlooks were as different as their technical apparatus and format. But they had in common, together with a handful of other publications, the experience of prior censorship. And they each generated a dual archive: a series of published issues and an immense quantity of vetoed material.[10]

THE CENSORSHIP OF THE *Estado de São Paulo*

The *Estado de São Paulo* kept the original proofs submitted to the censors. These pages, covered with the censors' red pencil marks, are the best record of the newspaper's prior censorship from September 1972 to January 1975. There are thousands of partially or entirely censored articles, usually several from any one day.[11] Some of the materials address topics that were consistently censored over the years; others were censored at particular times of crisis; and still others dealt with targets within the regime whose mention always led to a veto, regardless of the context or content of the material. Any news of or references to the censorship itself were also heavily censored. Some censored items offer clues to the practices of the censors and journalists involved.

Among the most consistently censored topics were disputes between the regime and the Catholic Church, living conditions and government treatment of the indigenous population, and student protests. The predominance of these topics may indicate a special sensitivity on the part of the regime toward these topics, or ample attention on the part of the *Estado de São Paulo*. Other frequently censored topics included prison conditions, government corruption, labor strikes, disruptions of transport services, and foreign criticism of the regime.

In addition to these regular themes, coverage of particular crises was extensively censored. In such instances absolutely any coverage—news, analysis, photographs, statements—would be censored. Such crises arose every few months. In 1973–1974, for example, they included the resignation of Agriculture Minister Cirne Lima in May 1973; General Pinochet's coup in Chile in September 1973; the sale of allegedly tainted meat from Uruguay in January 1974; the prosecution and imprisonment of Congressional Representative Francisco Pinto in 1974;[12] an epidemic of meningitis in São Paulo in July 1974;[13] the controversial wage policy of October 1974; and the November 1974 elections, which saw several important and surprising gubernatorial victories for the opposition. These topics received the most attention at the moment when they were most grave. It is very clear from the variety of the press coverage that was censored and the thoroughness of the cuts that the Federal Police order to the censors was to veto anything on these topics.

A third category of censored material concerned specific persons. This resulted in the elimination of references to isolated facts or particular individuals no matter how innocuous their context or use. Any mention was apparently forbidden. Such was the case, for example, with respect to Dom Helder Camara, archbishop of Olinda and Recife. News relating to him was censored whether he was discussing human rights abuses and poverty, being nominated for a Nobel Peace Prize or to the College of Cardinals, receiving an honorary degree, or simply saying mass. Congressional Representative Francisco Pinto was evidently another favored target, even long after his 1974 trial. Deletion of these names from articles, even when the person in question was not the main focus of the article, indicates the existence of what might be called a blacklist.

In addition to its topical content, the documentary record of prior censorship also contains some evidence on the practice and the relations of censorship. Some of the limitations and strategies of both censors and journalists are revealed in the record.

Federal Police censors were often charged by the press with gross incompetence and ignorance or with fear of their own superiors. The record does contain some puzzling material that would appear to result from the actions of shortsighted or nervous censors following the letter of their orders and not the spirit. During the 1974 elections, for example, censors were evidently ordered to eliminate anything on the government's controversial wage policy. Thus a progovernment candidate's speech defending that policy was entirely vetoed, while an opposition candidate's speech, full of criticism of every other aspect of the government excepting the wage policy, was permitted in its entirety. Such rule following defeated the purpose of the censorship orders.

Other instances, however, exhibit some care and skill on the part of the censors. The way cuts were made could produce different results: the absence or the distortion of information. In July 1974, for example, the *Estado de São Paulo* attempted to report the observations of U.S. economist Werner Baer (the censored portion is in brackets). Baer stated that the activities of the Brazilian state oil company Petrobrás were "reminiscent of the expansion of the state service of gas and oil in Italy [under the leadership of the deceased Enrico Mattei. The world considered Mattei a socialist pirate]." The censored version left the impression that in the estimation of a renowned economist Brazil was joining the ranks of the developed world, and it eliminated the suggestion of excessive statism.[14] The censor also did a careful job on a 1974 speech by MDB leader Ulysses Guimarães. According to Guimarães, as quoted by the *Estado de São Paulo* (the censored portion is in brackets): "First they used 'maintenance of the democratic regime,' and then 'democratic normality'; later it was 'political opening' [(although there was closing, censorship, torture, imprisonment, etc.)]; and now the phrase is 'political model,' maybe for export, who knows?" Guimarães was playing with the language, so that the *abertura* (opening) was actually an *apertura* (closing), but without the censored phrase one could have read his remarks as identifying a reasonable progression, or at worst maintenance of the status quo.[15] While there are many oddities in the documentary record, perhaps resulting from censors' inexperience or insecurity, there is also evidence of their care and skill.

Journalists and editors also left their mark in the censored documents. Clearly they were able to anticipate some of the censors' actions. The journalists and editors who have commented upon this period assert (and the documentary record substantiates their claims) that they did not rewrite material to pass the censor. Perhaps the clearest, but certainly not a unique, example of their approach is a completely censored editorial from early March 1974, when Geisel was about to take office. This was from a series in the *Estado de São Paulo* assessing the Medici administration, and looked at the Ministry of Justice under Alfredo Buzaid. It asserted, in part, that Buzaid "legitimated proceedings which made disrespect of the law routine. Buzaid danced upon the most elementary human rights, daily violated by the police authorities under his ministry. He denied the existence of torture when everyone knew that it had become common practice. And he defended as no one else did the necessity of censorship, while pretending later to be unaware of the practical consequences of its application." The editorial continued that if it was true that there had been a threat of terrorism, the threat had been confined to 1967–1970. Since then, even though the extremist movements had been dismantled, subversion had been "used as a bogeyman to justify disrespect toward the law, precisely by those who should be defending it." The editorial concluded that nothing good could be said about Buzaid's time as minister.[16] Who would have expected that to pass? There are many articles that no one would have written or submitted, had they internalized the censorship.

Another aspect of journalists' strategies was the almost absurd frequency with which some obviously targeted names appeared in the censored record. This suggests not only that these were definite sore spots for the regime, but that the reporters and editors knew it and were inserting them gratuitously. Recurring mentions of Dom Helder Camara and Representative Francisco Pinto, for example, seem to be beyond any genuine newsworthiness. They appear, rather, to reflect an effort to skirt the censorship, an assumption that names repeated again and again might eventually get through.

The documentary record reveals that burying the lead was another strategy for skirting the censorship. A common occurrence was an article full of descriptive detail about a Catholic Church ceremony and then, many paragraphs on, the words "In other Church news," followed by a reference to Dom Helder. One of the most pointed examples was an article entitled "Dom Helder May Go to the Sacred College" (the body that selects the pope), which was censored in July 1974. The article was entirely vetoed. On the following day there appeared an article entitled "Pope Chooses Dom Avelar" (to lead a Catholic board of education), from which just one brief paragraph was eliminated. The vetoed portion, however, stated that Dom Helder might become a member of the Sacred College. In this case it appears that the *Estado de São Paulo*'s journalists knew of the veto from the preceding day and were trying to bury the Dom Helder news within a tenuously related article—an article that would, and did except for this one portion, pass the censor.[17]

The censorship of censorship itself merits attention. The censorship of the press was indeed one of the most censored topics, occurring in the record consistently throughout the period of prior censorship. It also on occasion received crisis attention, for example during meetings of the Inter-American Press Association. Julio de Mesquita Neto, owner of the *Estado de São Paulo*, was president of the IAPA, and his addresses to the association were covered in full, together with related material. These reports, however, were very extensively cut. Mention of censorship was also a specific target. One finds many censored items such as the 1974 campaign speech by MDB candidate Orestes Quercia (the censored portion is in brackets). Quercia condemned "inadequate public transportation, [censorship of the press], indirect elections, and Decree Law 477."[18]

The censorship of censorship also left evidence of censors' foibles. One censor, who, it is clear, was dutifully following orders, vetoed a speech by ARENA Party senator Eurico Resende defending censorship, including the censorship of the *Estado de São Paulo*.[19] Evidence of journalists' strategies also appears, and reveals many attempts to slip in a forbidden topic. An extensive article on divorce law, for instance, included a section on "other law news" containing the remarks of a lawyer condemning press censorship.[20]

The *Estado de São Paulo* gave considerable coverage to press censorship in general, but particularly to its own censorship. In 1974, for example, it received the Golden Prize from the IAPA. Coverage of this never stopped. For months there continued to be articles on the prize, which were regularly censored. The most common sort of article was a statement of congratulations from a public figure praising the *Estado de São Paulo* for its steadfast commitment to freedom of the press and condemning the arbitrary restrictions under which it labored. The almost absurd extent of the coverage could have been part hubris and part self-promotion, but also part anticensorship strategy, frequent mentions being more likely to slip past the censors. And of course, the *Estado de São Paulo* could not have printed this praise had it not been offered in the first place, by members of Congress, other politicians, and business leaders. The very extensive record of censored congratulations from 1974 shows that many people were eager for the opportunity to register their support for the newspaper.

Remarks about the *Estado de São Paulo* found in the record also make it clear that if prior censorship was a secret, it was also a fairly public secret. The *Estado de São Paulo* had become a symbol, such that oblique references could be made to the censorship (although these were often censored). The following two examples refer to the *Estado de São Paulo*'s practice of publishing poetry, particularly the verses of Camões, in place of censored material. An MDB politician was censored when he remarked that "There will be liberty at the moment when the *Estado de São Paulo* stops publishing poetry except in its literary supplement." And on election eve 1974, just a phrase was censored from a final article (censored portion in brackets): "Quercia closed his speech [with a verse from Camões]."[21]

The very last entry in the archive of the *Estado de São Paulo*'s censored material, evidently the very last item censored, referred to censorship. The article described a ceremony of the Academia Brasileira de Letras (censored portion in brackets), "Barbosa Lima Sobrinho read from an article published in 1875 regarding freedom of the press [which because of its content could, according to him, have been written today or replaced by verses from Camões]."[22]

THE CENSORSHIP OF *Movimento*

There are several sources for studying the censorship of *Movimento*. One is the archive of original proofs sent from the journal's offices in São Paulo to the Federal Police in Brasília, reviewed and marked by the censors, and returned to *Movimento* for inclusion in that week's issue.[23] Another source is the brief bulletins that were prepared each week to notify staff members of what had been vetoed.[24] *Movimento*'s own evaluations of the censorship also provide important information. These appeared in the newspapers of journalists' organizations and unions during the censorship and in the several issues of *Movimento* following the end of prior censorship in June 1978. *Movimento*'s self-awareness in this regard can be contrasted with the *Estado de São Paulo*'s approach. *Movimento* was quite aware of its historic project as a journalist-owned publication, as well as of the experience of prior censorship. *Movimento* spent a relatively large amount of time documenting its own existence. There is thus a substantial historical record in the pages of the publication itself.[25]

For the period of censorship from April 1975 to June 1978 (153 censored issues), *Movimento* counted some six thousand articles and illustrations that were vetoed partially or entirely.[26] In addition, three whole issues were prevented from circulating. One on risk contracts for oil exploration by foreign companies (October 13, 1975) was simply prohibited from circulating at the final review by the Federal Police, after already having been censored. A special issue on the situation of women and their work in Brazil (May 10, 1976) had an unprecedented 80 percent of its material rejected by the censor. Not enough remained to publish an issue that week.[27] The third issue prevented from circulating addressed the need for a constituent assembly to draft a new constitution (September 19, 1977). It passed censorship and final review, but then was confiscated.[28]

Movimento also traced patterns in the intensity of the censorship (see fig. 2). It concluded that political tension and censorship went hand-in-hand and that sales declined as censorship intensified. The three peaks of censorship in 1976, for example, coincided with the opening of Congress in March and the immediate removal from office of three members, a corruption scandal that came to light in July, and the November elections. For *Movimento*, the pattern demonstrated "a certain general logic of censorship,

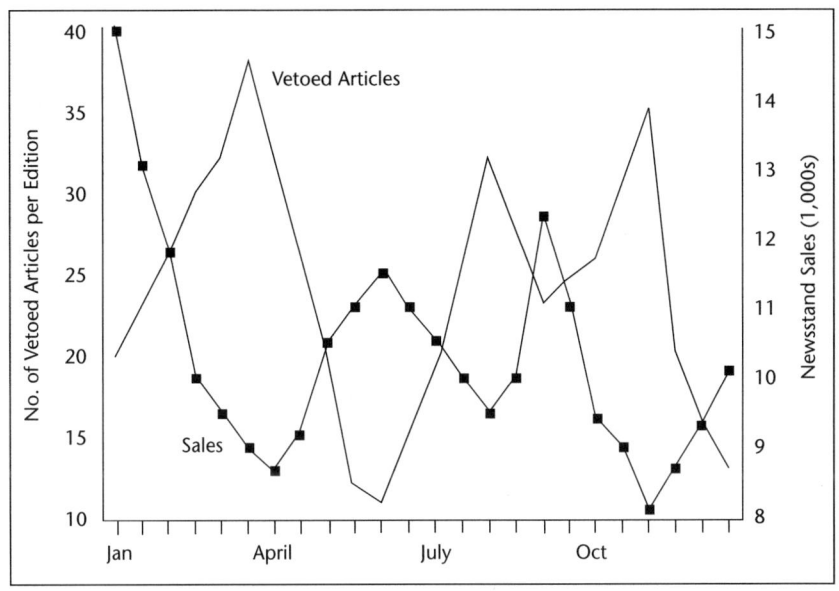

FIG. 2. Vetoed Articles and Newsstand Sales, *Movimento*, 1976
Source: Adapted from *Movimento*, no. 154, June 12, 1978, 14.

which despite having apparently nebulous criteria, always knew where to cut in order to impede *Movimento* from efficiently covering the important events of the nation."[29] Denied its coverage of such events, *Movimento* lost substantial newsstand sales.

Although the intensity of the censorship varied over time, the underlying message of the entire body of censored *Movimento* material, regardless of the topic, remained consistent: that current reality did not have to be the way it was. *Movimento* was providing coverage of existing viable alternatives, of other ways of organizing production, governance, security, and society. The content of this publication relativized almost every aspect of Brazilian experience and substantiated the feasibility and relevance of alternatives. The censored record reveals those same concerns as well as criticism of the people in power, be it political or economic power, at the local, national, or international levels.

As with the *Estado de Sao Paulo*, the censored material from *Movimento* falls into consistent topical and thematic categories. In addition, the censored material offers evidence of *Movimento*'s sources and style and of relations between the journal and the regime.

A prominent theme was the denationalization of the economy and the activities of transnational corporations in Brazil. The collusion of private business and government with foreign transnational corporations for private gain received regular attention. Vetoed articles examined the profit rates, tax exemptions, and investment patterns of international corporations and their domestic partners. Owners' wealth was contrasted with workers' poverty, hazardous working conditions, and low living standards. Pollution, violation of safety standards, and inadequate and unsafe consumer products were also reported upon—and censored.[30]

Movimento also addressed the misuse of public funds. An article entitled "The Price of Fame (and of the Publicity that the Mayor of Recife Uses to Publicize His Works)" was partially censored.[31] The mayor of Recife had a stairway built for a hillside slum, announcing it with great fanfare and providing detailed specifications on its cost, height, the exact number of steps, and so on. Subsequently, two local newspapers, the *Diário de Pernambuco* and the *Jornal do Comércio,* published in article form two paid advertisements containing the same material. *Movimento* noted the price of a paid advertisement in those newspapers, and the higher prices charged when advertisements were published as though they were pieces of regular reporting. It concluded that the mayor had spent a third of the total budget for the stairs on the article-style advertisement. The *Movimento* article was not totally vetoed, however. The censor approved the initial part, which described the building of the stairs. *Movimento* chose not to publish this.

The incompetence and corruption of the national government and the inadequacy of public policies were also regular themes in *Movimento*. The government was held responsible for avoidable disasters such as the shortage of basic foodstuffs or the crises produced by perennial droughts in the Northeast. Here the tone was one of irony: after four centuries, why do droughts always surprise the authorities? Agricultural policies, including the promotion of cash crops and the overuse and abuse of land, were identified as instances where state policy had aggravated natural disasters. Public health policies were also challenged in articles on infant mortality, malnutrition, epidemics, and contraception. In June 1976, when the government was considering initiatives to make contraceptives easily available, a censored article asked why, if access to birth control pills was going to be democratized and their distribution facilitated, beans, milk, housing, and schooling should not receive the same treatment.[32]

Many social conflicts received close attention in *Movimento*. Among these were conflicts over land between squatters, colonists, and ranchers, out of which emerged coverage of violence, slave labor, judicial indifference, and the power of large landholders and foreign corporations in the Amazon basin. An article censored in July 1976 quoted ARENA politician Herbert Levy's statement that it made no sense to permit rural workers to become owners of the land they cultivated, because "They don't have the psychological or economic conditions to make it productive" (this statement paralleled the regime's frequent charge that the people were not psychologically prepared to vote for their own representatives).[33]

Foreign news was also cut from *Movimento*, especially anything concerning criticism of military dictatorships or transitions from authoritarian to democratic rule. Coverage of disputes within the military in Pinochet's Chile was vetoed, as were many articles examining the transition from Franco to King Juan Carlos in Spain. Other censored foreign news addressed topics deemed sensitive within Brazil. For example, *Movimento* could not publish comments upon agrarian reform, student protest, labor organizing, or rape prosecutions in other countries. One undated article concerned Dutch soldiers being permitted to refuse participation in actions they disagreed with, such as a military raid on Moluccan activists who had seized a train.

Some of the material that *Movimento* prepared for publication was not timely news, but review essays and historical studies. A reassessment of Brazil's labor history included accounts of pivotal but not well-known strikes, and challenged the view of labor legislation as a gift from Papa Vargas rather than the fruit of labor's struggle. Another devastating historical article addressed Brazil's external indebtedness since the first international loans in 1824, Brazil's repeated inability to satisfy its debts, the consequent necessity of further loans, the pattern of seeking new loans to pay for old, and the generations-old burden of interest payments. These precursors to Brazil's contemporary fiscal crisis were offered as a series of lessons not yet learned.[34]

The denationalization of the economy, the incompetence and corruption of government, the inadequacy of public policy, the varieties of social conflict, and the social, economic, and political alternatives to be found in foreign news and Brazil's history are consistent themes in the documentary record of *Movimento*'s censorship. Also revealed there are some intriguing clues about the journal's sources. Many of these were unconventional. As an experimental publication, *Movimento* hardly depended upon "*o press release.*" There are some startling examples in the censored record of reliance upon alternative news sources, which shed light upon relations between this journal and the public, the regime, and the rest of the press.

Some of these sources were readily available, for instance from other published newspapers. In the censored archives are materials from all four of Brazil's major mainstream newspapers, *O Globo*, the *Estado de São Paulo*, the *Folha de São Paulo*, and the *Jornal do Brasil*. These materials include editorials and essays as well as news reports. The staff would often simply clip an article they wanted to reprint and paste it onto a *Movimento* proof-sheet. This format, and the inclusion of a source citation, would indicate to the censors that such articles were reprints. At other times *Movimento* would incorporate extensive quotations from prepublished material into its own articles and add commentary or analysis. Some of the quoted items, such as those dealing with scandals or corruption, were inherently controversial; others would be made controversial by the addition of *Movimento*'s critical commentary.[35] Despite already having been published, such material was frequently cut from *Movimento* by the censors.

Other sources that appeared in the censored parts of *Movimento* would have been readily available had Brazil had a public forum for dissent. Among the censored documents are many petitions and declarations sent to *Movimento* by student organizations, unions, doctors, rural workers, and relatives of prisoners. Copies of letters that were sent to officials were also sent to *Movimento*, as though to become part of the public record, even if winning no official response (although this too was frustrated by the censors). *Movimento* often seems to have been regarded as an alternative public forum.

Less publicly available were the materials submitted by other journalists. *Movimento* maintained only a minimal staff and depended upon the regular submissions of journalists employed by other publications. These journalists would freelance for *Movimento*, at times submitting material they knew would not be published by their mainstream employers, or handled in a fashion that would not be accepted by their mainstream employers. Thus the archive includes proof-sheets from nearly all of Brazil's major metropolitan and regional newspapers. This material was not secret, but would not have been distributed had *Movimento* not provided an alternative forum, albeit a censored one.[36]

No doubt the oddest and least public source in the censored material is a photocopied note from the leading security agency, the SNI. The note bears various stamps, including "urgent," "secret," and "reproduction of this document is prohibited." It was addressed to General Fontoura, former chief of the SNI and then Brazilian ambassador to Portugal. Fontoura was the subject of public protest because of widespread suspicion that he was conducting surveillance on Brazilian exiles in Portugal.[37] The note, dated September 24, 1975, would appear to confirm that suspicion. João Figueiredo, at that time chief of the SNI (and later Brazil's president) was sending Fontoura an update on two exiles, a military officer and a lawyer, both considered "grave risks" to Brazil's national security, against whom there would be a "Code 12 operation." The brief note was to confirm the SNI's recent twenty-three-page secret telex.[38] This never entered the public record, at least not through *Movimento*. One wonders how it even found its way into *Movimento*'s records.

The censored archive reveals some of *Movimento*'s unconventional sources. The journal was clearly an alternative outlet for members of the press and for a public frustrated with the lack of a public forum. The material offers tantalizing evidence on what might have become available about the regime had there not been press censorship. The censorship even of material already published elsewhere in the press also indicates that the content itself was not always key in determining whether veto power would be exercised. The treatment, style of presentation, and context of that material were also important.

As an alternative publication, *Movimento* engaged in many journalistic experiments. In addition to drawing upon unconventional sources, it also pursued new writing styles, topics, and subjects. These were as readily censored as straightforward news content. *Movimento*'s censored archive includes not only data, but also analysis, metaphor, and voice.

Plain data was often censored—figures on tuberculosis in Brazil, for example, or on participation of women in the work force. At other times, the data remained but the supporting explanation was eliminated. In the following example of a report upon economic growth, the portions in brackets were deleted by the censor: "In 1959, capital's share of industrial income was .571, while in 1970 this share had grown to .623 (data from the industrial census of 1960 and 1970, FIBGE). [That is, in the same period in which workers' real salaries were deteriorating, the profits of capital grew.] . . . One phenomenon is caused by the other and vice versa. The style of growth of the country in recent years enormously benefited the accumulation of wealth [among those groups that control the means of production]."[39]

Metaphor was also subject to censorship. For an October 1975 issue, Flavio Aguiar composed an allegorical representation of Brazil as "Marlboro Country" in which he assessed the power of cigarette manufacturer Philip Morris.[40] The essay disclosed the extent of Philip Morris's operations in Brazil and included references to official favors for foreign capital, from financial help to exemption from taxes. But more than that, the essay dwelt upon the enormous social impact of advertising—which, unlike political reporting or cultural expression, was uncontrolled. While all the data and much of the analysis remained uncut, the humiliating metaphor of Brazil as Marlboro Country, the fiefdom of a transnational corporation, was eliminated.

"Voices," by which I mean the perspectives of individuals rarely included in mainstream press coverage, were also readily censored. One of the subjects most often covered in both published and censored *Movimento* material was the everyday living and working conditions of average Brazilians. Attention to this was incorporated into almost every article, and was also the focus of a special section called "Brazilian Scene." These pieces, quite innovative at the time, examined daily life in poignant detail and always included the perspectives of the people affected. Often these were voices never heard in the mainstream press: prostitutes, slum dwellers, Indians, factory workers.

This type of writing validated the experiences of those immediately affected by whatever was being covered, giving their words equal weight by placing them beside the words of experts, policymakers, and other authorities. It also portrayed social groups as consisting of unique individuals rather than an undifferentiated mass. This approach made it clear that people spoke from their circumstances. As this was established for the poor and powerless, it could be heard in the powerful too. They were also located within their circumstances, so that their words were not presented as a singular enduring truth, but as a particular interested truth.

Another aspect of the inclusion of such voices was that it permitted the subordinate to address the powerful, even if only rhetorically, and even if censored. In one censored article a parent observed, "I'd just like to see the president of the Republic earn what we do, and manage to buy groceries or pay for school."[41] In another, colonists lamented having left Paraná for Amazonia. Lured by the government's false advertising and unkept promises, and then abandoned, they demanded accountability.[42]

What all these voices tended to communicate was both desperation and determination. Bleakness was twinned with anger. But it was not only the classically voiceless who were represented. In addition to the landless, the homeless, and the jobless, *Movimento* interviewed alternative professionals and alternative experts. Its censored pages included testimony from economists, architects, and engineers who did not speak for the government or a corporation. They offered criticism from an informed professional perspective on government policy and other aspects of social reality.[43] In *Movimento*'s pages one learned of the debates that could occur among trained professionals, a revelation that challenged the image of technocratic unanimity which characterized official policy discussion. Just the notion that there could be debate and disagreement among experts was not widely held; technocracy was supposed to supplant political debate. These voices were also censored.

A final example from the censored archive captures many of the elements characteristic of these documents. This is an undated article prepared by a journalist from Porto Alegre on the proof-sheets of the newspaper *Zero*

Hora. Evidently, the journalist concluded that the material would not be published by *Zero Hora*, or at least not with this treatment, so it was submitted to *Movimento*—but then vetoed in its entirety by the Federal Police censors.

The article addressed some of the key *Movimento* themes identified above: official incompetence, corporate greed, needlessly poor public health. The piece began, "Five children were resuscitated in Porto Alegre—or so it can be concluded from the information released by the Secretariat of Health." It explained that the secretariat office for Rio Grande do Sul had announced nineteen child deaths caused by dehydration in the first week of January. A few weeks later the secretariat reported only fourteen such deaths for all of January. The article went on to present comparative official data from several other cities and from previous years, pointing out that the data were incomplete. All of the figures were examined critically.

Next, the article discussed public health policy and the secretariat's campaign to prevent dehydration in children. The secretariat's posters of chubby children, which included advice to reduce meals from five to three a day and to drink plenty of milk, were "simply cruel," given most Brazilians' economic circumstances. Incorporating the voices of those involved, the journalist interviewed a nurse who wanted to know, "How can I say that to someone who's feeding her children once a day, if that?"

The article then turned its attention to the profits made from remedies for dehydration. The prices for those medicines tended to rise dramatically at the beginning of each summer, although production costs were very low. One version of the medication had ten ingredients, of which three were medicinal and the rest scents or coloring. Although the state could produce these remedies inexpensively, private pharmaceutical companies always charged much more.

With its attention to public health, public policy, the role of private corporations, alternative sources of data, and alternative voices, this article was a microcosm of much of *Movimento*'s censored content. Prepared by a journalist who evidently determined that it would not be published in a mainstream newspaper, it was submitted to *Movimento* as an alternative outlet. In prohibiting its publication, the Federal Police censors excised news, data, and critique, and further narrowed the fora available for presenting and sharing such information and perspectives.

As is revealed by the documentary record, the censorship conducted by the Federal Police eliminated important content from both the *Estado de Sao Paulo* and *Movimento*. Reports upon many events and issues worthy of coverage were vetoed. Much analysis and critique was also cut. Anything provided by certain individuals—whether single individuals such as Dom

Helder in the *Estado de São Paulo* or entire categories of people in *Movimento*—might be vetoed. All debate upon certain topics, including censorship itself, or any consideration of social, political, and economic alternatives, might be curtailed or removed from this public forum. Censorship had an enormous impact upon the content of the press. It also had a profound impact upon the daily relations of those involved with the press.

DAILY RELATIONS

During the years of prior censorship, a handful of publications produced a substantial physical record. In addition to this documentary record, prior censorship also produced a collection of personal relations quite distinct from those that characterized the much more common self-censorship. Journalists interacted with each other, confirming each other's experiences and developing strategies for coping with prior censorship or expressing frustration. Publications under prior censorship also related to their readers, seeking to alert them to the restrictions that were always publicly denied by the regime. Censored journalists also interacted with police censors, whom they saw or communicated with on a daily basis. And finally, they confronted the military regime, crafting expressions of rage or carefully planning legal challenges to prior censorship. None of the relationships was given. Members of the press under prior censorship applied effort and insight to the tasks of making sense of and perhaps resisting this illegal and secret practice.

Relations Among Press Actors

Press actors subject to prior censorship shared a minority experience. Understandably, then, their relations with one another were crucial for securing basic reality (despite the surreal denials of the government and the censorship of censorship), for interpreting events, and for validating experience. They shared the tension, anger, and frustration that resulted from being under prior censorship.

In more than one case, this sharing of subjective experience evolved into ritual. Marcos Sá recalled the "tea ritual" at *Veja:* "What started as a habit, a practice, to help one another stay awake through the many dawns of waiting for the censored material to be returned, became the tea ritual. For so many weeks, we stayed awake from Thursday through Saturday. At that time you could buy fancy imported tea. We added porcelain tea cups, linen tea towels, imported English teas. It was a way to keep awake, a game, a ritual, a being together in the middle of the night, sharing."

With the tea ritual, the journalists at *Veja* sustained one another with caffeine as well as camaraderie, both crucial to their dawn vigils. But the ritual had other consequences, as Sá later realized: "At *Veja* it was very participatory. So participatory that I think it wound up making us insensible to the problem we faced. I think this wound up harming us. There was anger, but we didn't take it seriously enough. It became a game, juvenile. And because of this, we made some errors."[44]

In their tea ritual, *Veja*'s journalists became caught up in the details and lost sight of the bigger picture. They were not uncreative, but they channeled their creativity and energy into elaborating this rite as a thing in itself. It seems to have strengthened their own friendships, but it isolated them from other purposes they might have pursued upon reflection, and insulated them even from their own anger.

A different ritual, according to Raimundo Pereira, then editor of *Opinião*, was followed at the close of each week's issue at that journal's Rio de Janeiro office: "We stayed together all the time, and on Sunday, when the next issue was ready, we would all go to my house for coffee. Afterwards, we would all go to the beach, everybody together . . . in the game that we used to play at the beach, extremely symbolic, we would all get in the surf and try to push the waves back. It was a game; you would be so tense and would need to do something physical. And then everyone would jump in the surf as though it had been . . . a catharsis."[45] Pushing the waves back. What better symbol could there be for *Opinião*'s endeavor? It is a startlingly apt metaphor for their situation: engaged in a joint effort against ridiculous odds, against the political tide, but insisting upon engaging that tide. At least as Pereira recalled it, this game had a cathartic rather than numbing effect.

Relations with Readers

All of the publications under prior censorship sought to alert their readers to its existence. This can be seen as an effort to communicate directly with readers but also to reach the state. If readers were made aware of the prior censorship, this would foil the regime's careful efforts to keep it secret (or at least deniable) and to maintain a facade of commitment to press freedom. Perhaps unmasking the censorship would have harmed state legitimacy. By its actions, the regime evidently proceeded on this premise.

Often the content of a censored article would not give any indication of censorship. For example, there were many cases similar to the coverage of a secret meeting in Argentina of leftist guerrillas "from Argentina, [Brazil], Chile, Bolivia, and Uruguay." Only the mention of Brazil was censored (as indicated by brackets) from this article. A reader would get the impression that indeed all topics were being covered by the press, even secret guerrilla meetings.[46] Thus the press devoted some creativity to alerting readers to prior censorship. These efforts met with only limited success. They were stymied both by continued reader ignorance and by further state intervention.

In trying to communicate the fact of prior censorship to its readers, the *Estado de São Paulo* used a number of stratagems. It sought to establish a sign that would immediately be recognized by readers as indicating prior censorship. This was a frustrating process for editor Oliveiros Ferreira, who came to realize through this exercise just how limited the newspaper's rapport with its readers could be.

The editors first attempted to change what was to them sacrosanct placement of subjects covered in each edition, switching international news to an inside page and putting local news on the front page, for example. When this elicited no response, the editors tried printing Brazilian poetry in place of the censored material. The works of Gonçalvo Dias, Machado de Assis, and Manoel Bandeira began appearing on the news pages.[47] These were hardly in line with the usual content of the newspaper, yet again there was little response. Ferreira then fabricated and printed on the front page some ludicrous spoofs of letters to the editor, regarding, for example, gardening in São Paulo. These were met by earnest replies from interested readers.[48] Likewise, printing recipes for inedible dishes generated queries from dissatisfied cooks, but no one seemed to guess anything further was intended.

The final tactic was to choose one text and consistently print selections from it whenever the newspaper wanted to indicate censorship. The text chosen was the classic Portuguese epic poem, *Os Lusiades,* by the sixteenth-century poet Luiz Vaz de Camões. Cantos from the poem regularly began to appear anywhere in the newspaper—on the international news page or in place of an editorial—and often with the parenthetical note, "(continued)." Sometimes the regular news headline would remain but the text would be replaced by poetry, such as "Conflict at Mackenzie University" followed by lines from the ninth canto:

> . . . the lovely
> Nymphs and their sailor lovers,
> Adorning them with enchanting offerings
> Of light and gold and abundant flowers . . .
> They promise eternal companionship,
> In life and death, of honor and happiness. . . .[49]

Coverage of the meetings of the IAPA was always heavily censored, including speeches by the newspaper's owner, Julio de Mesquita, who was also president of the IAPA. The edition of April 5, 1974, bore an uncaptioned photograph of the readily recognizable Mesquita, with "Ninth Canto" in large print substituted for the headline. The entire text of the censored article was replaced by lines of poetry:

Because of the grand deeds of the daring,
Strong and famous, the world is waiting.
The prize comes at the end, well deserved,
With great fame and high exalted name. . . .
Better to deserve it without possessing it
Than to possess it without deserving it.[50]

It should be emphasized that the *Estado de São Paulo* could use Camões's poetry in this way not only because of its own ingenuity and commitment but also because it could get away with it. Other publications found themselves prohibited by the regime from using such ruses (*O São Paulo* from printing the Lord's Prayer; *Opinião* from printing the United Nations Universal Declaration of Human Rights). Editor Oliveiros Ferreira asserted that if the regime had prohibited the *Estado de São Paulo*'s use of Camões, the newspaper would have found something else and kept on trying. That is undoubtedly true, given the newspaper's determination. But it is also true that the regime did not prohibit the use of Camões, that it granted the *Estado de São Paulo* a leeway which it did not grant to others.

The Camões poetry appears to have been widely recognized as a ploy to indicate censorship. References to Camões in Congress were understood to be references to censorship (and were themselves therefore censored). Everyone now cites this as the classic story of the period's censorship. It has become such a famous story that it is now difficult to know just how readily the ploy was recognized by the average reader of the *Estado de São Paulo*, for there is no independent evidence on this point.[51]

Readers of *Opinião* or *Movimento*, on the other hand, were perhaps much more likely to have suspected or to have heard of the prior censorship of those publications. Vani Moreira Kenski has produced an intriguing study of *Opinião*'s readers entitled "The Fascination of *Opinião*." She tells of each copy passing through many hands, of people being afraid to subscribe because they did not want their names on lists that might fall into the hands of police agents, and of readers carefully purchasing copies from different newsstands to avoid being recognized. Some readers recalled the sense of vicarious engagement and identification with an active opposition gained simply from reading the journal. Some noted their own feeling of daring from such acts as pointedly reading *Opinião* in a public place, for instance a bus or ferry.[52]

The history of *Movimento* includes similar accounts, which suggest that reading and subscribing to the journal were complex acts. One staffer sought subscriptions at the government economics research institute, IPEA. Fifty people wanted to subscribe, but only one was willing to put his name on the subscription list. And so for years, fifty subscriptions would be delivered to that single individual, who would then distribute them among his colleagues.[53] These were people who, in this climate, could be expected to be on the alert for clues of prior censorship or other restrictions. They would have presumed that there was more than met the eye in any edition.

This predisposition on the part of readers perhaps gave alternative publications some leeway in indicating when prior censorship had occurred. On the other hand, *Opinião* and *Movimento* also faced harsher restrictions from the regime in their attempts to do so. Furthermore, representatives of both publications testified that the sense of solidarity was not enough to make readers buy an emptied edition.

Opinião and *Movimento* each had many stratagems to indicate censorship and to encourage readers to read between the lines. They would leave gaps where phrases or names had been deleted by the censor, leave a sentence unfinished, or alter punctuation or verb agreement where changes had been made. *Opinião* would change the typeface within a censored article to indicate the location of breaks, or chop an article into ten pieces scattered throughout the edition, each piece corresponding to an interruption created by the censor. *Opinião* also printed sections of the Universal Declaration of Human Rights in place of prohibited material, until that practice, too, was prohibited. *Movimento* would print footnote numbers in the text and at the end of an article, even when the content of the footnote had been censored. Large bands of black could frequently be found in both publications, in place of a headline, at the close of a partially censored article, or as a thick border around a page.

A simple advertisement, "Read and subscribe to *Opinião*," or "Read, subscribe, and publicize *Movimento*," often appeared in white letters within the black bands, or in marginal spaces.[54] *Movimento* also used a more elaborate slogan: "Read, subscribe, and publicize *Movimento*; in defense of democratic liberties, national independence, and the improvement of workers' living conditions." This appeared everywhere—in conventional advertising spaces, in large bold print across an entire page in place of a censored editorial, or in headline type in place of a vetoed headline. The slogan was also frequently inserted into the text of censored articles. Sometimes a part would be inserted midsentence, adding to the abruptness while hiding the slogan in the regular type of a normal column of print. All of these measures were prohibited by the Federal Police. Censors vetoed the use of blank space, and then vetoed what the publications selected to fill that space.

Were these tactics clear indicators of censorship to the readers? Argemiro Ferreira, editor of *Opinião*, doubts it now, although he found the practice gratifying then.[55] *Movimento*'s staff were also aware of instances of readers failing to catch the clues they planted. When they were prohibited from using large black spaces and therefore began to insert their slogan, some readers canceled their subscriptions, fed up with the publication using so much space merely to advertise itself. A translation of a *Movimento* article used by a European magazine also translated the slogan, edited to make some sense of the sentence into which it had been inserted.[56]

The final objectives of both publications, however, were to undertake opposition and critique and inform readers, not to engage in exercises against censorship. As Raimundo Pereira, editor of *Opinião* and then *Movimento*, recalled, "We decided to leave a mark only because the publication was so very mutilated. The purpose of the publication was not to indicate censorship, but to publish information, to make a good journal."[57]

One measure of their lack of success in this endeavor was their sales, which declined sharply with censorship.[58] The staff at *Opinião* and *Movimento* were well aware of the affective relationship, the "fascination" that many readers held for these publications. But they were also quite clear that this was not sufficient to compel regular purchases of publications that had been so deprived of their content by the censors. To ensure sales they had to offer real content. As Argemiro Ferreira observed, "No one is going to buy a skinny paper. It doesn't do you any good to have people feeling sorry for you because nobody buys just for feeling sorry for you, week after week." Raimundo Pereira, editor of *Movimento,* likewise asserted,

You needed to forget the censorship in order to buy it. Some say that people bought *Movimento because* it was censored. That's complete nonsense. People bought it because it said things. And we wanted people to buy it. The censorship meant low sales. . . . A reader is a reader, not a supporter. A reader is looking for content, for information. Of course there were some giving contributions, but not in general. If it has nothing new or important to say, why buy it?

Even if *Opinião* and *Movimento* could expect a better rapport with their readers, could expect some sophistication in detecting the clues that they offered, this did not necessarily help them in their larger projects of publishing alternative information about the regime and Brazilian reality, or in remaining viable businesses.

In attempting to alert its readers to prior censorship, *O São Paulo* shared some of the strategies of other publications. In place of censored material, it at first left blank space, and then switched to inserting psalms or other passages from the Bible or the Lord's Prayer, or advertising for itself. But as in the experience of other publications, each of these tactics was prohibited. The newspaper then embarked upon a much more direct approach.

Boletim CIEC was a mimeographed Catholic Church bulletin produced by *O São Paulo* that was slipped inside each issue of the newspaper. As this was merely an internal mimeograph, the authorities paid no attention to it. And this is where *O São Paulo* put the censored material. At first, the censored articles would be reprinted in full, with an explanation that they had been prohibited from inclusion in *O São Paulo*. Later, when there was too much material to reproduce, *Boletim CIEC* would simply include a quick summary of that week's censored articles.

Even if the readers of *O São Paulo* were not reading any other newspaper, with respect to censorship they had to have been some of the most aware readers of any newspaper in the country. And indeed, *O São Paulo*'s records include letters to the editor asking for copies of the censored articles. In a reader survey, 26 percent of the respondents complained about lack of access to the censored material (as well as requesting more accessible language; they did not want to be excluded).[59]

Being subject to prior censorship was a confusing experience. Considerable effort was expended just to communicate the fact of censorship and to acknowledge the experience. From *Veja*'s tea ritual to *Opinião*'s struggle against the waves, press actors needed to develop some means of expressing their experiences and sharing them with each other. In reaching out to their readers, they could be highly creative, though not necessarily successful. But they never seemed to give up. Each new regime prohibition led to a new press tactic. These may have absorbed excessive energy, and been poorly designed, but they do indicate the commitment of these press actors to continuing to struggle against prior censorship, in contrast to the behavior of those subject to self-censorship (see chapter 7).

Press Relations with Censors

Direct interactions with Federal Police censors could make a difference when items were being considered for a veto. Some censorship decisions were discretionary, even arbitrary, and in these cases personal relations could make a difference, as could tricks such as eluding, exhausting, or fooling the censors. As the obvious and immediate agents of censorship, individual censors became the target of many such efforts.

This was not a pointlessly narrow way to proceed. Because prior censorship itself was publicly denied and debate about it in public fora therefore unlikely, one way to attack it was through personal relations rather than public legal or bureaucratic procedures. These attacks represented efforts to liberate specific materials, not to challenge prior censorship as such. The affected publications constructed varying ways of dealing with their censors.

Although censors had a daily presence at the *Estado de São Paulo* for years, no one recalls an effort to write in order to pass. Vetoes might have been anticipated, but they were left for the censors to make. Ricardo

Kotscho, who was in charge of the reportorial staff, noted that "During the prior censorship at the *Estado de São Paulo,* there was no self-censorship. You wrote the whole. You did your work, the censors did theirs. You didn't do the censors' work."[60] Carlos Alberto Sardemburg, reporter and news editor, concurred: "At the *Estado de São Paulo* the writing and preparation was always done properly, as though it were going to be published, even if you doubted it. You knew it might be censored, but you did the whole process." Editor Oliveiros Ferreira was vehement that "We wrote the news, all of it. Cutting it was their problem."[61]

Journalists could anticipate the censors in other ways. Kotscho, for example, knew that the volume of material produced was such that the censors could not read everything: "So we reversed standard journalistic procedure, put the lead in about the tenth paragraph."[62] This would be what appears in the censored record following such catch phrases as "in other Church news" or "in other police news." From its appearance in the censored record, however, it is clear that Kotscho and his colleagues did not win with this tactic every time.

In addition to strategies applied to the writing itself, there were also continual efforts to negotiate agreements on particular topics or articles. These occurred at many levels, from the reporter who dealt with the censor on duty to the editor who engaged police authorities in discussion. In these negotiations, press actors used whatever they could (personal contacts, arguments about lack of time and the extent of the cuts) to try to lighten the censorship. It appears that a difficulty they all faced was the underling censors' reluctance to take independent action even in small matters and tendency to transfer responsibility to centralized superior powers.

At the lowest level of negotiations were the senior journalist and the censor on duty in the newspaper's offices. Kotscho recalls many late hours spent with the censors:

We were always trying to negotiate with the censor in the offices of the *Estado de São Paulo.* The later it was, the better chance we had. There would be five or six of us from the newspaper, trying to win by pushing for time. By 3:00 A.M. the censor would be so exhausted you had a better chance of getting something by. We got a good bit more through that way. Or you could say to the censor, "Look, you've cut a whole page. We can't publish an entire page of Camões." And the response would be, "Wait, I'll call Brasília."[63]

Why not a whole page of Camões? The regime would want to avoid the really peculiar, the utterly obvious. Revealing press censorship would damage its legitimacy, and this was a weakness for the newspaper to exploit. Deferral to higher authorities also occurred when editor Ferreira would call the Federal Police in São Paulo about a particular problem. Occasionally he too would get the response, "Wait, I'll call Brasília." Ferreira interpreted this as fear on the part of underlings, fear of reprisals if they exercised their own judgment in executing the not very clear directives on censorship. At other times the response would be, "All right, because of personal relations, you can do it."[64]

Personal relations among the elite eased the restrictions on the *Estado de São Paulo* from time to time. But they also must have narrowed the newspaper's leeway for action on other occasions. Not wanting to jeopardize those at times helpful personal relations would have removed certain strategies from the *Estado de São Paulo*'s range of action. There was evidently a fine line here, a crucial ambiguity, resulting from the newspaper's historical prestige and membership in the elite, despite its temporarily oppositional status.

Opinião and *Movimento* also sought to liberate censored material by indirectly undercutting or directly negotiating with the censors. Given the distance to Brasília (where the prior censorship of these two publications was conducted) as well as their relative lack of friends in powerful places, their opportunities for negotiation were limited, but not nonexistent. In contrast to the actions of publications under self-censorship, they never stopped devising methods to undercut censorship. As in the case of the *Estado de São Paulo*, the goal was always the liberation of a particular article, not the defeat of prior censorship as such. And these alternative publications could likewise try to take advantage of the space created by the regime's pursuit of legitimacy and consequent desire to keep censorship discreet. As *Movimento*'s editor Pereira asserted, "*Movimento* never negotiated, never made offers, so as to be freed of prior censorship, or to get softer prior censorship. The opening was the government's desire for legality. We used that. We never negotiated. We were going to make the publication, and they could do as they pleased."[65]

One of the most basic artifices for getting material passed was simply to submit it more than once. They would send in a photocopy, and when this was rejected they would remove the cover sheet with its "vetoed" stamp, affix another, and submit the article again the next week. Argemiro Ferreira, editor of *Opinião* after Raimundo Pereira left to start *Movimento*, recalls resubmitting articles so frequently that sometimes there would be a note from the censor scribbled in the margin, "Look, don't send this one again!" But he viewed this as not only a maneuver to get material passed, but also as an expression of obstinacy, a refusal to cooperate. At least, Ferreira shrugged, "we could oblige them to read it again."[66]

This was in line with the similar practice of slightly altering graphic material after it had been passed. In one instance, an approved photograph of an opposition politician was torn in half before being reproduced on the cover. A graphic approved in one size would be made larger. Ferreira also recalled dripping red ink onto an approved sketch of a dove. He was obeying the letter of the censors' "law," publishing only what was approved, but simultaneously sabotaging the censors' control.[67]

Another regular strategy at *Opinião* was directed not toward liberating a specific item but getting an entire issue's worth of material liberated. With half or more of its material censored each week, the journal had a serious problem just filling its pages. Rather than reduce the number of pages, and thus appear quite thin and flimsy on the newsstands, the staff would submit extra foreign news to the censors. This was less apt to be cut and thus helped *Opinião* present the same bulk during what would otherwise have been rather lean weeks.[68]

In contrast with the practice of self-censorship, opportunities for negotiations were few, but did exist. Some of the journalists responsible for collecting the material from the Federal Police in Brasília recall negotiations over particular articles, especially when so little was left that it would have been difficult to mount an issue that week. Jaime Sautchuk recalls one censor agreeing to take a second look, "just because my face was so sad." It was from such experiences that he concluded that the regime did not want to close the censored alternative publications, but wanted to maintain them in a highly controlled fashion.[69]

The effort to fool the censors by exhausting them seems to have been the elementary tactic most readily available to publications under prior censorship. It was, however, a game that could be played by both sides. Federal Police censors could refuse to release material until the last moment, thus requiring the staff of censored publications to labor into the early morning hours to make their publication deadlines. Marcos Sá recalls going without sleep at the end of each week for years, as the magazine staff and their censor, Ricardo Bloch, faced off in this way.

Sá also believes that the journalists at *Veja* were losing sight of their public and writing more and more to fool the censor. This had a distorting effect:

Perhaps in a way we were writing for the censor. And when you write to evade the censor, what remains is incomprehensible to the reader. Our relationship was with the censor. The censor became the focus, became the goal; to elude him, to challenge him. We weren't writing for the reader any more. We couldn't see the reader.

It was an error to write for the censor, to mask things in metaphor or twists. It's obvious: if you managed to write in a way that passed the censor, then 90 percent of the readers didn't get it, couldn't get it. And yet we were so proud, independent of the result—forgetting that 90 percent, forgetting the results of our strategies.[70]

Other journalists from the period recall seeing another approach in the pages of *Veja,* one consistent with Sá's observations. This was to publish calumnies or to repeat accusations against certain individuals (Dom Helder, for example), so as to be able to report anything on them at all. However, it was up to the reader to distinguish the strategic calumny from the intended news, and this could backfire.

Just how badly their deceptions could backfire Sá himself discovered when he came to write a retrospective on the 1970s for a special issue of *Veja.* This involved months of research and the preparation of dozens of articles. Sá began the research by consulting back issues of *Veja,* for that was the newspaper where he had experienced the decade. He discovered, however, that he could not reconstruct the period from back issues, and was deeply chastened by that realization:

> It was a shock. I thought our work had been so significant, but I could not reconstitute the decade from *Veja.* The only thing there was what they had let us say. It had the feel, the flavor, the ideas; but the facts (of censorship, torture, disputes over succession, real crises of the regime) were completely missing. I had to go to *O Globo,* to any other basic newspaper, for which I had had no respect at the time, to find the basic information, the names, the dates, the news.
>
> This changed my thinking very much, about censorship, about the newspapers that I had considered weak in that period. Despite all the self-censorship, the data and circumstances were there—no critique, but the basic information. While for all the struggle at *Veja,* the expertise—there was nothing. Despite all the craziness, there had been a method to the censorship. For all our expertise, the censorship had been efficient, had removed what was essential to the regime.
>
> And so I began to "respect" censorship. Now I know the censorship made me a fool; at the time I thought we were making a fool of the censorship. In the end, who had been the greater idiot?[71]

Journalists' relations with the Federal Police censors took several forms. Sometimes this was through writing quite strategically, trying to hide meanings or information, seeking to elude the censor's rubber stamp and black marker. At other times journalists negotiated directly with the censors, aiming for a more lenient reading of a censored article. The following poem, by José Carlos Dias, represents another way of addressing and challenging the censor. Entitled "Poem to the Censor," it was barred by the censor from publication in *O São Paulo* in August 1977.[72] It reads, in part:

> What'll it be, Censor?
> Sit here by my side . . .
> forget the censored material.
> Try something: put on the paper,
> the paper accustomed to your rubber stamps,

a poem, the lyrics of a song
an editorial, an essay, a story, a play,
something of your own. . . .
Come on, create, create and say what you feel
but speak only
of that which beats
in your heart, in the streets of your people . . .
add something of yours, of ours,
of our time.
Do this, Censor,
You who read so much,
You who see so much,
You who know the heat of the printing rooms
who already sensed the smell of the paper being born
who aborted it in that instant . . .
go on, create something
and later, later, maybe even unconsciously
reach into your pockets—your art is ready—
and stamp it, out of habit or out of disgust,
"vetoed."

And the censor in charge of reviewing the material for *O São Paulo* that night—reached into his pocket and stamped the poem, "vetoed."

Relations with the Regime

In the greatest contrast with self-censorship, those subject to prior censorship also sought to confront the regime directly, to condemn prior censorship and even challenge it in court. Their route was strenuous. The military regime was of course far stronger than the press. Using the public as a resource was difficult, for prior censorship remained largely hidden and denied. Using legal institutions was also tricky, when up against a regime willing to issue Institutional Acts, Decree Laws, and other convenient casuistries.

Indeed, all the efforts by press actors to halt prior censorship failed. Nonetheless, those efforts were not futile. They were often both creative and courageous, and generated very different relations, identities, and legacies than complicity would have created. The ability to directly challenge prior censorship, even if unsuccessfully, sets these press actors far apart from their colleagues in the self-censoring press.

The *Estado de São Paulo* belonged to the elite. Its owners were among those who had sought and supported the 1964 coup; political congruity as well as personal friendships connected them to powerful individuals in the regime. This is part of why their newspaper's being censored is puzzling, and why their anger about the censorship has a tone of indignation—not only at the violation of liberty of the press, but that they in particular, as long-standing members of the elite, should be subject to this affront. At issue was how to define the ruling elite, the people who would be included in determining Brazil's course. The *Estado de São Paulo*'s status was threatened here, and it responded with pique and fury.

It did so, however, in a suitably restricted elite manner, with targeted conversations and internal messages rather than a public show. In confronting censorship, the *Estado de São Paulo* did not seek a public revelation of the censorship. It proceeded, rather, through private communications to members of the Cabinet and Congress. Its only relatively public forum was the IAPA, where the *Estado de São Paulo*'s owners made speeches to the owners of other newspapers in the hemisphere.

While these approaches were traditionally elitist and aimed at restricted audiences, their content was hardly polite or restrained. The *Estado de São Paulo* vented its full rage. Below is the text of a telegram sent by Ruy Mesquita to Justice Minister Alfredo Buzaid in September 1972, when prior censorship began:

Mr. Minister, upon hearing of the orders issued by Your Excellency, my sentiments were those of profound humiliation and shame. I felt ashamed, Mr. Minister, for Brazil, degraded to the level of a little banana republic, to any old "Uganda," by a government that has now lost its composure. While using force against your very partners in revolution . . . you have not considered for five minutes the judgment of history. You, Mr. Minister (who will one day cease to be so) and all those who are in power today but one day shall step down, will have to realize then . . . that the truth cannot be contained.[73]

This was not the only telegram of its kind.[74] In addressing the regime, the *Estado de São Paulo*'s owners made sure to include references to their own participation in the revolution and to the temporary quality of the government's power. The contrast, obviously, was with the *Estado de São Paulo*'s almost one hundred years of existence, deeper historical perspective, wisdom, and superior judgment and prudence.

In another piece of theater, the newspaper's owner again assumed the stance of a wronged but not humbled member of the elite, and got away with it. Julio de Mesquita Neto had been summoned to testify at a military police inquiry set up to determine who was responsible for the publication of a prohibited news item. Editor Ferreira recounts the story:

Formally identified, Julio de Mesquita Neto was questioned: "The gentleman is the director responsible for the *Estado de São Paulo?*" Answer: "No!" A gasp of surprise in the headquarters of the Second Army. "How is that? Then who is?" Mesquita's reply is still remembered: "The director of the *Estado de São Paulo* is the minister of justice, Alfredo Buzaid, who has a censor in the typography room of the newspaper." Silence and discomfort among the generals. Afterwards, nothing else was asked, they exchanged civilized compliments and the case was closed.[75]

The efforts of the *Estado de São Paulo* were frustrated. Promises made to the newspaper by others within the elite (such as that Geisel would surely end prior censorship upon taking office), went unfulfilled for a long time. And while its allies in Congress were raising the issue of censorship, duly supplied with documentation by the *Estado de São Paulo,* other members of Congress were declaring the charges false and denying the existence of censorship. The Mesquitas nonetheless continued to try to engage the regime on this level of elite interchange, of private conversations and personal telegrams. Their goal seems to have been twofold: to secure liberty of the press, but also to ensure their continued privileged inclusion among the elite (and to merit that privilege by maintaining appropriate elite behavior).

Opinião took a very different tack. It chose to call the regime's bluff on legitimacy, to play upon the regime's simultaneous continuation and violation of the Constitution. Despite all the "devertebrating" changes to the judiciary made by the military regime, *Opinião* determined to take seriously, at least for strategic purposes, the regime's claim of respect for traditional institutions, including the judiciary. It decided to assert the constitutional illegality of censorship by following formally correct legal procedure and filing a case against the government.[76] *Opinião* began to look for an opportunity to do so soon after prior censorship was established.

The case arose out of the April 14, 1973, issue (no. 24). *Opinião* submitted its materials for censorship as usual. When these were not returned at the appointed time, and the journal could delay no longer and still meet its production deadlines, it decided to print the full uncensored issue. This was immediately confiscated, and the journal's owner and editors were imprisoned. Once released, they inquired about publishing an issue of *Opinião* using the material that had passed the censors. This they were permitted to do, and they therefore prepared and distributed a second issue no. 24, dated April 18, 1973. It was these two issues that provided the evidence with which to challenge the censorship in court.[77]

The lawyer who volunteered to argue the case was Adauto Lúcio Cardoso. He had been a congressional representative, president of the House of Representatives, and a justice of the Supreme Court. He had resigned the latter position precisely over a ruling regarding the legality of censorship.[78]

Opinião had the physical proof and a lawyer of substantial repute. Next, it needed allies in the press. *Opiniao*'s owner, Fernando Gasparian, was sure that the weight of the case would be immeasurably greater if his little opposition weekly were joined by the likes of the *Estado de São Paulo*. This would keep the issues of legality and constitutionality in sharp focus, not blurred by *Opinião*'s political stance or diminished by its small size and recent founding. When Gasparian approached Ruy Mesquita, however, he was rejected. Mesquita acknowledged Cardoso's reputation but gave several reasons for refusing to join the case.[79]

The Mesquitas had heard, most likely from their friend Governor Paulo Egydio, that Geisel intended to end prior censorship of the *Estado de São Paulo* upon taking office. They refused to jeopardize that possibility by becoming involved in a lawsuit, instead preferring to wait and take advantage of the expected favor.

Mesquita also asserted that he had a primary responsibility to his business as a business, and did not want to run the risk of a victory in court. Such a victory would bring an end to prior censorship but also invite retaliation from the regime, which had so many avenues for putting financial pressure on the newspaper. As a straightforward businessman, Mesquita was not interested in becoming party to a legal case, and certainly not to a legal victory.

Finally, there were status differences. The Mesquitas allegedly viewed themselves as members of a "republican aristocracy" unwilling to join forces with anyone of lesser social or political status.[80] Gasparian was aware of their hesitation on such grounds, and even suggested that Mesquita bring the suit, with *Opinião* as coplaintiff. When the *Estado de São Paulo* refused this proposal as well, *Opinião* decided to go its own way.

Opinião's action sought a *mandato de segurança* (an injunction) against the government.[81] The case was argued in May 1974. *Opinião*'s lawyer set out the illegality of prior censorship, the inappropriateness of existing moral censorship legislation for a publication such as *Opinião*, and the "shameful arbitrariness" and "capricious stupidity" with which the censorship was conducted. He also noted *Opinião*'s detailed objections upon technical grounds to the delays and interruptions caused by censorship. In his arguments, which quoted *Opinião*'s letters earlier addressed to the Federal Police and the Ministry of Justice, the lawyer frequently cited comparisons between his client's procedures and those of weekly magazines of international reputation such as *Time, Newsweek*, and *Der Speigel*. By asserting parallels between itself and such publications, *Opinião* was building up its own stature, rhetorically requiring respect from and suitable behavior on the part of the regime.

In addition to providing numerous examples of censored materials, the brief argued that censorship was a "notorious fact" as defined by article 211 of the Code of Civil Procedure, and therefore that its existence did not need to be proved to the court. "The notoriety of political censorship of the press in Brazil is incontestable to any person of straight conscience," Cardoso asserted, citing examples of censorship from the *Estado de São Paulo* and discussions of censorship in IAPA publications.[82]

Cardoso insisted not only upon the illegality of prior censorship but also upon how the censorship detracted from the legitimacy of the regime as a whole, even on the regime's own terms. He cited the censorship as one example of the violence, arbitrariness, and illegality "which has taken possession of a revolutionary movement whose declared commitment was to 'restore in this country the rule of law and the respect of democratic institutions' (inaugural speech, President of the Republic Castello Branco to Congress, April 11, 1964)."[83] He then taunted the court with a quotation from the 1937 Constitution of Vargas's Estado Novo, charging that the current regime's practice of censorship had resurrected its sinister predecessor. Cardoso further accused the regime of violating its own constitution, which he also quoted.

As the judicial voting began, one of the eleven judges requested and was granted a recess. When the voting resumed, the prosecutor announced that he had obtained a letter from the minister of justice affirming that the censorship was conducted by order of the president under AI-5, not Decree Law 1077, and hence could not be reviewed by the court. Cardoso interjected that the arguments in the case had already closed and that new material could not be presented once voting had begun. The court accepted his position and the voting was concluded. By six votes to five, the court declared the censorship of *Opinião* unconstitutional.

Opinião's jubilation lasted one day.[84] On June 20, 1973, President Medici issued a brief dispatch annulling the judicial decision and reaffirming censorship upon the basis of AI-5. Placing the censorship squarely within the purview of AI-5 meant that it could no longer be challenged in court. The most fascinating aspect of this dispatch, however, was its reference to an until then unknown dispatch of March 30, 1971, in which Medici had adopted article 9 of AI-5, which permitted prior censorship in defense of the revolution. Until that moment it had been presumed that article 9 would be invoked only in a declared state of emergency, as specified in the Constitution. This dispatch made the discrepancy between AI-5 and the Constitution that much more evident.

There appears to be no doubt in anyone's mind that this dispatch, ostensibly from 1971, was actually prepared in 1973 in response to the crisis of the *Opinião* trial. Rather than simply announcing that the censorship followed from AI-5 and was therefore beyond the reach of the courts, the government apparently went to the extreme of fabricating a backdated document authorizing the use of article 9. The regime of exception was again mimicking the rules of due process. This exercise both emphasized appropriate legal formalities while also demonstrating that the regime's power was above the law.

Opinião's victory had lasted one day; its subsequent defeat was definitive. No further appeals could be made. Despite the drama of the story, the case was neither a juridical nor a political milestone. News of it was for the most part censored, and there were no repercussions in the press or in society at large.

Prior censorship was an elaborate system with set schedules, established procedures, and assigned personnel. If it lacked a proper legal basis, it was supported by an executive branch willing to fabricate legality by backdating dispatches. Its documentary record is immense, providing parallel archives of prohibited news, analysis, voice, and perspective. The impact of this censorship was felt not only in higher production costs and lost coverage but also in the identities, rituals, and strategies of targeted publications, and in their loss of basic freedom.

Who the antagonists were was clear: the censors in newspaper offices, with their red pencils, black markers, and "vetoed" stamps, and the Federal Police in Brasília. Against these antagonists the press response was often creative and courageous. That its efforts did not even impede, much less overthrow, prior censorship had more to do with the regime's excessive power than with any failure on the part of the press to recognize, condemn, and devise strategies against prior censorship.

Prior censorship is generally considered to have been more severe, invasive, and onerous than the system known as self-censorship. Although prior censorship affected very few publications, these were important symbolic reference points for the press. Prior censorship was indeed costly and coercive, and there was no effective recourse against it. Yet the fact that those under it nonetheless found the means to resist, even ineffectually, suggests that they did maintain some power. Faced with an external agent, the press found the resources to reject and condemn the restrictions of prior censorship. Those against whom self-censorship was exercised were in a very different situation, as we will now see.

7
SELF-CENSORSHIP

> Liberty is not granted out of mercy or tolerance. One must deserve it or demand it. As long as there are the souls of slaves, there will be the vocations of masters.
> *Aliomar Baleiro, Member of the Supreme Court*

> The sound of the driven leaf will put them to flight. Fleeing as though from the sword, they shall fall though none pursues.
> *Leviticus 26:36*

THE TERM *self-censorship* suggests a practice originated by the souls of slaves, eager to participate in their own enslavement or perhaps falling though none pursues, but this was not the case with respect to the Brazilian press. Self-censorship was imposed by the regime, not by the censored upon themselves. From 1968 to 1978, the Federal Police issued illegal prohibitions against reporting specific news items and monitored press compliance with those prohibitions. Although this process was called self-censorship, the term was a misnomer. Nonetheless, the press did comply, with almost no resistance. The relative responsibility for the censorship is thus difficult to discern.

Whatever the relative roles of press and state in the practice of censorship, it is clear that there was much more at work here than slavishness on the part of the press. An established police personnel with a definite chain of authority and an elaborate set of procedures undertook a daily practice of repression that resulted, in addition to the gross limitation of public information and curtailment of constitutional freedoms, in an ample documentary record as well as a new set of relations. These do indeed suggest that there was a sword which put the press to flight, but a concealed sword wielded in a peculiar fashion, so that pursuit remained in doubt or at least deniable.

THE TERMINOLOGY OF REPRESSION

Certain concepts and vocabulary are key to examining the situation of the press in Brazil under the military regime. In general, the term censorship denotes the instrumental prohibition of information, analysis, and debate from appearing in public media.[1] It restricts the availability and circulation of information (plain objective data), and also impedes communication (in the strong sense, including formation of identities and interests). It is intended to serve the interests of those in power by causing ignorance and distortion, by weakening or incapacitating a subordinate populace. It impairs both informed assessment of the existing order and the conceptualization of alternatives to it. Censorship prevents scrutiny, curtailing efforts to make those who rule accountable. Under censorship, the comprehension of social and natural reality, of one's position in the world, and often especially of those who hold power, are manipulated.

Self-censorship is a subcategory of censorship. There is something to say, you know it, and you don't say it. This is not the silence of ignorance or poor judgment, but rather of cognizant withholding. The results for the public are similar to censorship in terms of the manipulation of knowledge and understanding, but often with the added element of the public's not even knowing that they are being denied information. This is a further level of distortion to which they are subject. For the public, overcoming the effects of press self-censorship involves not only gaining access to denied information, but first discovering and appreciating that their information about reality has been grossly limited or tampered with.

The public is a clear victim of both censorship and self-censorship. Although the press is a victim of censorship, the puzzle of self-censorship is in discerning whether—or better, to what degree—the press is victim or accomplice.

A charge of self-censorship raises two immediate issues: first, the correctness of imposing those restrictions upon oneself and sharing in the responsibility for the harm that results from those restrictions—in other words, the ethical issue of complicity; and secondly, the truth of the claim that those restrictions are indeed self-imposed—in other words, the epistemological issue of whether there is substantial or significant coercion exercised by another. The two issues are related. The press is much more deeply implicated if it has a choice.

In Brazil, as perhaps in most cases, there is no single account of the self-censorship. The censorship was not initiated or perpetuated by the press, but imposed by the regime. Yet the press was not completely weak, cowering in utter fear of the regime. There were instances of avoidance, sabotage, and scorn that would not have occurred had the press been either genuinely supportive of the restrictions or paralyzed by fear. Nonetheless, it is also true that compliance was the overwhelming norm. For years, the press accommodated an entirely illegal process that violated its basic professional and constitutional freedoms. Self-censorship continues to be the name given to that ambiguous practice.

In Brazil, the use of such terms as censorship and self-censorship was often somewhat muddled or misleading. "Censorship," for example, was used very broadly. Many press actors asserted that censorship was always occurring, whether by an editor or by the government. Raimundo Pereira, editor of *Movimento,* cited Freud in insisting that all writing included censorship. Journalist Sergio Buarque, also citing Freud, likewise affirmed that everyone practices self-censorship all the time—newspapers, businesses, government, individuals.[2] Members of the regime echoed this view. Representative Nina Ribeiro of the ARENA party offered the following defense of press censorship in Congress in 1973: "To begin with reality, censorship simply exists.... What would become of our personalities if there were no internal censorship? ... censorship exists in order to pass from an idea, a feeling, the flow of our id, of our subconscious, where terrible secrets exist, into facts, into behavior."[3] The only distinction that Walter Fontoura, editor of the *Jornal do Brasil* during the period of self-censorship, could make, had to do with whether there was one censor for all the newspapers: "Look, in normal times the function of the editor of a newspaper is to censor. The editor censors. It's the editor who decides this is going to be published, that is not. Not the reporter.... [On the other hand, under the military regime] when there's censorship, then there's someone deciding for all the newspapers."[4] There were other reasons for not publishing: lack of sufficient corroborating evidence, not wanting to damage one's other interests, congruity with a publication's larger project, even lack of space, lack of interest on the part of readers, or questions of taste. None of these resulted from a denial of liberty, an exercise of domination, an imposition of another's interest, or a use of force. The term censorship should be used to refer only to relationships of domination, to cases where someone has been denied freedom. Evaluating the self part of self-censorship has precisely to do with how masked this denial of freedom is.

The term self-censorship *(autocensura)* is used here to refer to the process of receiving and complying with prohibitions issued by the Federal Police from 1968 to 1978 because this was the term used throughout Brazil. It was used by members of the regime as well as by members of the press and their readers. This was the common and commonly identified experience of censorship, and its accepted label was self-censorship.

One further term calls for attention. *Bilhetinho* was the name for the prohibitions that were prepared and delivered by the Federal Police. *Bilhete* translates literally as "note" or "ticket." The diminutive -*inho* suffix makes it a "little note," as in the informal tone of "just thought I'd drop you a little note." They were not called prohibitions (*proibições*) or orders (*ordens*). The innocuous diminutive *bilhetinho* disguised the objective character of what were, in fact, news prohibitions that originated from the authoritarian regime.

But of course the press was not receiving them as "just a little note" from a friendly neighborhood police officer. The *bilhetinho* label also incorporated absent legal status. If on the one hand the label masked the force and authority that were behind the *bilhetinhos*, it did not mask their illegality by claiming another legal status.

The term *bilhetinho* was not contested. It was and is the label used by everyone, in the regime as well as in the press. But it was undoubtedly heard and used in different ways by different actors. The term remains one of the artifacts of the ambiguous status of these "suggested prohibitions," one of the representations of the ambiguity of the relationship between the state and the "self-censoring" press, of the ill-defined mixture of cooperation and coercion. The Portuguese *bilhetinho* will be used here rather than any inadequate English substitutes so as to retain this ambiguity.

THE PROCESS OF SELF-CENSORSHIP

The process of self-censorship in 1968–1978 had many identifiable external characteristics. It had an established bureaucracy and personnel responsible for preparing and distributing the *bilhetinhos;* a distribution system with strict rules; and a pattern of circulation within each newspaper. Patterns of compliance and enforcement also became standard.

The People Responsible

Despite being unconstitutional, self-censorship was administered by a centralized bureaucracy. Although the bureaucracy and hierarchy were established, there were many permeable places where others became involved as well.

As with prior censorship, self-censorship was under the purview of the Ministry of Justice, which determined the overall orientation of the censorship and the content of the prohibitions. The Federal Police were in charge of implementation. Again the key personnel were Special Advisor Helio Romão and a small staff of assistants. From Federal Police headquarters in

Brasília, they issued the *bilhetinhos,* which were sent to regional and local police offices throughout the country for distribution to all local media. The Federal Police both handled the distribution of and monitored and enforced press compliance with the *bilhetinhos.*

Although these people were the core personnel, others were involved. The content of the *bilhetinhos* originated primarily but not solely in the Ministry of Justice. The *bilhetinhos* themselves infrequently cited their sources, especially in the early days. In the record that remains, those sources included the president, CIEx, the Second Army, and the military police.

Even in cases where no source was cited, the close working relationships between the Federal Police and their military colleagues in CIEx and the SNI as well as the regional armies suggests that orders came from those sources as well. In an interview, the former chief of the Federal Police, Moacyr Coelho, explained its close working relationship with CIEx and the SNI as being "like this," as he pressed the palms of his hands together.[5]

Further corroboration of the involvement of the security and military apparatus comes from the content of the *bilhetinhos* themselves. These were often so sensitive or so timely that they could only have emanated from the security forces. Only the security forces would have known about some of the matters that were prohibited, such as clashes with guerrillas or street confrontations, sometimes identified in detail in the *bilhetinhos.* A final confirmation is that so many journalists recalled regularly hearing of events for the first time through the very *bilhetinhos* that prohibited their coverage.[6]

Many actors, other than the federal authorities and members of the security apparatus, evidently attempted to gain access to this process of censorship. These included not only local police and other local authorities but also politicians and other public figures.[7] Chief Coelho asserted that "Many people tried to take advantage of political censorship to exercise influence, to avoid that disagreeable things be known about them. Whenever a journalist was doing a piece which displeased a certain politician or national personality, we would get requests that it be prohibited. We didn't do it, but this was very disagreeable to us."[8] This, of course, is the chief of the Federal Police speaking, putting himself in the most responsible light, casting politicians as traditionally and inherently corrupt. Journalist Carlos Chagas believes that access to censorship was abused at times, that it was available to members of the regime or people with friends in the right places.[9] Others, when rebuffed by the national government, tried exercising influence at the local level. Clout with the local police office was sometimes sufficient for getting someone either to exercise censorship or apply pressure in another form. The fact of this unsanctioned involvement on the part of dispersed authorities is corroborated by a *bilhetinho* signed by Coelho and issued to the *Jornal do Brasil* on May 29, 1974:

> So as to avoid tendentious use, distorted information, frustration, and improper preferences, I recommend that the media of social communication be alerted that liberations and authorizations to divulge matters under censorship will be made only through the Federal Police, including distribution of official notes. Any communication attributed to other authorities which are contrary to the orders of prohibition should be communicated immediately to the director general of the Federal Police.

Another route, besides having access to the established process either through the centralized authority or its local branch, was simply to know how the system of censorship operated, and to abuse it by using that knowledge to masquerade as a person with censorship authority. Some publications found themselves the targets of such masquerades.[10] In an environment in which the state did not take public responsibility for all its actions, and indeed was not responsible for all the actions taken in its name, it was possible to become the target not just of the unconstitutional acts of the "constituted" authorities but also of anonymous counterfeiters.

Thus the system of self-censorship was formally in the hands of the Ministry of Justice and administered by the Federal Police. The military and security forces, however, were also clearly involved in determining the content of the *bilhetinhos*. Most *bilhetinhos* appear to have come from these sources. Where access became dispersed, there may also have been instances of local officials influencing the prohibitions. Evidence of involvement on the part of the upper-level military indicates that censorship was one of the valued tools of control and repression. Evidence of involvement of lower-level or local officials as well as masqueraders indicates that the upper levels could not maintain a strict monopoly on this tool—as they also could not on other forms of repression.

Delivery of the Bilhetinhos

The *bilhetinhos* had no legal basis, and this was reflected in the manner in which they were distributed.[11] The Federal Police issued prohibitions via telephone, telegram, or written document. The paper was plain and bore no official seal or stamp—a practice highly unusual for Brazilian officialdom, and duly noted by many journalists. Thus the document itself would give no clue about the origin of the prohibition. The written *bilhetinhos* were brought to each newspaper by a lower-level police officer. Although the plain paper concealed the authority behind the order, the uniformed police agent would make that authority quite clear.[12]

The *bilhetinho* would be given to a member of the newspaper's staff,

```
                    PROIBICXO

        Fim evitar deturpações e interpretações tendenciosas, reitero/
        determinações digo determinação superior sentido manter total/
        posição divulgação, através meios comunicação social, qualquer
        matéria relativa a DOM HEDER CÂMARA
                        SIGAB/DG/DPF


        BRASIL HERALD      ........ Rj Rezende, 65
        OPINIÃO
        '. Últime Hora     ........ R.
        A Gazetas de Notícias .... R. L. Martins, 72
        O Cruzeiro         ........ R do Livramento, 189
        O Jornal do Comércio ..... R do Livramento, 189
        O Pasquim          ........ R. Saint Roman
        O Jornal do Brasil,        Av. Brasil, 500      6666
        xxxxxxxxxxxxxxxxxxxxxxxxxxxxxxxxxxxxxxxxxxxxxxxxxxxxx
        O Diário de Notícias ... R. da Constituição, 11
        Rádio Roquete Pinto R. Erasmo Braga,118
        Rádio Vera Cruz,   R. B. Aires. 160
        Radio Rio de Janeiro ... R. Teodoro da Silva-
        Rádio Mauá ... Ed. o Ministério de Trabalho
        T.V. Rio .... R. Alberto Campos 12 - Leblon


            666_____   ///  _____

                   Rio de Janeiro-sm, 19 de julho de ' 7?'

        Nos papéis contendo as proibições oficiais funcionários dos jornais
        eram solicitados a colocar suas assinaturas, tomando ciência. Mas não
        havia assinatura de qualquer autoridade e nem timbre da Polícia Federal.
```

FIG. 3. Police *Bilhetinho*
Source: Ferreira 1985b, 101.

someone with a degree of responsibility.[13] The individual receiving the *bilhetinho* would copy its contents. Photocopying was not permitted, even for the longer prohibitions. *Bilhetinhos* had to be copied carefully, and they evidently were, for identical wording occurs in the records kept by different publications around the country. Newspaper employees must have known that they were taking orders, or they would not have copied the documents word for word.

When the newspaper representative had finished copying the *bilhetinho*, however, that person had to provide evidence of having accepted it. This was done by signing at the bottom of the *bilhetinho,* on a line designated for that purpose. Below the content of the prohibition there would be a list of the names and addresses of the newspapers to whom the police agent would be carrying the prohibition. Beside each was a line for the signature of the person taking responsibility for receiving the police order on behalf of the newspaper. It was all quite thorough and formal. By signing you were taking responsibility in the presence of the Federal Police agent. After delivering the *bilhetinho* and collecting the signature, the police agent would always take the *bilhetinho* away. No physical evidence was ever left behind.

The asymmetry of this process could not have been more expressive. Public responsibility was being avoided or kept deniable by the police, who, if they arrived in uniform, were bearing "a little note" on plain paper, conveying a usually unsigned order, and carefully taking it with them upon departure. Journalists, on the other hand, had to indicate their responsibility directly and explicitly by signing and providing complete precise information (the name and address of their institution and a signature of a registered employee). The degrees of publicness, of accountability, of responsibility were entirely asymmetrical, with only the representative of public authority permitted secrecy and anonymity.

A further aspect of the way *bilhetinhos* were delivered was the relation among all the publications as they faced the police. When presented with a *bilhetinho,* you saw the signatures of those complying or lines where signatures were to appear. One way your professional community was being defined was through seeing this. A *bilhetinho* was one of the places where you saw yourself listed with your counterparts. It was one of the descriptions made of you, to which you had to respond by accepting or rejecting. And who would be your allies, if others signed? Were you being unreasonable to resist, when all the others were complying? The content of the *bilhetinhos* has been fairly well documented and analyzed. This aspect, however, of the required signatures and prepared blanks, has received much less attention, perhaps because there are no examples of *bilhetinhos* in any public records. Thus to see one of the few photocopies someone managed to make at the time is quite illuminating (see fig. 3).[14]

Internal Circulation

Once delivered to each newspaper and duly copied, the *bilhetinhos* had to make their way to the relevant desks. To facilitate compliance, as more than one interviewed editor or journalist asserted, most newspapers collected the *bilhetinhos* in what came to be called black books. This permitted coordination among the editors of the newspaper's topical sections, who would be able to consult the compilation. Circulation or consultation appears to have stopped at this level in these vertically structured organizations.

Somewhat different stories are heard from the different newspapers, or from different posts within the newspapers, but everyone—from editors-in-chief to junior reporters—agrees that there was no formal or informal discussion, no announcement or bulletin board making the *bilhetinhos* generally available or public within any newspaper. There was no open recognition on the part of a newspaper's hierarchy or among the employed journalists that *bilhetinhos* were arriving and being obeyed.

Any discussion of the prohibitions occurred among the top editorial staff during the meetings in which the editors of the different sections of a newspaper would discuss the content of that day's edition. Consulting the *bilhetinhos* would be part of their general coordination of the newspaper's production. Thus those at the highest levels in the newspaper's editorial structure, those who would be participating in such meetings, were the ones who regularly saw the black books.

The process at the *Jornal do Brasil* appears to have been typical. Its editor at the time, Walter Fontoura, recalled this as a straightforward routine. When asked about the nature of the discussions on the *bilhetinhos*, he interpreted the question literally: "There would be two daily meetings of editors, at 2:00 P.M. and 6:00 P.M. The economics editor would learn of prohibitions dealing with economic news, et cetera." Director Waldir de Góes also recalled ample discussion among the top staff: "We, the cupola of the editorial staff, had daily meetings in which we evaluated what we were publishing, what care we needed to take." With respect to circulation or discussion of the *bilhetinhos* beyond the top staff, Fontoura felt that "Everybody knew. There was no intent to hide anything. Whoever wanted to know, knew." But not hiding is different from discussing, debating, or making available.[15]

Nuinio Spinola, economics editor at the *Jornal do Brasil* from 1967 to 1974, considered the vertical organization of the newspaper to be highly relevant to the practice of censorship. To explain the newspaper's internal functioning, he delineated the lines of authority in that period: "The structure of the *Jornal do Brasil* was this: (1) Brito, owner; (2) Alberto Dines, editor-in-chief; (3) Carlos Lemos, head of the editorial staff. Below him there were editors for each section: politics, economics, sports, city beat. I decided what I could publish; Lemos decided what I couldn't publish." Spinola pantomimed Lemos prancing into his office, waving a *bilhetinho* in the air, and singing, "Look what I've got for you." For Spinola, there was no way around the newspaper's own hierarchy, and this was what immediately determined his experience of censorship. As number four in the hierarchy, he accepted what came down from number three. Spinola felt that he had freedom within a circumscribed space, and that was how he operated.[16]

Journalists who were not privy to the meetings of the editorial staff nonetheless might know of the *bilhetinhos* in general, and sometimes their content.[17] José Neumanne Pinto was at the *Folha de São Paulo* from 1970 to 1975, during the period of the *bilhetinhos*. In the early 1970s, as a junior reporter, Neumanne knew that there was censorship, that orders were arriving via telephone, and that they were coming from the Federal Police: "Everybody knew. But there was a code. You knew up to what point you could go; ... the *Folha de São Paulo* would get messages over the telephone, the prohibitions. There would be no general meeting to say, 'We've been prevented from publishing the following.' There was no explicit communication, no communication between editor and reporters. Period. If you happened to be standing by, you heard the *bilhetinho* too."[18]

Jaime Sautchuk was likewise a junior reporter, but at the much smaller *Diário de Brasília,* and therefore was given greater responsibility. As a subeditor, he would close the newspaper in the evenings, and was well aware of the *bilhetinho* process. In his view, most press owners and editors-in-chief were "conniving" with and "subservient" to the military regime, and were therefore distrusted. Discussion between journalists and editors was cautious and restricted, while discussion among journalists was veiled: "Well, a *bilhetinho* might come by my desk by mistake. I would turn to my neighbor and say, 'Look, this came to my desk and it belongs on yours. Let's let it fall in the wastebasket.' We would publish everything, and the next day, when confronted with the *bilhetinho,* say, 'Gee, I never saw it.' This wasn't done openly. It was secret, secretive, informal. There was a climate of distrust, and no space to create otherwise."[19] Sautchuk could apparently expect some degree of tacit agreement and trust from the journalist at the next desk, but this was never developed openly, and certainly did not extend to the editors.

Journalist Carlos Lins da Silva reflected similarly upon the lack of discussion regarding the arrival and content of *bilhetinhos*. To account for the lack of discussion he suggested two factors, fear and newsroom organization:

I think first there was fear. Fear of being fired or of being arrested right there, because of police in plain clothes or informants. There was a general lack of confidence. You didn't know who could be beside you. Anyone could be a nonjournalist policeman faking it as a journalist.[20]

The second factor is that the newsroom is so dynamic, so noisy and busy. The workplace is not where journalists talk with each other. There was no time or leisure to discuss. So those were the two factors that impeded discussion, but fear, of course, was the most important factor.[21]

Commenting upon why editors would never intervene to call a general meeting, Lins da Silva argued: "It never happened. They were even more scared. They had more reason to be fearful than the reporters. They were more eminent and more well known by the police and the owners of the newspapers."[22]

Denis de Morães, then a journalist at *O Globo*, considered whether there were any disagreements between journalists and editors about accepting the *bilhetinhos*. He answered, "No. The rules, the lines of authority, were so clear that you were intimidated from challenging, from asking. You accepted your part. The limits were so clear and it wouldn't get you anywhere to push. Where would it get you? Kicked out."[23] So no disagreement was expressed, but that did not mean that there was agreement.

The structure of the workplace—from the pace in the newsrooms to the vertical organization that divided the top editorial staff from the journalists—combined with distrust of both police and superiors to impede discussion of the receipt and content of the *bilhetinhos*. The different actors in this process were relatively isolated.

Result: Preempted Coverage

Once the *bilhetinhos* arrived in the hands of the appropriate editor at the meeting of the top staff, the most frequent manner of complying was simply to fail to assign a reporter to cover an event. Only rarely were any articles cut or investigations halted. In many cases, the very first time that a newspaper would hear of a news item that was the subject of a *bilhetinho* would be from the *bilhetinho* itself. In that situation, the newspaper would simply not send anyone to cover the story.[24]

It is therefore moot to ask anyone about the experience of having an article censored. In most cases this did not happen. Neumanne Pinto, for example, recalled that as a reporter at the *Folha de Sao Paulo*, "Sometimes you learned of the censorship from your work being cut, but far more often, issues were just never covered. The *bilhetinhos* would come in immediately, before the editor knew independently, so the editor simply didn't send anybody out to cover that story." Waldir de Góes of the *Jornal do Brasil* recalled that "Frequently the *bilhetinhos* were on topics we didn't know about: the death of so-and-so in a confrontation with security forces at such-and-such a place. And we wouldn't have known anything about it. But it would remain our internal knowledge. We just couldn't do anything more with it." Fontoura assessed the harm caused by the censorship as follows: "It was not financial, as in wasted materials, because prohibitions would come and we wouldn't cover. No. The harm was intangible, a moral damage."[25]

Awareness of the process was avoidable or avoided as a result of three things: the ambiguous manner in which *bilhetinhos* were delivered by the Federal Police, who disguised and removed the evidence yet simultaneously displayed their authority; the lack of general availability or open discussion of the *bilhetinhos* in newspaper offices; and the manner in which the press complied, which led to coverage being preempted. It was possible to operate within self-censoring newspapers without ever choosing to confront, or being confronted by, the censorship. Ignorance was possible. The modus operandi recalled by Denis de Morães was shared by many other journalists: "As a journalist you handed in the material, and there ended your responsibility. The implicit law was: don't ask."[26]

Compliance, Monitoring, and Retaliation

Very little straightforward data on compliance with self-censorship is available. Much of the *bilhetinho* process that has been described here was denied and concealed. There were no public debates of censorship as a policy decision, and there are no official records of the orders and proportions that were obeyed. Similarly, there is no complete accounting of confiscations in retaliation for noncompliance.

Also lacking are detailed accounts of single spectacular cases of resistance or retaliation—because there were no such cases. Unlike prior censorship, there were no lawsuits, no sarcastic telegrams, no stunning acts of coercion, no harsh threats, no grandiose confrontations, and thus no dramatic and didactic stories of retaliation. There are, rather, unanimous expressions of the common knowledge that the press complied completely. All recollections confirm that compliance with the *bilhetinhos* was the overwhelming norm.

The Federal Police monitored compliance through their offices in Brasília. Special Advisor Romão claimed that his office read every newspaper every day, "to make sure everything was just right." And if it was not, they would order confiscation. While both Romão and Federal Police chief Coelho recall numerous confiscations, neither could provide estimates of their number or frequency.[27]

Certainly, the press felt closely monitored. Waldir de Góes of the *Jornal do Brasil* was well aware of the presence of the police: "Possibilities of resistance were absolutely null, because it was an open dictatorship. And the police accompanied the rolling of the presses. If there was anything there that shouldn't be—well, they were the police. They could order the presses to stop, and the newspaper would not circulate. So either we followed orders or the newspaper would not circulate, with considerable financial damage."[28] From a business standpoint, confiscation of an edition would be sufficient retaliation to ensure compliance.

Jornal do Brasil's editor, Fontoura, also considered any potential retaliation to be sufficiently dire, even if the threat was vague: "Prohibited material was not published. If it were, no one knew what might happen—perhaps invasion of the newspaper, I don't know, imprisonment."[29] His speculations were not unfounded, and were part of the context of compliance.

From the overall record of compliance, it would seem that discipline and reprisal occurred frequently enough to enforce the *bilhetinho* process and underscore authority, and infrequently enough to imply that the system did not need much enforcing.

Demise of the Bilhetinhos

The number of *bilhetinhos* began to dwindle after 1974; the last one was recorded in 1978. The return to press freedom, such as it was, occurred within the framework of the *abertura* and mirrored that movement's progress. There were no dramatic breakthroughs, no wholesale rejections of the past. Rather, the process was for the most part slow, gradual, and controlled—the descriptions most often used by the regime. But it was also subject to uncertainties. Two forces pulling the dynamic of *abertura* away from its preprogrammed path (whether the issue was the press, direct elections, political amnesty, or judicial reform) were the regime's internal disputes and the increasing organization and activity of civil society. These forces affected the return to press freedom, with hard-liners seeking to maintain forms of press censorship while press organizations, such as the ABI and the journalists' union in São Paulo, became more vocal and critical. Thus, as with the *abertura* as a whole, the return to press freedom was gradual and halting, a process of retreats as well as advances. The *bilhetinhos* may have dwindled in number, but they were never challenged or repudiated.

One further force promoting the return to press freedom was that press freedom itself could be used by the Geisel faction in their continuing struggles with the hard-liners. By permitting press coverage of hard-line actions and positions, Geisel transferred these into the public arena. By doing so, he strengthened his hand, adding public pressure when his own factional resources were insufficient to subdue or discipline his hard-line opponents within the regime.[30] By permitting press coverage, he greatly increased pressure for some sort of accounting for hard-line actions. Celina Rabello Duarte analyzes this aspect of the *abertura* and concludes that relaxation of censorship of the press was "fundamental to making the project of *abertura* viable, to increasing the state's capacity to govern, and to strengthening the Geisel group in power." She cites a journalist well aware of the delicate symbiosis, the potential for mutual manipulation in these circumstances. It was not, the journalist noted, a debate on "how to define liberty of the press, but rather a use, by groups within the system, of reciprocal vulnerabilities."[31] In leaving behind the self-censorship of the *bilhetinhos*, the press did not move into a period of absolute independence. Rather, with the end of the more explicit forms of control, press and state settled once more into the historically familiar relationship of reciprocal vulnerability.

THE CONTENT OF SELF-CENSORSHIP: THE *Bilhetinhos*

The existing collections of *bilhetinhos* provide crucial information on the military regime. They contain some of the still untold news stories of the time. They also reveal certain aspects of the censorship bureaucracy as well as some of the chief concerns of the regime. Yet the archive also has important limitations. Compilations were maintained by newspapers primarily to facilitate compliance, not to secure the historical record. These compilations, known as black books, were typically begun a few years into the period of *bilhetinhos,* and are therefore incomplete. Despite these limitations, the language and content of the *bilhetinhos* preserved in several black books have been analyzed by a number of researchers, who offer fairly consistent conclusions.

The Collections: Sources, Quality, and Frequency

The collections derive from several sources. Two important collections were maintained by the *Jornal do Brasil* and the *Folha de São Paulo.* The black book kept by the *Jornal do Brasil* was begun in September 1972, continued until October 1975, and eventually contained 256 *bilhetinhos.* The *Folha de São Paulo*'s black book was begun in March 1972, continued until December 1974, and eventually contained 286 *bilhetinhos.* In addition, participants at a 1978 ABI conference on freedom of the press placed in the conference record collections from Radio JB (Rio de Janeiro) and TV Bandeirantes (São Paulo). Journalist Paulo Marconi compiled a set of 308 different *bilhetinhos* from various media outlets in the city of Salvador, Bahia, including the newspapers *A Tarde, Tribuna da Bahia,* and *Diário de Notícias.* His record dates from 1969 to 1978. These are the most comprehensive collections of *bilhetinhos.*[32] No such collection is held by the Federal Police, or at least none is publicly available, but the content and frequency of the *bilhetinhos* can be sufficiently assessed by examining the material just mentioned.

The *bilhetinhos* found in the black books were, as discussed above, not the originals, but quick copies made by the journalists who received them. This would have created opportunities for error, one source of divergence among the collections. Yet they were obviously copied with great care, as if by people who knew they were taking orders, for the same wording is found in copies from São Paulo, Rio de Janeiro, and Salvador.

An important limitation is that none of the black books are complete. Years went by before these records began to be kept regularly at any of the publications. The *Jornal do Brasil* black book, published in full and one of the best known, is wrongly considered complete. It does not begin until September 1972, whereas prohibitions were being issued (although irregularly and without recourse to all of the previously described elaborate channels of communication) from the end of 1968.

TABLE 1. Number of *Bilhetonhos* Issued in Brazil, 1969–1978

	Salvador, Bahia (several publications)	Unidentified Collection	*Jornal do Brasil*
1969	1[a]	—	—
1970	27	27	—
1971	52	67	—
1972	80	107	25
1973	159	222	106
1974	162	194	117
1975	18	—	8
1976	12	—	—
1977	25	—	—
1978	15[b]	—	—

a. Contains 17 prohibitions.
b. Marcon's Salvador collection included 308 different *bilhetinhos*. The total recorded here is greater because it includes duplicates received from different media outlets.

A comparison of the black books suggests that censorship was applied with roughly equal force to all newspapers. The total numbers found in each collection are very similar. The *Jornal do Brasil* recorded 256 and the *Folha de São Paulo* 286 from roughly the same period. The collection from several sources in Salvador, which covers a slightly longer period, contains 308 different *bilhetinhos*.

It is also clear that the *bilhetinhos* reached their numerical peak from 1970 to 1975. Table 1 presents data from several collections. The first column is from Marconi's compilation of 308 Salvador *bilhetinhos*, the second is from an unidentified collection examined by Glaucio Soares,[33] and the third is from the black book of the *Jornal do Brasil*.

The pattern in each collection indicates the intensity of the censorship during the Medici administration, particularly 1973, and in 1974, the first year of the Geisel administration. Of the 117 *bilhetinhos* issued to the *Jornal do Brasil* in 1974, 84 followed Geisel's March inauguration. Other aspects of repression, such as political disappearances, also reached their greatest intensity during these years. Although both phenomena declined dramatically after 1974, they remained available as tactics for several more years.[34]

Language

As a documentary record of self-censorship, the *bilhetinhos* can be analyzed for both their language and content. Certain patterns in the language, such as its elaborateness or indications of authority, suggest aspects of the relationship between the regime and the press.

Occasionally the language of the *bilhetinhos* was brief and to the point, as in the following succinct prohibition:

Don't touch on the presidential succession (delivered to the *Jornal do Brasil*, January 3, 1973).

The language of the great majority of *bilhetinhos*, however, was heavily formulaic and burdened by elaborate set phrases. There was no economy of language:

By order of the director of the Federal Police, it is prohibited throughout the national territory to disseminate via the written, spoken, or televised press any news or commentary referring to external financing destined for the acquisition of arms by the Brazilian Army (delivered to the *Jornal do Brasil*, March 20, 1973).

By superior order, it is definitively prohibited to disseminate via the written, spoken, and televised means of social communication any news, interviews, references, transcription, photographs, and other materials about the adherence of Patricia Hearst to terrorism (delivered to the *Jornal do Brasil*, March 5, 1974).

By superior order, it is definitively prohibited to disseminate via the written, spoken, or televised means of social communication any news, commentaries, transcription, reference and other materials about the declaration of Representative Mario Teles attributing to Minister Golbery do Couto e Silva information regarding the suspension of censorship and complete *abertura* (delivered to the *Jornal do Brasil*, June 20, 1974).

The pattern was already established in 1973 and remained consistent through the tenure of several directors of the Federal Police. Every medium and form of coverage was fastidiously specified. Even on days when there was more than one *bilhetinho*, the entire formula was repeated.

Although the regime delineated the content and scope of the *bilhetinhos* in elaborate language, it was quite willing to be rather vague and terse about the authority from which those documents emanated. This too was embedded in the language of the *bilhetinhos*. On this issue, Marconi has done some numerical analysis.[35] Marconi took the 308 different *bilhetinhos* that were delivered to the media in Salvador from January 1970 to September 1974 and examined how frequently the anonymous phrases "by superior order" and "it is prohibited" occurred. While at the beginning of the period there were references to the censoring authority, such as the Ministry of Justice, the Federal Police, or even the president, in time these declined in number, and eventually disappeared. Marconi found that the share of *bilhetinhos* lacking references to a particular authority rose steadily, from 47 percent in

1970 to 63 percent in 1971, 81 percent in 1972, 98 percent in 1973, and 100 percent in 1974. Marconi considers the increasing use of such elusive constructions as "it is prohibited" proof of the arrogance and impunity of the censoring authorities.

The anonymous "by superior order" that came to characterize the language of the *bilhetinhos* was complemented by other aspects of their delivery. They were presented on plain paper, with no official seal or stamp, and often with no signature even by a local authority (although the recipient had to sign), and were removed after being copied.

When challenged on this pattern of increasing anonymity, both Moacyr Coelho, chief of the Federal Police from 1974 to 1985, and Helio Romão, Special Advisor to the Federal Police and the man responsible for overseeing the censorship's operation, asserted that no one had been attempting to hide anything. The prevalence of such phrases as "it is prohibited" was to them simply the result of the process's routinization. Because *bilhetinhos* were issued so frequently, there was no reason to continually identify the exact authority. Everyone knew who the authorities were, and it was merely a matter of saving time to omit such information. There was nothing sinister about it. Indeed, they affirmed there was no need to hide their actions.

Where Marconi sees impunity and arrogance, an intent to hide behind anonymous phrases, former Federal Police officials downplay the *bilhetinhos*' coercive nature by stating they were akin to casual conversations, gentlemen's agreements. There is substance, moreover, to Romão's assertion that it all became very routine, including in language. The linguistic routines, though, were quite the opposite of those Coelho and Romão wanted to assert. Far from dispensing with officious formulas, the *bilhetinhos* were encased in elaborate terminology, prohibiting "via written, spoken, and televised means of social communication any news, commentary, interviews, references, transcription, photographs and other materials." Such formulas may not have been the result of the sinister arrogance that Marconi sees, but neither did they indicate the chummy familiarity and mutual understandings between police and press that Coelho and Romão would like to claim.

The language could have resulted from fastidiousness. It also revealed a lack of trust. In being so careful to specify the particular forms of prohibited communication, the regime seemed to be indicating that if they were not specified, the press would find a way to disseminate its views. The implication was that the regime assumed that the press was looking for a way to skirt the prohibitions, and therefore that the regime needed to be thorough in specifying the particulars of the prohibitions. If there was little confusion in the communication, it was not because of shared points of view or a shared vocabulary, but rather because the regime had made its commands so explicit. Furthermore, the thoroughness of the specifications made it evident that the regime considered itself to have authority over every newspaper, radio station, and television station, every source of news or interpretation, indeed every detail.

Like the manner in which they were delivered, the *bilhetinhos*' language both hid and revealed the authority upon which they rested. The anonymous "it is prohibited" did disguise the identity of the censoring authority, but at the same time the elaborate formulaic phrasing signaled the degree and scope of authority the regime claimed.

There was more to this language, however, than fastidiousness, arrogance, or the assumption of authority. A further issue was the manner in which authority was assumed. The language of the *bilhetinhos* fit the pattern of the regime's pursuit of legitimacy.

The question for the regime was, how to phrase a baldly illegal news prohibition directed at a nominally free press, while continuing to claim to uphold constitutional press freedom. The answer: by mimicking legal formulas. The regime always went about breaking the rules in an extremely lawlike fashion. Its Institutional Acts, which contradicted the Constitution, were presented as central documents establishing the rules of governance. The elections it held, characterized by limited candidacies, restricted campaigning, and canceled mandates, were nonetheless presented as though they were free. The regime purged Congress and curtailed its powers, but nonetheless kept it open, maintaining its status as a continuous traditional institution. In all these practices, legitimate institutions were mimicked but not truly respected. Indeed, they were overridden or contradicted during the execution of this very process of mimicry.

This same mimesis occurred in the language of the *bilhetinhos*. Despite being illegal news prohibitions, they were presented in full legalistic language, almost as a spoof of legalese. Despite constant repetition, they always included the same elaborate officious formulas. There was an assertion of legal rectitude, propriety, and due formality in the ornate, mannered phrasing. Indeed, there was an incantatory or ritual aspect to the language, in that it was clearly accomplishing a dual function: delivering information via the content of the prohibitions while also asserting, through mimicry, not only the actual capacity but also the full legal authority to do so.

Whenever possible, the regime concealed, denied, and eliminated the evidence of censorship. When this was not possible, the regime conducted itself as though it had due authority to issue news prohibitions, as though the practice were entirely legitimate. It did so by mimicking traditional norms of legal language and the format of official orders.

Content

The documentary record of the *bilhetinhos* can be assessed for content as well as language. Several content analyses have identified the topical categories in which the *bilhetinhos* clustered.[36] These topics included repressive acts, opposition activities, and the regime's internal problems. The essential and unsurprising finding is that in all the years for which there is a record, the issues most censored had to do with protecting the state and hiding its authoritarian nature. As Glaucio Soares concludes, "The censorship was, principally, an authoritarian instrument of protection for the state itself. It sought to hide the authoritarianism in an authoritarian manner, as well as hiding resistance to it."[37] The following selection of *bilhetinhos* illustrates their most frequent themes and topics, including state repression, the presidential succession, the regime's internal disputes, the Catholic Church, and censorship.

With respect to incidents of state repression, some *bilhetinhos* were very specific, and must have been the first indication that newspapers had of these events:

About the shootout on the viaduct of Parada Lucas, in which police were wounded, the only thing permitted is the official statement of the First Army (delivered to the *Jornal do Brasil*, November 11, 1972).

Other *bilhetinhos* were very general, although still explicit:

By superior order any news on the action of security organs in the states of Bahia, Sergipe, Alagoas, Pernambuco, Paraíba, Rio Grande do Norte, Ceará, Piauí, and Maranhão is prohibited (delivered in Salvador, February 1, 1972).

Daily newspapers, weeklies, magazines, radio and television are prohibited from covering news on the death, imprisonment, detention, or any activities of subversive elements, in whatever circumstances, except when there is specific and direct authorization from the director general of the Federal Police, so as to avoid a breach of secrecy or exploitation of publicity regarding facts of this nature (delivered to the *Jornal do Brasil*, April 10, 1973).

Prohibition of anything regarding the presidential succession was another frequent theme of the *bilhetinhos*, just as it was a consistent theme of prior censorship. The prohibition was restated frequently enough to make it appear that succession was both a regular concern of the regime and a highly sensitive issue that it would have expected the press to report upon:

By order of the Ministry of Justice, all newspapers and magazines are definitively prohibited from publishing any commentaries, criticisms, suggestions, or analysis respecting the presidential succession, accepting *[sic]* only transcriptions of parliamentary speeches, without, however, treating these items sensationally (delivered in Salvador, August 22, 1972).

The prohibition of the publication of any news referring to the succession of President Medici is reiterated. This restriction includes the transcription of speeches or pronouncements made in the city councils and state assemblies (delivered in Salvador, August 24, 1972).

By superior order we reiterate the maintenance of the prohibition against news referring to the presidential succession, principally to avoid divulging the names of possible candidates (delivered in Salvador, May 16, 1973).

By superior order the prohibition of news referring to the presidential succession is maintained, including transcriptions from other newspapers, principally to avoid divulging the names of probable candidates (delivered in Salvador, June 8, 1973).

By superior order it continues to be prohibited to present news regarding the presidential succession, principally the indication of the names of probable candidates (delivered in Salvador, June 18, 1973).

By superior order, commentaries and editorials regarding the presidential succession are liberated. Only criticisms of the system for choosing the new president and of the person indicated as candidate are vetoed. The official news release of the president of the Republic regarding the succession may be disseminated (delivered in Salvador, June 19, 1973).

Disputes within the regime's civilian and military establishments were also a regular topic of the *bilhetinhos,* and again there was a parallel with prior censorship. Disputes were one of the topics most consistently censored. The censorship continued until the very end of the period in which *bilhetinhos* were issued:

VERY URGENT. By superior order, it is definitively prohibited to disseminate via whatever means of communication, press, radio and television, the interview, memorial, letter, or any other manner of statement by or referring to General Albuquerque Lima (delivered in Salvador, March 3, 1971).

URGENT. By superior order, all media are prohibited from disseminating any commentary on the pronouncement of General Albuquerque Lima, even if it is in Castello's column in the *Jornal do Brasil.* And also whatever challenge to the regime, notably to AI-5, whatever critique of the government that would be injurious or defaming or that is aimed at provoking dissension in the heart of the armed forces, or whatever material of an analogous nature. For any violation, newspapers will be confiscated and other media taken off the air (delivered in Salvador, March 18, 1971).[38]

One issue that arose, particularly in the case of policy disagreements between civilian officials, was that of press leaks as a resource for members of the regime engaged in internal disputes. With the press censored, using leaks as tools for shifting a debate was no longer an option. It is possible that the minister of agriculture intended to leak the secret plan referred to in the *bilhetinho* below, but was thwarted by the Federal Police. This was another fine moment in the history of Brazilian public debate:

The following are prohibited: news about the dispute between the Ministry of the Treasury and the Ministry of Agriculture, and news about the secret plan to combat inflation, which the Ministry of the Treasury has delivered to the president of the Republic (delivered to the *Jornal do Brasil,* January 17, 1973).

The last *bilhetinho* in the black books examined here also concerned the regime's internal divisions:

By order of the Ministry of Justice, radio and television stations are prohibited from disseminating news, interviews, and commentaries of military officials or civilians relating to the situation of General Hugo Abreu (delivered in Salvador, November 9, 1978).

Another prevalent *bilhetinho* topic, again mirroring the concerns of prior censorship, was the Catholic Church, as represented by the National Conference of Brazilian Bishops, and in particular Dom Helder Camara. Sometimes the Church was the only topic for several weeks.[39] The *bilhetinhos* on this topic were striking for their frequency and repetition, for the virulence of their language, and for the paranoia and sense of betrayal they expressed. The following are only a small selection:[40]

By order of the Ministry of Justice, it remains prohibited for the spoken, written, or televised press to make any statement whatever against or in favor of Dom Helder Camara. This prohibition extends to those time periods on television reserved for political campaigning (delivered in Salvador, October 9, 1970).

By superior order, it is definitively prohibited to disseminate via any media, newspapers, radio, and television, the following news item: "Federal Police invaded the Metropolitan Curia, imprisoning priests and seizing a vast amount of documentation. Dom Helder protested vehemently and etc., etc., etc." (delivered in Salvador, July 8, 1971).

Not one reference to Cardinal *[sic]* Helder Camara, whether in favor or against (delivered in Salvador November 8, 1972).

By superior order it is definitively prohibited to publish, transcribe, comment upon, or make any type of reference to, through organs of the written, spoken, or televised press, the Manifesto of the Bishops of the Center West, considered a violent piece of political contestation (delivered in Salvador, June 13, 1973).

By superior order it is definitively prohibited to disseminate any news, transcription, commentary, information, or reference to foreign coverage linked directly or indirectly to Dom Helder Camara, as well as other materials on [Dom Helder Camara], through the written, spoken, or televised means of social communication. Observation: I [General Antonio Bandeira] recommend to superintendents, directors, and others responsible that they exert themselves personally and with all rigor to see that this determination is complied with. Confirm receipt and indicate measures taken (delivered in Salvador, February 5, 1974).

By superior order, I reiterate the total prohibition, for undetermined time, of whatever material, via the written, spoken, and televised means of communication, on Dom Helder Camara (delivered in Salvador, February 8, 1974).

Interspersed throughout the record, as in the record of prior censorship, are a number of *bilhetinhos* prohibiting mention of censorship. Not only was the press being censored, but the fact of this censorship was itself censored. The press could not tell its readers that it was being censored and that they were reading censored news, or anything about the official debates concerning censorship:

By superior order it is prohibited to publish any news or commentary on the measures imposed upon newspapers, including confiscation of editions, if there are any. I recommend attention to the dispatches coming from foreign news agencies (delivered in Salvador, August 25, 1972).

It is prohibited to publish the decree of Dom Pedro I, from the last century, abolishing censorship in Brazil. Any commentary regarding this decree is also prohibited (delivered in Salvador, September 6, 1972).

The Federal Censor prohibits the dissemination of the speech of the Majority Leader, Senator Filinto Muller, denying that censorship exists in Brazil (delivered to the *Jornal do Brasil*, September 19, 1972).

The InterAmerican Press Association released a statement regarding restrictions upon the press in Brazil and four other Latin America countries. By order of the minister of justice, it is prohibited to divulge only the part of this statement concerning Brazil (delivered to the *Folha de São Paulo*, January 3, 1973).

A few final examples of *bilhetinhos* will suggest the range of the remaining topics. Occasional topics included bus strikes, riots on trains, land invasions, corruption cases, oil sales, and streaking (the fad for running naked through a public place—the subject of the sole *bilhetinho* issued on March 15, 1974, the day of Geisel's inauguration). Some of these topics were also covered by prior censorship, such as the outbreak of meningitis in São Paulo and the importation of rotten meat from Uruguay. A number dealt with public health issues and included justifications for the prohibitions:

By superior order it is prohibited to disseminate by any means of communication the news relating to the accident of the leak of the pipeline in Cubatão (delivered in Salvador, April 27, 1972).[41]

By superior order it is prohibited to disseminate any news referring to the matter covered in the telex transcribed below: "The Government has already taken all cautionary measures regarding the mosquito-related outbreak of hemorrhagic fever among children in the Amazon region, this population being immunized. It is of great importance that this fact not be disseminated in the country's press, giving pretexts for improper and inopportune attacks to all types of opponents to transamazon policies. The dissemination of any news regarding this matter should be prohibited" (delivered in Salvador, May 22, 1972).[42]

It is prohibited to disseminate news of the poisoning of a reservoir in Alameda Santos (SP), because this could get in the way of police investigations (delivered in Salvador, April 29, 1974).

By superior order and so as to avoid doubts and interpretations, it is reiterated that the dissemination of numerical data, graphs, and statistics about meningitis as well as about the quantity of vaccine imported is prohibited. It is equally prohibited to disseminate via the press sensationalist material or tendentious exploitation of any subject relative to meningitis (delivered in Salvador, July 28, 1974).

By superior order, so as to avoid speculative favoring of some meatpackers and ranchers, who are inclined to finance a tendentious campaign aimed at provoking an increase in the price of fresh meat, it is prohibited to disseminate news, commentary, reference, transcription, and other materials via the means of social communication, giving negative attributes to frozen meat or establishing comparisons between the quality of frozen and fresh meat. Equally prohibited are any news items accusing the governmental authorities of protecting foreign meatpackers (delivered in Salvador, August 8, 1974).

Other *bilhetinhos* are significant not for their topical content but for what else they may reveal, such as possible disputes within the censorship bureaucracy, careful monitoring of the press, and manipulation of the public record through the use of prohibitions. A few odd echoes also invite one to consider what it was like to be a newspaper editor responsible for reading *bilhetinhos* together with the more conventional press releases that crossed one's desk.

The following very thorough, obviously carefully considered order was rescinded the very same day it was issued. Was this the outcome of a dispute within the censorship bureaucracy, or, as will be discussed below, perhaps a response to complaints from editors? Whatever the reason, the capriciousness captured in this example would clearly have made complying with the *bilhetinhos* difficult:

It is prohibited to publish any commentary, news, interviews, or criticisms of whatever nature on the *abertura* and democratization as well as related matters; amnesty for or the review of the cases of those whose rights have been canceled; editorials, commentaries or unfavorable criticisms in the financial and economic field; presidential succession and respective implications. These determinations apply to everyone, even ministers of state or persons who have occupied any function in public activity. It is prohibited to transmit speeches made in Congress or in state assemblies, in whole or in part (delivered in Salvador, November 1, 1973).

By order of the Federal Police, editors should disregard the previous communication (delivered in Salvador, November 1, 1973).

Another issue was the closeness of the monitoring and the care with which orders were communicated. On certain topics, there was to be no leeway for error or interpretation. The two-part prohibition below included references to national and foreign sources as well as statements to be made in the future, and was followed by a further clarification, probably by telephone:

1. Do not publish any news or commentary about the apprehension of journalists today in Porto Alegre, even if this news comes via foreign news agencies.

2. Amnesty International earlier announced that the Brazilian subversive Manoel da Conceição was assassinated. This news item is not true, and the authorities in Fortaleza will present this individual today.

Officer Carlos Alberto clarified the point that any news on Amnesty International is vetoed, with the exception of this news about the subversive Manoel da Conceição, which is liberated (delivered to the *Jornal do Brasil*, September 20, 1972).

The degree to which the authorities could distort the public record, with no redress for those affected, is also suggested by some of the *bilhetinhos*. In the case of the prohibition transcribed below, it is clear that there had been a private meeting and an account of it by one participant was about to be reported in the press. The other participant, however, had the power of censorship. He might not have been able to control the private dialogue, but he could determine its appearance in the press, which would have had far greater effect:

Bishop Dom Ivo Lorscheider, after a meeting with the Ministry of Justice, yesterday gave an interview in which, in part, he affirmed that the minister "had promised to order an inquiry to investigate irregularities that Dom Ivo had denounced." This passage is false and is therefore prohibited from publication or dissemination, and should not appear in the text of the interview (delivered in Salvador, January 20, 1972).

Some of the oddities that occur in the *bilhetinhos* are artifacts of language in passages that may have been hastily or poorly written or incorrectly transmitted or recorded. Nonetheless, they are striking. Consider the final phrase of this *bilhetinho* and the dual nature of *bilhetinhos* as instruments of concealment and sources of information:

It is prohibited to publish the protest of the Brazilian Bar Association against the arbitrary imprisonments and kidnappings of persons, which have been occurring (delivered to the *Jornal do Brasil*, July 13, 1973).

Finally, imagine being an editor with any sense of professional responsibility or personal vulnerability, and reading this:

By superior order, it is definitively prohibited to disseminate via any media, press, radio, or television, the news transmitted by UPI and Agence France-Presse about torture in Brazil, with the recommendation of the International Commission of Jurists for the intervention of the United Nations in our country (delivered in Salvador, March 23, 1971).

DAILY RELATIONS

The institutions, practices, and procedures of censorship also generated a set of relations within the press itself and between the press and the regime. Often these were in striking contrast to the relations that emerged from prior censorship. They were characterized more by nonconfrontation and avoidance than by the direct and strategic assertions of prior censorship.

Two kinds of relations were simply missing from the *bilhetinhos*. The first involved relations with readers. While publications under prior censorship undertook numerous tactics to alert their readers to censorship, such as inserting black boxes, blank spaces, inedible recipes, and romantic poetry into their pages, there were no parallel efforts in publications subject to self-censorship, no strategies for indicating to readers that the dissemination of information was being prohibited.[43]

The other absent dimension was the immediate relationship with police censors, the individuals whom those under prior censorship could seek to cajole, fool, or exhaust. In the case of self-censorship, the contact was with the police officer as messenger responsible for presenting the *bilhetinho* and collecting the receipt. Contact was minimal and anonymous. There was no further relationship at that level.

Relations Within the Press

Relations within the press under self-censorship were in stark contrast to the relations that characterized prior censorship, which included such gestures of solidarity and identification as *Veja*'s tea ceremonies, *Opinião*'s wave rituals, and the shared self-knowledge among the staff of the *Estado de São Paulo* ("we wrote; *they* censored").

For the publications under self-censorship, vertical organizations and hierarchies were key in the formation of internal relations. At every level, members of the press under self-censorship were aware of their position in a vertical structure and of the consequent degree of their responsibility and authority. There was a pervasive sense of being a subordinate with limited power, and thus of not being the one responsible. Everyone, in whatever position, could identify an authority to whom he or she had to defer, who properly had responsibility for and the power to make decisions. These decisions had already been made, or were being made by others higher up in the hierarchy.

Thus junior reporters might feel constricted by decisions of the editorial staff, but the editors had the power to make decisions, and the reporters were expected to follow instructions. As Denis de Morães remarked, "you handed in the material, and there ended your responsibility."[44]

It was not only among reporters, however, that this perspective was found. Lower-level editors deferred to their superiors, and top-level editors to the owners. The *Jornal do Brasil*'s economics editor, Nuinio Spinola, for instance, knew that he was on the fourth tier, knew the degree to which his professional liberty or judgment was consequently circumscribed, and operated within that designated space.

Evandro Carlos de Andrade, as editor-in-chief of *O Globo*—a position that one might think carried significant power—described his situation thus:

The orientation of *O Globo* comes from Dr Marinho [the owner]. The political position of the newspaper is his. The newspaper is edited according to his orientation. About this there has never been the least doubt. There is no question of autonomy. He determines the line of the newspaper. Of course after nineteen years I can go for a month without talking to him, and continue to edit the newspaper as he wishes. But he determines absolutely, no discussion.[45]

Everyone fit into the scheme in a way that deferred responsibility to others. This pattern of hierarchical obedience with respect to obeying news prohibitions, accepting writing assignments, and making editorial decisions helped to shape the response to censorship. No one had a sense of full responsibility for complying with or responding to the censorship, and there was little solidarity within each publication to help forge such a response. The press's vertical organization was directly relevant to its experience of and response to state-imposed self-censorship.

Relations with the Regime

Relations between press and regime were also quite different from those that grew up under prior censorship. Publications subject to prior censorship sent angry telegrams to Cabinet ministers and initiated lawsuits to challenge the constitutionality of the regime's actions. The journalists who received the *bilhetinhos,* by contrast, appear to have had little to say, for no protests were made against the *bilhetinhos.*

This passivity had several probable ingredients. First, the vertical organization of the press meant that only the top editorial staff had regular contact with the process. Had more people been involved, there might have been a greater chance for response. The diversity of responses under prior censorship (slipping a lead into the middle of an article, altering an approved graphic, resubmitting material, keeping censors up late) was in part the result of so many people being involved in the process. By contrast, the *bilhetinhos* were received, read, and implemented solely by the editorial staff.

Another factor was the gradualness with which the prohibitions began. There was no announced policy, no public decree on the part of the regime. Prior censorship was not underpinned by public regulations or announcements, but at least the manner in which the affected publications learned of it was unequivocal: police notification that from that point forward all material would have to be submitted for review. In the case of self-censorship, on the other hand, there was no indication of what to anticipate—how elaborate or regular the process would be, what topics would be covered, what leeway would be permitted, how long the censorship would last, what might be the penalties or repercussions for refusing. Instead, there would just be a "little note" delivered by a uniformed agent, and then a second note, and a third, gradually falling into a pattern, and eventually providing enough notes to fill a black book. (In the eyes of police censor Romão, "There weren't so many things cut, three or four occurrences in the course of a week. Over the years, they pile up, but at any moment there were not so many.")[46] Decisions could have been made one at a time, *bilhetinho* by *bilhetinho.* It is as though only later the editors found themselves in a situation of general compliance with a rather routinized but entirely illegal system of state censorship. Because of this gradual beginning, and despite the fact that self-censorship began more or less at the same time for many newspapers, there may not have been one pivotal moment when the editors were directly confronted with something immediately and undeniably recognizable as the initiation of a system of state censorship—a moment that would have required an overt decision, a conscious strategy, a direct response.

Another factor contributing to the pattern of nonconfrontation was the widespread perception among journalists that the censorship would not last forever. This was not an unreasonable view, and it was one that many people held about the regime itself. People said that Brazil had been through dictatorships before, that they had passed, and so too would the regime. Several members of the press believed that they were receiving signals from the government that the censorship would end soon. It is possible that some publications were manipulated through the planting of rumors; it is also possible that some officials in the Geisel government in particular gave such signals in good faith but then were overridden by the hard-line faction that wanted controls upon the press to continue. Even if members of the press believed that they were complying with something manifestly illegal and illegitimate, they could take some solace from the thought that this was only for the time being.

There was some negotiation, some pursuit of maneuvering room. As with prior censorship, this varied with from publication to publication. The prestigious newspapers could make use of their elite contacts; those less well connected could not. What was different from prior censorship was that the negotiations could occur only at the higher editorial levels, because the lower ranks of journalists had virtually no contact with the *bilhetinhos* or the people who were the sources of those documents. Furthermore, it is not clear whether the journalists involved in such contacts sought to abolish the restrictions—as *Opinião*'s lawsuit sought to abolish prior censorship—or fine-tune them.

Boris Casoy, editor-in-chief of the *Folha de São Paulo,* had a good relationship with the Federal Police censor for São Paulo, Ricardo Bloch. On occasion Casoy would call Bloch if he felt that a prohibition was unworkable, and Bloch might agree. "I would call and say, 'Look, this is ridiculous, our whole front page is gone.' And he would respond, 'Yes, I just got a call from Oliveiros [Ferreira, editor of the *Estado de São Paulo*] too. I agree. I'll see what I can do.'"

But although Casoy would request reconsiderations, he was adamant that the *Folha de São Paulo* never exchanged favors with the regime, and insisted that the *Estado de São Paulo* and the *Jornal do Brasil* never did, either. There was compliance and negotiation, but no favors were offered to the regime. Fontoura emphasized that his newspaper obeyed the *bilhetinhos,* but no more than that; the *Jornal do Brasil* would not extend self-censorship beyond the exact wording of the prohibitions.[47]

O Globo, conspicuously absent from Casoy's list of newspapers that never exchanged favors with the regime, was edited by Evandro Carlos de Andrade. Asked to describe his relations with the regime in the matter of censorship, Andrade would only reply, "What relationship? There was no relationship!" He went on to explain that he never took a *bilhetinho* from the hand of a police agent. Asked then to consider what might have been the owner Roberto Marinho's relationship with the regime, Andrade emphasized the very close personal ties between Minister of Justice Falcão and Marinho (since publicly broken). Evidently, in *O Globo*'s case any negotiation would have gone on at that level, and not between the actual editor and censor.[48]

Even with *O Globo,* compliance went just so far and no farther. One case of its following the letter and not the spirit of some tacit agreement on press control concerns the employment of João Sant'anna. This professional journalist had been a political militant and a member of the Dissidência Comunista, and had spent a year and a half in prison. In addition to extensive involvement in various alternative publications, he eventually sought work at *O Globo,* accepting the argument of a colleague that it was "better to go to work in *O Globo* than just insult it from a distance." Sant'anna was hired and given a good salary and full benefits, but his *O Globo* employers would not sign his work card. They nicknamed him "Red Guard" and refused to make his employment official. Sant'anna paraphrased their refusal as follows: "We've already filled our quota of subversives. If we put your name on the list the SNI will come by." On the day of the Amnesty Law they called him in and signed his card, four years after he had begun working for the newspaper.[49] *O Globo* accepted that an SNI blacklist of "subversives" existed, and reacted by refusing to sign the work card; yet it did employ Sant'anna. This action fit the larger pattern of compliance without endorsement.

Although there was virtually complete compliance with the *bilhetinhos,* there does not seem to have been eager cooperation. The regime believed it necessary to monitor, threaten, and occasionally confiscate publications, and frequently repeat its verbose *bilhetinhos.* The press complied fully with the illegal prohibitions and its relationship with the regime was entirely nonconfrontational. Yet it also claimed to follow only the exact wording of each *bilhetinho* and was willing to hire those it would not register. Nothing suggests that compliance amounted to endorsement.

The system of self-censorship was not initiated or perpetuated by "slavish souls" in the press. The regime indeed wielded a sword against the press, although that sword was concealed and its existence denied. News prohibitions, disguised by their very name as "little notes," were delivered by the Federal Police to every press outlet in the country. Yet they were never left behind in newspaper offices, and the police always required a receipt. The *bilhetinhos'* language was anonymous but authoritative, and achieved that authority by mimicking proper legal forms. These orders were distributed minimally within the press, via the black books shared only among the top editorial staff who would comply by simply not investigating a potential news item. Failure to comply might be met with confiscations or imprisonments, enough to make the threat effective, but not so frequent as to suggest that there was any pattern of noncompliance.

In contrast to prior censorship, characterized at every level by confrontation with an outside agent of censorship, the relations of self-censorship were nonconfrontational. The vertical organization of the press meant that contact with the censors and responsibility for complying with the censorship occurred at the higher levels. There were no rituals of shared recognition, identity, or solidarity within the press. In place of furious telegrams and carefully crafted lawsuits was the expectation, at least on the part of some journalists, that the *bilhetinhos* were a passing phase. And in the meantime there was negotiation and accommodation. But though the accommodation was consistent, it was also limited—neither eager nor resentful.

The pattern, then, remains obscure. The regime did wield a sword. But there is still some doubt about the nature of the press's flight. That doubt was best expressed by Waldir de Góes: "It was self-censorship, in that we accepted it, but if we hadn't the newspaper would have been shut. . . . More could have been done than what was being done. There could have been greater resistance. The fear was greater than the ferocity of the animal. One could have resisted more, no?"[50] The perceptions and experiences of censorship that gave rise to that lingering doubt are explored further in the next chapter.

III

"A FORCED AGREEMENT"

8

REPRESENTATIONS AND REFLECTIONS

NO ASPECT OF THE CENSORSHIP was straightforward. There were contortions in its process: the unsigned "little notes" delivered by uniformed Federal Police agents. There were contortions in its content: the prohibition of a senator's speech denying the existence of censorship. There were also contortions in people's perspectives, understandings, and interpretations. The representations and reflections of press and state actors did not necessarily form logical and coherent wholes. Firm convictions sometimes dissolved into second thoughts and qualifications. Closely held commitments did not always yield the expected actions or conclusions.

Representations and reflections were themselves areas of contestation, as different actors sought to control and manipulate their own images and the perceptions of others. The military regime wielded substantial power in this regard. It not only could practice censorship but also could conceal the censorship from the public. In dealing with the press, it could present the illegal *bilhetinhos* as though they were fully legal artifacts. But while the regime could dominate and distort, it could not determine or dictate others' views and interpretations. In some areas the regime made no effort to do so. In others its efforts at manipulation were ineffectual or had unintended consequences.

Many representations and reflections are revealed by the statements, documents, and actions of the period. Others were formulated later by journalists, editors, censors, and police agents when they considered the record of compliance and repression.

THE PRESS'S SELF-PERCEPTION

When the press looked at itself it saw opposing fragments. There was a significant lack of solidarity within the Brazilian press. Rather than joining together to confront the regime, members of the press were often busy attacking or criticizing one another. Multiple cleavages, including class divisions, business competition, and political and personal differences impeded the formation of a common identity and blocked potential alliances.

Certainly, solidarity itself would not have equipped the press with the resources to confront the regime. As Boris Casoy, editor of the *Folha de São Paulo,* stated, "They had the guns; we didn't." Solidarity would not have changed the full array of resources available to the press, but it might have made a significant difference in particular situations and with respect to overall strategies. What if the *Estado de São Paulo* had joined *Opinião* in its lawsuit against prior censorship in 1974?[1] What if other newspapers had protested when General Abreu prohibited all state advertising in the *Jornal do Brasil* in 1978?[2] Solid alliances within the press would have contributed to a different situation from the one the press confronted in their absence.

Some potential for solidarity did exist: between the owners, editors, and journalists within a given publication or between peers at different publications. But with the few exceptions of internal solidarity found in publications subject to prior censorship, such alliances never formed. The obstacles to press solidarity were not created, enhanced, or exploited by the regime; lack of solidarity was a handicap of the press's own making.[3]

Although divisions within the press existed on multiple levels, the strongest and most consistent kind arose out of class differences. Throughout the 1964–1985 period, journalists and editors faced each other across opposite sides of a class divide. Collective action, which required the existence of a common interest among journalists, editors, managers, and owners, was therefore inconceivable. The rhetoric of class division was dominant and unavoidable, and set the terms of debate for any consideration of collective identity or action.[4]

In this environment, editors and management sought to block the presence of union representatives in newsrooms, and journalists characterized themselves as employees, as *mão de obra* (manual laborers) who shared an identity with the industrial proletariat. In journalists' eyes, owners, editors, and managers were the bourgeoisie, standing in necessary and total opposition to journalists' proletarian interests.[5]

One of the most revealing sources on this issue is the record of the proceedings of the National Congress of Journalists for the Liberty of the Press, which met in October 1978 and attracted participants from journalists' unions and associations throughout Brazil. The conference was held just four months after the end of prior censorship, at a time when *bilhetinhos* were still being issued (although their number had dwindled substantially). Of the more than twenty presentations to the congress recorded by the Brazilian Press Association, more than half discussed not the regime's censorship but the economic censorship practiced by owners. The journalist's enemy was almost always identified in these presentations as the bourgeoisie, the newspaper owners, and not the military regime or the Federal Police. Some contributors prefaced their remarks by acknowledging state censorship, but then went on to identify private economic censorship as the primary threat. Wholehearted attention was given to the restrictions on freedom of the press that resulted from journalists operating within a capitalist system that supported private ownership of the media. Only minimal attention was directed toward the restrictions imposed by the military regime, and none to the proposition that these would have been imposed even if the press had been organized into collectives and cooperatives.

The charges leveled by the journalists were sometimes quite specific, as in the charge that it was the editors who determined work schedules and decided whom journalists would interview. Often, however, the charges were general and deductive. Several essays cited Marx and Althusser to support the argument that because the ideas of the ruling class were the ruling ideas of the age, it followed that all information was in the hands of the ruling class.[6] Because newspapers were operated for profit, the argument went, they could do nothing but serve the class interests of their owners. One expression of this view was put forward in an essay entitled "The Social Right to Information":

It is imperative for journalists to be aware that their function of freely informing [the public] is frontally opposed to the economic, political, and ideological interests of the owners of the means of communication, who are linked to the dominant groups in society, although in some cases these may even appear similar. This contradiction with the owner exists as much with regard to the function of the journalist to inform (in opposition to the censorship by the owner) as with regard to the position of the journalist as a salaried worker.[7]

There was no parallel exhortation for journalists to make themselves aware of concealed police censorship, to expose the illegal restrictions practiced by the regime, or to open a debate on the *bilhetinhos*. This was at a time when *bilhetinhos* continued to be delivered by the Federal Police, the National Security Law still singled out the press for harsh punishment, and prior censorship of *Movimento, O São Paulo,* and the *Tribuna da Imprensa* had only recently ended. The conference essays preserve, as in a time capsule, journalists' views of the period. These views permitted no room for compromises or new alliances, even if temporary or primarily for strategic purposes.

The class analysis was not incorrect. There were plenty of objective reasons for criticizing the economic power of owners as weilded within the press. But with "worker" and "owner" as the sole terms of analysis, attention to other relevant issues was precluded. By casting owners as the primary and permanent enemy, journalists deflected attention away from the military regime. Because class oppression was presumed fundamental, no efforts were made to explore the actions of the regime itself. The class analysis was not necessarily false, but it was inadequate to other relevant aspects of the situation.

Of the many divisions in self-representation of the press, that of class was the most striking. Other perceived divisions arose out of political differences, personal animosities, and business competition. A long-standing animosity existed, for example, between the *Jornal do Brasil* and *O Globo,* both of which were based in Rio de Janeiro. *Jornal do Brasil* owner Nascimento Brito was clearly referring to his archcompetitor Roberto Marinho at *O Globo* when he said, "We never had the plasticity that certain newspaper owners have. I know the game, understand? It's just that I never wanted to play it." Asked, with respect to pressure from the regime, whether the press could not have exhibited more solidarity, Brito responded, "Any unifying of the Brazilian press is very difficult because not all have the same formation. Some are more prepared, others less. There are very different visions of what the press is, of what it is to love certain values . . . and besides, to unite businesspeople engaged in the same activity is always very difficult."[8]

This lack of solidarity was also evident to journalist Carlos Chagas: "During the dictatorship itself, during the censorship, *O Globo* was at the service of the dictatorship. It didn't pursue an understanding with anyone. The *Jornal do Brasil* considered itself an aristocracy for the intellectuals of Rio de Janeiro. The *Estado de São Paulo* and the *Folha de São Paulo* were competitors in São Paulo, so they too weren't going to create an alliance. There was never this type of unity."[9]

If these multiple divisions created by class interests, political differences, personal animosities, and business competition seemed self-evident, they were not predetermined, nor did they need to be accorded paramount importance by the press. But they were. In constructing their self-representations, press actors articulated a vision so profoundly splintered that they could not unite against the restrictions imposed by the regime, could not formulate shared strategies to oppose those restrictions. What they had in common as journalists subject to state censorship was never acknowledged or made use of. These divisions were neither created nor manipulated by the regime.

PRESS VIEWS OF THE REGIME

The regime was the subject of many different representations by the press. Competing and even contradictory views of the regime coexisted within the press as a whole, and were also held by individual journalists. General evaluations did not result in particular decisions or actions that would appear consistent with those evaluations. It was possible to wholeheartedly support the regime and yet not endorse press restrictions. It was also possible to fear the regime and yet join the targeted press and create new platforms for expression. Often the regime and its actions were difficult to evaluate at all because they seemed so all-encompassing and became invisible in their ubiquity.

Support

There was considerable support among Brazilians for the authoritarian regime.[10] Brazil's national motto, emblazoned on the country's flag, is "Order and Progress." By the regime's own criteria—criteria shared by many Brazilians, including some who were its victims—the regime had considerable success achieving those two goals.

Within the press one could find varying degrees of support for the regime, or at least a readiness to cooperate with it. Some journalists offered reflective, informed, conscious support. Others provided measured support so as to gain favors in return. Still others perceived that they had little room to maneuver and concluded that it was best to cooperate with the regime as a way of protecting some limited capacity for action. Changing political and other circumstances gave rise to many permutations in the forms support for the regime could take.

Reflective Support

Within the press, no one expressed support for the regime more sincerely or with greater self-awareness than Boris Casoy, editor-in-chief of the *Folha de Sao Paulo*.[11] Casoy has never claimed that he was ignorant of the regime's repressive nature, nor has he suggested that knowledge of its abuses would have altered his views.[12]

The basis for Casoy's considered and heartfelt support for the regime was simply that it upheld the world as he knew it, a world he was convinced was under a dire and immediate threat from communist guerrillas. Casoy vividly recalled cars being set on fire in the *Folha de São Paulo* parking lot and newspapers hiring security guards for the first time. But beyond the immediate danger there was also, for Casoy, the earth-shattering possibility that the guerrillas would gain real political power. This possibility threatened not just his economic and personal security but the basic order of the universe.

As he said, "The guerrillas weren't against the dictatorship, they were against our way of life."

Casoy is a particularly well-informed and articulate individual, yet in discussing the guerrilla threat, his account turned uncharacteristically vague: "It was a threat that was beyond measure. . . . Look, no one knows the size [of the guerrilla forces] for sure, but yes, the newspapers did feel threatened, the middle class did feel threatened. I think even the military didn't know the extent for sure, but you knew they were around. They were called terrorists." The unknown dimensions of the supposed terrorist threat increased its scariness. This was not a measurable objective identifiable threat, but a threat of another order, a metalevel threat. In Casoy's opinion, as in the opinion of many others, only the military regime had the capacity to meet this threat.[13] The regime's repressive practices were viewed as necessary, and in the fight against terrorism even press censorship had its place. Speculating upon the reasons why there was press support for the regime, Casoy offered the following explanation: "What I'm trying to say is that there were points of contact [between the views held by the press and by the regime]. Newspapers are businesses, linked to capitalism, to anticommunism, and were never in favor of guerrillas, indeed approved of the repression of the guerrillas. The rest we didn't approve of but we accepted. Deep within my heart, I supported them. I *supported* them!" The points of contact were sufficient for Casoy to continue his support for a manifestly repressive regime that protected his way of life. He identified with the regime's goals and accepted its means. Although it is unusual today to hear such deep expressions of support for the regime, Casoy believes that many in the press held the same view.[14] His ardent support for the regime, however, did not translate into an endorsement of censorship. He would go no further than the statement that "we didn't approve but we accepted" press restrictions.

Pragmatic Opportunism

In contrast to Casoy's reflective support was a stance of pragmatic opportunism. By playing along with a powerful regime, one could take advantage of many business and professional opportunities, including easier access to bank loans, broadcast licenses, state advertising contracts, press agent jobs, and news. A few members of the press assert this position about themselves; many more are ready to attribute it to the press in general and to newspaper owners in particular. No ideological commitment is implied by this kind of support; this was straightforward opportunism.

Carlos Chagas, a well-respected journalist with Estado de São Paulo, unequivocally condemned the pragmatic opportunism of the press at every level—owners, editors, and journalists. He lamented the existence of a dichotomy between "journalistic consciousness" and "business consciousness," and charged many in the press with being purely business oriented and failing to recognize other responsibilities. In Chagas's estimation, the press did not perceive a dilemma in balancing a commitment to freedom of the press against one's business interests. In the press's eyes, business interests were simply the primary concern, and were frankly acknowledged as the basis for accepting restrictions upon the press. For press actors, favors from the government, whether loans from the Banco do Brasil or appointments as press advisors, were business as usual: "As long as all that continued to function, [the press] offered news as a bargaining factor."[15]

Journalist João Sant'anna asserted that Brazil's newspapers enriched themselves under the military regime, particularly as a result of increased advertising by state companies. Some newspapers benefited from the damage the regime did to their rivals. Sant'anna cited the example of the *Jornal do Brasil* gaining a much more secure financial footing after the destruction of its Rio de Janeiro rival the *Correio da Manhã*. According to Sant'anna, newspapers profited from the regime, and that was the extent of their concern: "They weren't interested in the rest."[16]

The disdain in these assessments is clear, but neither Chagas nor Sant'anna charged the press with bribery or corruption. The press, according to some observers, was simply taking advantage of what was available in an environment largely controlled by the state. As long as its business interests were not hurt, the press made no effort to challenge illegal restrictions.[17] When one hears disdain, it is for the press's lack of principle, not for wrongdoing.

Yet few press decisions were motivated purely by profit. In a period when noncooperation could be punished by confiscations, suspension of crucial state advertising, and cancellation of journalists' credentials, there obviously were sound business reasons for cooperating. As journalist Carlos Castello Branco remarked, under an authoritarian regime the press "couldn't very well indulge in a romantic gesture."[18]

Circumscribed Autonomy

In addition to offering genuine support for the regime or following a course of pragmatic opportunism, a third way that the press approached the regime was by acknowledging the regime's immense strength and then seeking some degree of autonomy, some room to maneuver, within the limitations set by the regime. In this approach the press neither endorsed nor confronted the restrictions imposed by the regime, nor did it seek advantage from them, but rather hoped to take advantage of the limited freedom that remained.

In the opinion of the journalists who chose this course, quiescence was better than confronting the regime and being silenced, or choosing to shut down so as to pressure the sanctity of one's free speech—and being thereby silenced nonetheless. Seeking limited autonomy within the restrictions did indeed take Chagas's "journalistic conscience" as its starting point, but pursued it to a very different conclusion. One journalist whose actions were grounded in this perspective was Luis Alberto Bettancourt, at the time a reporter for both *O Globo* and *Repórter*. Casting himself after the fact as a savvy political observer, journalist, and businessman, Bettancourt presented his path as demonstrating the acumen of a survivor:

Reality is never monolithic. It was a brutal dictatorship. But I have come to the understanding that it's better to have a General Good Guy, who lets me work a little bit, than a General Rotten, who doesn't let me work at all. If I don't work, I can't get out of my own intimate circle, can't further any social relation. I don't establish any contact with reality . . . to transform it, to change it. I don't have social expression for my indignation. Now if General Good Guy says, "Oh, let the fellow make his little criticism"—this alters the situation, establishes a reality. There's a brutal difference between General Good Guy and General Rotten.[19]

In this view, paradoxically, self-censorship became a situation of relative control. By cooperating with the regime, one maintained some autonomy, albeit within a restricted scope. The potential danger was that the autonomy could become so restricted as to be meaningless.[20]

These ways of going along with the regime—by offering reflective support, by engaging in pragmatic opportunism, or by accepting circumscribed autonomy—often existed in shifting combinations rather than as discrete motivations. Statements made by two journalists in 1977 suggest some of these shifting and partial perspectives. Both Castello Branco and Chagas were successful and respected in their profession and acknowledged as leaders of the press. Both had stood their ground against the regime with some degree of courage, Castello Branco when running for union office on an opposition slate and Chagas when facing national security charges. Both were also entwined in the compromises made by the mainstream press with the regime and Chagas had held an official position. Their statements, issued on International Press Freedom Day, bore very different connotations. The statements were made several years into Geisel's term, when *Movimento, O São Paulo,* and the *Tribuna da Imprensa* were still subject to prior censorship, and *bilhetinhos* were still being issued by the Federal Police.

Castello Branco had this to say: "The manifesto signed by twenty-five hundred journalists, presented in a public event held by the ABI on International Press Freedom Day and already well publicized, should not be taken as a criticism of President Geisel but rather as a stimulus for his policy of gradual liberalization for the media."

Carlos Chagas's remarks went as follows:

The passing of International Press Freedom Day brings into consideration the fact that, because of the sui generis moment experienced today in Brazil by force of a regime of exception, we have a little bit of liberty, we have moments of liberty, and thus we do not have liberty, because liberty cannot be meted out in homeopathic doses or distributed in tiny morsels. The majority of the newspapers in this country are able to print criticisms, commentaries, denunciations, and simple news about current events, but only because that is how those who hold power see it, just as they also see that other means of social communication need to be discriminated against, including other newspapers, radio, and television, which do not possess these same prerogatives.[21]

Chagas thus scoffed at the mere morsels of liberty doled out to the press, while Castello Branco praised the morsels and offered encouragement for their continued supply. But probably neither journalist would have unqualifiedly endorsed the positions contained in their respective statements. Chagas worked with the regime for a period as presidential press advisor, and Castello Branco confronted the regime when he ran for office as an opposition candidate in journalists' union elections. In the daily exercise of their profession, in their daily judgments, both men displayed a variety of motivations and commitments.

Fear

Fear also figured in press representations and reflections. Members of the press feared for their livelihoods and their lives. People were detained, tortured, and murdered by the regime. Although, as was noted above, the data gathered for the Nunca Mais project demonstrate that the press was not a primary target of state terror, no one could feel entirely safe. Even those who applauded the regime could also be frightened of it.

Boris Casoy, for example, was as articulate about his fear as he was about his support. Casoy became editor-in-chief of the *Folha de São Paulo* in September 1977 in the midst of an episode of tension and fear that provides a vivid example of the precariousness of the press's situation under the regime. Brazil was in the midst of a crisis-prone process, the presidential succession. The political battles between the regime's moderate and hardline factions were quite heated,[22] and the press became one arena for the airing of political disputes,[23] as well as a pawn of the disputing factions.[24]

At that time the *Folha de São Paulo* was a small and unprestigious publication. It was owned by Otavio Frias, a businessman not primarily identified with the press. Its editor-in-chief was Claudio Abramo, a mainstream journalist who had worked for many publications and had been editor-in-chief at the *Estado de São Paulo* for many years. Abramo was also identified—by the military regime and by himself—as a Marxist.[25]

The newspaper had never run editorials, but in 1976 it decided to begin an editorial page, in part as a marketing ploy. The idea was to publish polemical guest editorials that would cover a broad political spectrum, and thus attract sales because of their controversial nature. Although the editorials were signed, and their authors were people from outside the newspaper, they appear to have solidified Abramo's reputation as a leftist. Casoy remarked that "The newspaper, like myself, has always been in favor of market capitalism, liberalism, the bourgeoisie. But with some of these editorials, the newspaper acquired the image of being a little left of center. Probably anytime there was anything that irritated the military, they attributed it to Claudio Abramo. I had greater facility, a more right-wing image, which it was possible to hide behind."[26] In this time of tension between different factions of the regime over the presidential succession, and confusion over the role of the press in that dispute, the *Folha de São Paulo* began to receive complaints about the editorials from certain authorities.

Among the newpaper's staff was Lorenço Diaféria, who wrote human interest pieces for the back page (belittled by Casoy as "ingenuous little pieces" and by Abramo as "mediocre").[27] In September 1977, during the annual week of military parades commemorating Independence Day, Diaféria wrote about an off-duty army officer who had recently saved a child's life at a zoo by pulling the child from a sea lion's cage at the cost of his own life. Diaféria contrasted this genuine and much appreciated act of heroism with the general standing of the military in the eyes of the populace who, he wrote, urinated on the statue of the military hero Duque de Caxias.

This article passed unnoticed except by some in the army, who were outraged.[28] Army Minister Frota was evidently furious. Casoy, through his personal connections, heard of this and informed Frias, who immediately dispatched him to Brasília to try to calm the situation. What could have happened?

No one knew! No one knew! I went on a diplomatic mission, ran to explain, to explain it away. I knew everybody—advisors to the president, military officers, ministers. What could have happened? The suspension of the *Folha de São Paulo*, the imprisonment of Frias. I got to Brasília and was told, look, Sylvio Frota has ordered Lorenço imprisoned under the National Security Law. And he was imprisoned by the Federal Police. I came back with my tail between my legs, and Lorenço was imprisoned. After that, I was very tired, very tired, and went on holiday. Frias said yes, go. I got in my car and drove nine hours to Minas Gerais.[29]

One did not return from unsuccessful negotiations with the hard-line faction of the military merely "tired." Casoy, clearly, was fleeing, getting out of the way until the storm blew over.

The rest of the editorial staff then debated what to do, and it was decided to leave Diaféria's usual space in the newspaper blank as a gesture of protest. Abramo, who in Casoy's estimation "was no fool," opposed this action, which he feared might be seen as provocative. Frias embraced it as a bold, heroic gesture.[30] The *Folha de São Paulo* thus began publishing the newspaper with Diaféria's space left blank, and included a statement that it would remain so while Diaféria was in prison.

It was at this juncture that General Hugo Abreu, leader of the Military Cabinet and of the hard-line faction, summoned Frias to a meeting. Abramo claims that Abreu ordered Frias to remove him as editor, which Frias did. Casoy provided this account of the meeting, which he heard about from both Frias and Abreu:

Abreu told Frias: "I'm talking to you as chief of the Military Cabinet, not as a friend. One more white space, and you'll be punished. You will put in motion a process of punishment." It was a threat, an imprecise threat. There had already been other warnings from the grapevine—informal, "off the record." These . . . off-the-record statements were even more frightening, even more the basis of fear. Frias was scared: for himself, for his family, scared of being imprisoned, scared they would suspend the publication of the *Folha de São Paulo* for a period of time, which would be its end. So Frias pulled Claudio Abramo, pulled Alberto Dines (an aggressive columnist), pulled the editorials, pulled his own name from the masthead, and sent a plane after me in Minas Gerais (hence I knew how serious the matter was).[31]

Abramo was interrogated by the Federal Police. In tears, Frias appealed to Casoy to assume the editorship, and then left for an extended tour of Europe.

There are different versions of this story, but none that alter the basic facts.[32] When questioned further about the different versions, especially those parts relating to events that he knew only secondhand, Casoy stated that he had first heard Frias's version, and then had asked Abreu for his account. According to Casoy, "Abreu confirmed the threats. No, Abreu said that he warned Frias, but that Frias overreacted, took it too strongly."[33]

It is exactly in situations of arbitrary and disproportionate power, and of the possibility of an abusive use of that power, that serious misperceptions about the nature or extent of a threat can arise. It may have been a miscalculation, but a miscalculation on the safe side, for Casoy to drive nine hours into the mountains. Likewise, Frias's evident terror, as he pulled his name from the masthead of his own newspaper, fired its top staff, and left the country, was perhaps based upon a misperception, but a reasonable one. And Abramo, a proud Marxist who nevertheless voted against the use of white space in the newspaper, must have felt he had ample reason to avoid being seen as provocative.

Fear seems to have been the overriding element in crises such as that which occurred at the *Folha de São Paulo* in September 1977. But what constituted a crisis? This was a very difficult question to answer when faced with an authoritarian regime capable of arbitrary action. It was that much more risky because the regime was divided into factions, all ready to take advantage of actions that might seem rather innocuous. A back page article mentioning people urinating on a military statue would not in most assessments be grounds for putting in jeopardy the existence of a mainstream daily newspaper and the careers and possibly the physical safety of several reporters and editors. But that is what it became. Despite the data from the Nunca Mais project indicating that the press was not a primary target of state repression, fear was evidently hard to banish.

Only one journalist—Luis Alberto Bettancourt, a self-identified pragmatist in search of circumscribed autonomy—asserted that fear was not an issue, that it was completely irrelevant to his decisions and actions. Indeed, he derided those in the press who spoke about the importance of fear, and argued that this was merely an excuse for their "servile psyches." Bettancourt himself faced twenty-two legal proceedings, including several under the National Security Law, and saw issues of his alternative journal, *Repórter*, confiscated numerous times. Nonetheless, he affirmed that fear "never touched me. I was never afraid." But then in the course of the interview he too changed his mind: "'I was never afraid'—well, that's nonsense. I never subordinated myself to it, that's it. It still let me do something. The fear—always. It weighed heavily upon my behavior, but it never justified my inertia."[34]

Whether in the reflections of junior reporters or senior editors, ardent supporters or outspoken opponents of the regime, self-confident pragmatists or cautious businessmen, fear figures as one part of press experience. It coexisted with many different assessments of the regime and many different responses to restrictions upon the press.

Routinization and Powerlessness

Although threads of support and fear are woven into all press representations of and reflections upon this period, the basic fabric of the press experience under censorship was routinization. No matter what their political perspective or position in the press hierarchy, it is the banality of the illegal press restrictions that dominates the recollections of press actors. The regime's system of news prohibitions functioned smoothly throughout the nation. The daily procedures were well established and unswervingly adhered to by the censorship bureaucracy. The same patterns recurred everywhere. There was nothing ad hoc in the process by which *bilhetinhos* were issued to the press, transcribed, and removed. The routinization was underscored by the repetition of officious legalistic language in the *bilhetinhos*. Furthermore, this form of censorship involved little in the way of observable discretionary action by agents of the state, such as censors marking one's drafts with a red pen. The same established procedures were repeated daily, and the press could not observe their creation.

Routinization was the primary characteristic of the way the regime conducted the so-called self-censorship. It also came to dominate how the press experienced that form of censorship. José Neumanne Pinto, then a junior reporter at the *Folha de São Paulo*, described it thus: "There was a bureaucracy of repression and it functioned industrially, automatically. The felt experience was like Arendt's banality of evil. You experienced it as a system. It was impersonal, large, distant. There wasn't a direct relation. You just stopped using the phone, or changed the way you used it. You incorporated that into the daily experience."[35] The system of self-censorship was experienced as general, impersonal, ubiquitous. No one was directly or observably responsible for it. There was no refuge where it did not reach. Censorship was seen as automatic and complete, without specific limits or sources.

This was in contrast to the experience of prior censorship, to which a small handful of publications were subject. For these publications, the practice of censorship was far more personal, and gave rise to direct confrontations with the agents of censorship. Press recollections of that form of censorship and their actions include representations of their own possible effectiveness against the restrictions. Journalists who worked for the *Estado de São Paulo* and *Veja*, for example, recall how they made censors less alert by keeping them up late. Jaime Sautchuk remembers his negotiations with the censor who had cut so much from *Opinião* that it could not mount an issue. Argemiro Ferreira certainly had a sense of the individual censoring *Opinião* when he resubmitted vetoed material just to oblige the censors to read it again. And José Carlos Dias, who wrote the poem "To the Censor," which was vetoed from *O São Paulo*, also had a distinct conception of the person censoring that publication. These were relevant relationships, involving bureaucratic agents who might be susceptible to negotiation, cajoling, and exhaustion, and who might even have consciences. In looking back upon the period, many of the journalists who were subject to prior censorship exhibit some sense that their anticensorship actions were at times effective, or at least that opposition to censorship was a worthwhile exercise.

By contrast, those journalists who were subjected to self-censorship indicate that censorship for them was a much less direct and personal experience. The prohibitions they received originated in anonymous "superior orders" and often were simply telephoned in. Because newspapers were vertically organized, only the editorial staff saw and discussed the text of the prohibitions. Moreover, because the prohibitions almost always arrived before an event had been investigated or an article written on it, journalists working for newspapers under self-censorship almost never had the experience of seeing something they had written vetoed. Instead, they were not sent to cover the prohibited story. Thus the lack of a direct, personal relation which characterizes many journalists' reflections on the system of self-censorship is quite understandable.

Journalist Antonio Carlos Pereira echoed Neumanne Pinto in finding the routines impersonal and mundane. Pereira recalled that "The means of communication functioned normally . . . You knew telephones were tapped, and telexes were always intercepted. All this wound up entering into our routine. It wasn't something that reached you, grated against you personally. . . . The thing about small pains is that you wind up accustomed to them. And you had no personal means to react against it. . . . You worked, and you waited for it to end."[36] To be functioning "normally" came to be defined as being tapped, intercepted, under surveillance. Because the prohibitions were ubiquitous and automatic, there was nothing personal in them, and no personal way to respond.

Against these seemingly automatic, all-encompassing, self-perpetuating routines, the press came to the conclusion of its own powerlessness. A lack of relevant means to fight or confront the press restrictions was a frequent press commentary on the routinized system of censorhip. The system was conveyed by the regime and perceived by the press as so large, so automatic, and so seamless that by far the most common interpretation within the press was simply that "it would do no good" to challenge it.

This, too, contrasted somewhat with the experience of the handful of publications under prior censorship. There were no illusions of power under prior censorship; all involved knew that they were up against the enormous capacities of an authoritarian military regime. But nonetheless, there was a more frequent assertion of at least some power: the power to keep the censors up late at night, to make them read the material twice, to have them reconsider a decision. This was not the power to escape censorship or overthrow the system, but neither was it a self-representation of complete powerlessness.

Those who suffered under self-censorship, however, were almost unanimous in their opinion that they were powerless. Many factors contributed to their powerlessness, from the actual power of the regime to the various sources of the press's internal weakness, such as the impact of vertical organization or the lack of solidarity among different press groups. But whatever the factors that contributed to the imbalance of power, the press under self-censorship perceived its powerlessness as complete. Press actors could see no strategies, no choices, no opportunities to combat the censorship. Nothing seemed likely to make a difference, and any action could have negative consequences. It therefore made no sense to try.

Such assessments are heard from people who worked at every level of press organization, from junior reporter to editor-in-chief. Denis de Morães, then a reporter with *O Globo,* observed, "It wouldn't get you anywhere to push. Where would it get you? Kicked out. . . . You didn't have a way to start. Mostly you were so convinced that it would do no good."[37] This was the perspective of a junior reporter, someone relatively powerless within the vertical organization of *O Globo.* But that sense of powerlessness, caused by the pervasiveness of the system of restrictions, by the creeping routine and inescapability of it all, was remarked upon as well by Walter Fontoura, then editor of the *Jornal do Brasil:* "The press was forced to take this. Well, not forced. In the end it wound up being because no one knew what could happen if you didn't obey. There were confiscations, et cetera. . . . It was an intolerable situation." An intolerable situation that was nonetheless tolerated? "Yes. There was no way out. What could you do?"[38]

Their conclusions are not inaccurate. The skeptical questions were fair ones to ask. Against the strength of an authoritarian regime and the immensity of the censorship system, what could they do? Where would it have gotten them? Perhaps nothing; perhaps nowhere. What is significant here is the unanimity of that representation.

The press experienced a deep sense of powerlessness, and attributed that powerlessness above all to the routinization of the censorship system. While there were instances of a sense of powerlessness caused by fear, the much more frequent experience was that of powerlessness caused by the banality of the system. This sense of powerlessness was produced not by the terror of the system, but rather by the *normality* of it, the routineness of it, such that one would identify tapped telephones and intercepted telexes as "normal." Against a pervasive, impersonal, automatic series of bureaucratic routines, the press believed that there was no way to develop a relevant critique, useful strategies, or proportionate power.

Legitimacy

That sense of powerlessness against the restrictions did not, however, yield to a sense of the legitimacy of those restrictions. Restrictions, prohibitions, and surveillance became normal, but that did not make them right. The press did not generate the resources, alliances, or commitments needed to reject or resist the illegal restrictions it faced, but it nonetheless did not view them as natural, just, or legitimate.

Some journalists made their views of the illegitimacy of such restrictions clear by their actions, skirting the restrictions when possible and looking to alternative publications for outlets for their work. Other members of the press could articulate specific grounds for the illegitimacy of the restrictions. They denounced the restrictions in no uncertain terms, even while abiding by them. Most journalists simply became accustomed to them. But even if customary, this did not make them correct.

No one in the press was prepared to directly challenge the *bilhetinhos*. They followed the *bilhetinhos* to the letter, but no more. They did not anticipate or generalize from the exact prohibition received. At least one journalist recalled avoiding or neglecting *bilhetinhos*, and then claiming ignorance of their existence. If the restrictions had not only been complied with but also accepted as legitimate, such would not have been the case.

It was very common for journalists at mainstream newspapers to submit articles to alternative publications when they could not print in their own newspapers. The archives of *Movimento* include many such articles. The *Zero Hora* journalist whose essay on children dying from dehydration was quoted in chapter 6 was presumably convinced of the veracity and importance of that material. The specific restrictions faced by the press, and the general state of relations between the press and the regime, meant that such an article would never have been published in a mainstream newspaper. Unable to publish it in the mainstream, self-censoring newspaper that employed him, he sent it to *Movimento*. For that journalist—and for many others whose work appeared in such newspapers or in censored newspaper archives—the inability to publish in a mainstream newspaper did not make the story unimportant, untrue, or of questionable value. Rather, it made questionable the newspapers that refused to publish such stories, just as it made questionable the restrictions imposed by the regime. If the restrictions had been legitimate, publication in an alternative forum would not have been pursued.

Press actors also explicitly denounced the restrictions. These denunciations were not akin to the formal statements occasionally issued by publications under prior censorship, such as were found in speeches to international press associations or telegrams to Cabinet ministers. Instead, they were informal but articulate observations. The condemnations were dispensed, coming from mainstream as well as alternative publications, from supporters as well as opponents of the regime. They were based upon several kinds of arguments, and might encompass issues of legality and morality.

Despite the many trappings of legality associated with the press restrictions—the officious language of the *bilhetinhos*, the requirement that recipients sign to indicate receipt—they were fundamentally illegal. This was known to many in the press, and was one basis for asserting that the routinized system was illegitimate. The press was historically part of the elite and as such more likely to have experienced some degree of the rule of law. As McDonough's research indicates, the commitment to certain aspects of the rule of law was indeed what different sectors of the elite all shared.[39] That which was illegal was, consequently, illegitimate in the eyes of the press; at least that argument was readily available to all.

O Globo was well known for its support of the regime. Though its editor, Evandro Carlos de Andrade, favored the regime and many of its goals and methods, and complied with the system of *bilhetinhos*, he never considered the censorship legitimate. He attributed his disapproval precisely to the censorship's illegality:

It's not that I ever was against the military. I never was; never. But I was against—well, above all, I was against censorship. Censorship was never formally instituted. It couldn't be, because of the Constitution: there cannot be censorship of newspapers. Never did an agent of censorship leave an order here [physically]. Never did an agent of censorship direct himself to me [personally]. Never. They entered, showed the paper to whomever they encountered first, a secretary, a third-level employee, and left. And this person would say—this arrived, the message is, you may not, et cetera. Because, in truth, censorship was a farce. The Constitution permitted prior censorship of books and magazines upon moral grounds, but not of newspapers.[40]

Even someone who supported the military regime could not view as legitimate a practice that was blatantly unconstitutional. He complied with it, but would never deign to come in direct physical contact with it.

Oliveiros Ferreira, editor of the *Estado de São Paulo*, likewise condemned regime actions against the press because of their illegality. One of his most vehement outbursts of utter indignation was over the timing of the seizure of his newspaper on December 14, 1968. AI-5 had been signed at 11:00 P.M. on December 13, but would not become legally valid until properly published in the *Diário Oficial* the next day. Nevertheless, troops entered the offices of the *Estado de São Paulo* and seized the issue at dawn on the 14th. In Ferreira's account, this action would have had some legal basis a few hours later, but it most certainly did not at dawn! Ferriera therefore viewed this as a gross violation of proper legal procedure.[41]

Ferreira's expression of fury at the authoritarianism, injustice, and illegitimacy of AI-5 turned upon the legal treatment of that Institutional Act, proceeding through arguments based upon the proper exercise of the rule of law. Of legality he had no doubts; therefore it was solid ground from which to denounce the illegitimacy of the regime's actions against the press.

Attacking the press restrictions by focusing upon their illegality was also an approach adopted by the alternative press. When an issue of *Movimento* that dealt with the sensitive topic of risk contracts for petroleum was confiscated, for example, the journal denounced the confiscation by condemning the lack of a written and signed order of authorization. Even after having duly submitted the issue for prior censorship—and having an inordinate amount of it vetoed—the entire run was seized by the Federal Police. The journal remarked that "The double arbitrariness took us by surprise: despite having been liberated, the publication was confiscated and no explanation was given to us, no right to defense, no document giving any type of legality to the decision (if it is possible to legalize the arbitrary)."[42] Even if *Movimento* was using the absence of a signed order only as a pretext for objecting to the confiscation, it is still noteworthy that this was a strategy available to them, and one they would be likely to select.

Another way to denounce the illegitimacy of the restrictions was to point to their immorality. The press, as press, seeks truth. It searches for facts, pursues corroboration, and tries to make truth public. This, of course, is an ideal, only occasionally approximated, for the press also seeks sensationalism, attention, and notoriety. But fact-finding and the reporting of events remain essential to the press's self-definition. The regime's lies and distortions were blatant and were often recognized as such. The censorship order prohibiting publication of the statement of Senator Muller asserting that censorship did not exist in Brazil was just one of many examples.

If the press as an institution had no choice but to publish official lies and omit the truth, this did not mean that many in the press did not experience this glaring deception at a visceral level. The lack of fit between reality and the official version was another reason for seeing the routines of press restriction as illegitimate. One journalist who was painfully aware of official deception, and focused upon in it in his recollections later, was Neumanne Pinto:

The greatest trauma of the whole experience was to know that something was going on, know that the official version was not true, and not be able to find out the truth. Knowing that what you had was false, and that you couldn't get the truth, and as a reporter. . . . We would receive official bulletins (a suicide in a prison), know something had happened, but not know what. . . . you had not the least conditions to find out what had really happened. You were reading in the newspapers stuff that you knew wasn't true.[43]

Neumanne Pinto expressed his ongoing angst over a situation he fully knew he could not change. It was an extremely uncomfortable self-awareness; he was quite conscious of the bind he was in.

For the press, whose daily work supposedly consisted of fact-finding, whose profession painted itself, at least in an ideal sense, as a vehicle establishing public truth, this self-awareness could be excruciating. Official deceptions and distortions were an immoral practice well beyond the specific routines of censorship. In serving those distortions, censorship itself could never be legitimate.

But not everyone had such a difficult time living with official distortions. Not all expressed the illegitimacy of the restrictions by actions, complying as narrowly as possible with the *bilhetinhos* or publishing their articles in alternative publications. Not everyone could be sure of the lack of a legal basis for the restrictions, especially when laws were changing in content and nature with the creation of such "superlaws" as AI-5 and the National Security Law. And clearly not everyone was as sensitive and perceptive as Neumanne Pinto in his awareness of official mendacity (which Neumanne Pinto also experienced as profoundly banal). Many press actors simply went along with the system.

In their reflections, however, that is just what they communicate: that they went along. These are not expressions of fright or support. Rather they are statements of having become accustomed to the restrictions, accustomed to what one had no power to reject. The basis of that powerlessness was the routinization, the automaticity of the system as a whole. Because it functioned as an immense, automatic, bureaucratic routine, the censorship seemed unassailable and incomprehensible.

The previously quoted journalist Antonio Carlos Pereira did not represent the restrictions as illegitimate upon specific legal or moral grounds. He said, rather, that it did not get to you, that it did not touch you personally. And he also said that you worked "and you waited for it to end." If this is not clearly articulating illegitimacy, certainly it is expressing some degree of it. One does not wait for the end of something that is correct, natural, and just. If he lacked the resources to condemn it, let alone resist it, Pereira nonetheless did not represent the censorship as legitimate.

Censorship by *bilhetinho* was experienced as an impersonal, automatic, routinized system. The experience of that system generated a particular kind of powerlessness. One might act against a specific agent or policy, but not against an impersonal routine or a smoothly functioning, all-encompassing system. The sense of powerlessness, however, did not lead to an acceptance of the restrictions. They were tolerated and complied with, but they were not seen as legitimate.

REGIME REPRESENTATIONS AND REFLECTIONS

Members of the military regime also generated varied understandings and accounts of the restrictions that they imposed upon the press and then sought to conceal and deny. The restrictions clearly presented an image problem, whether for immediate instrumental purposes of avoiding foreign disapproval or forestalling domestic protest, or for some larger project of their own legitimacy, however conceived. There was an apparent need for self-justification, for an ongoing assessment of censorship's legitimacy. Ample reflections by regime actors concerning the restrictions imposed upon the press were recorded then or are voiced now.

Some of these views assert the legitimacy of censorship; others seek justifications for its practice, even if it was illegitimate. Some of these accounts are more convincing than others, not only in the historical record but to the individuals themselves. Included in what follows are the comments of members of Congress, the military, and the Federal Police, as well as of press actors who have made an effort to examine the period from the regime's perspective.

That careful efforts were made to justify censorship is unsurprising. The restrictions were hardly straightforward uncontroversial measures, in line with construction projects or trade agreements. If their success depended in part upon acceptance and cooperation, and if they were recognized by the regime as being to some degree unwanted, there had to be some attempt at justification. No one in the regime ever seems to have suffered from such a radical case of self-deception as to think that the censorship was welcome or legitimate. There were several different accounts.

Dirty War, Dirty Means

Many in the regime shared the belief that they lived in such extraordinary times that extraordinary means were required. The national security doctrine was premised upon a threat of internal subversion. This threat was used to justify Dirty War tactics in Brazil as well as in Southern Cone nations.

According to the regime, national security could not be compromised; it outweighed all other concerns. The regime portrayed itself as battling communism and fighting for the salvation of Western Civilization. Illegal and coercive measures to control the press were subsumed within the imperatives of this mandate.

Federal Police chief Moacyr Coelho used the following analogy to explain the need for illegal measures against the press: "It was a war, a Dirty War. It had to be fought with dirty means. . . . There were excesses in combating this; but there wasn't time. You couldn't spend days and days looking into something, because the assassinations would occur by then. So a process was used that can only be justified—or rather, explained—in the perverse and inhuman context of this type of irregular war."[44] For Coelho, the extreme nature of the times explained—although it did not justify—the regime's use of dirty measures. It was in the context of the Dirty War that press restrictions made sense.

Progovernment members of Congress also cited the imperatives of the larger fight against communism in their defense of press censorship. In a 1973 debate in Congress, Senator Eurico Resende referred to the need for exceptional measures and called upon the press to do its patriotic duty by accepting censorship for the sake of the larger national project: "The fundamental characteristic of a revolution is its interventionist character, and our superlaw [AI-5] established the simultaneous existence of traditional democratic norms and norms of democratic exceptionality. . . . [Censorship] is a sacrifice that the press truly is suffering, for the benefit of the country under the prudent judgment of the revolution; . . . why can't the journalists and newspapers put up with this sacrifice for the benefit of the country?"[45] Resende acknowledged that press censorship was an extraordinary measure, but argued that it was justified by extraordinary times.

Even in asserting the necessity of the practice, however, Resende did not entirely relinquish a claim to democracy. To Resende, this democracy was "exceptional" rather than "traditional," but it was still democracy. Likewise, in finding a way to overturn *Opinião*'s legal victory, the Medici administration maintained a facade of proper administrative practice. The decree that it fabricated as a response to the victory was carefully predated to the beginning of *Opinião*'s prior censorship. The continuation, or apparent continuation, of such practices and norms was important for the regime.

The Vulnerability of Foreign and Domestic Audiences

Other justifications invoked for both the censorship and its concealment related to the press's potential audiences, particularly foreign audiences and the supposedly ignorant masses at home. Both of these audiences, the regime believed, could easily be led astray by the press, foreigners because of their lack of information or their tendency to believe the worst of Brazil, and the masses because of their ignorance and simplicity.

On the occasions when censorship was openly admitted by the regime's supporters, the justification perhaps most frequently heard for both censorship and its concealment was the need to protect Brazil's image abroad. The reasoning was that without such controls, the irresponsible press would publish calumnies against Brazil, and such calumnies would be readily believed.

The prior censorship of the *Estado de São Paulo* provided the basis for several congressional debates upon the press and Brazil's international reputation.[46] Members of the MDB would read into the record a speech by the newspaper's owner to the IAPA or a telegram to the minister of justice, and a debate would ensue.[47] At one of these, held on September 6, 1973, MDB Senator Nelson Carneiro proposed a law that would have required all publications under prior censorship to bear on their front page the statement, "This edition was approved by the censors of the Federal Police Department." His idea was to make the censorship public. Resende condemned this proposal as a "mockery," saying that it would be criminal to consider such a law and that it would be humiliating and harmful to Brazil's image. He claimed that censorship in Brazil was not practiced systematically, but when it did occur it was because the security forces deemed it to be in the national interest: "What the government aims at with these restrictions is to avoid the projection of tendentious news, injurious news, distorted news . . . onto the marketplace of ideas abroad."[48]

Another explanation that the regime developed to justify its efforts to control the press was popular vulnerability. In the regime's view, the Brazilian people were ignorant, unprepared, and culturally backward. The remedy was not to educate them or foster debate and critique, but to protect them from manipulation by preventing them from gaining access to certain information or hearing certain arguments. Two members of the regime who supported this view were Federal Police Chief Coelho and Jarbas Passarinho, an army colonel who served as minister of labor and minister of education. Their rationalizations sometimes come perilously close to full circle, as they bemoan not the false claims of injustice but the actualities of gross inequality throughout Brazil.

Coelho was appointed chief of the Federal Police by Geisel in 1974. He remained at his post under the Figueiredo administration and into the beginning of Jose Sarney's term in 1985. Coelho thus presided over many years of Federal Police censorship. He insists that he never liked the censorship, but that it was necessary because the "tremendous cultural backwardness" of Brazilians made them vulnerable to demagoguery, be it from the Catholic Church or from the communists. Although he did not like censorship, he undertook it as part of his responsibilities:

I consider myself a nonmilitarist military officer. I did many things not because I enjoyed them, but because I recognized the necessity of preventing news that could harm our government at that time, as we determined. . . . We had to censor because it's so easy to work the people, these Brazilian people who are without culture. . . . The cultural level of the people is very low, and therefore they are very vulnerable to mystification . . . Because of the profile of income concentration in this country, we are vulnerable to extremists. So censorship was a way to protect the population from being exploited. Income concentration here is lamentable.... The people can put up with anything as long as they have hope. What we couldn't permit was that the people lose hope. There were people working to destroy the hope for better days."[49]

Coelho offered no account of whether or how better days would come. His remarks put the Federal Police in the best possible light, as protectors of the vulnerable, even if his explanation would seem to justify the overthrow of the system that the police protected.

Passarinho echoed Coelho's assessment: "The communists are so tiny and weak in the United States. But in Latin America, the injustice is so profound, the misery and the poverty are so profound, that it all fits. The Marxist image is very attractive."[50] Censorship was intended to prevent this attractive—and, in this account, apparently reasonable—message from reaching those who would be most vulnerable to it.

Consistency and Authenticity

Another approach to justifying the regime's censorship and other actions was by pointing to the regime's intrinsically authoritarian character. It was a common assertion that consistency and "authenticity" were the most important standards by which to judge any government. This view was voiced best by two individuals of very different background and standing. One, General Meira Mattos, now holds a doctoral degree and is a professor of political science at Mackenzie University in São Paulo. He would be expected to have elaborated some standard for regime evaluation. The other, Helio Romão, was a lower-level police bureaucrat. He had been a police officer, then worked in the censorship office in Brasília, and then returned to active policing without much exposure to approaches of evaluation. Yet these two shared an understanding of the paramount value of consistency.

According to Meira Mattos, consistency was the most important standard of regime performance: "A government is to be evaluated by whether it is true to its identity. An authoritarian government must be authoritarian in order to survive. It must be authentic to its own—you have an identity and are true to it.... The government was authoritarian and had as its instruments authoritarian laws, the Institutional Acts One, Two, Five, et cetera. All of these were approved by Congress. Ergo, no one can say that they are illegal. Authoritarian, yes; illegal, no. Censorship is part of authoritarianism."[51] For Meira, this was sufficient.

Romão's opinion of his work was that he was just doing his job, just following orders, and therefore that he was not responsible for the consequences of his actions. When asked to reflect further, he asserted that the censorship was appropriate for its time, and consistent with the government's orientation:

> At that moment it was valid, within the designs of the government. But whoever was not here, who did not live it, who is not familiar with the mentality [cannot understand its validity] . . . In this context, this was the orientation. . . . It was a period of exception. Things were going on that today could not be done. Today there isn't a press law, there isn't censorship, so today it would be a manifestly illegal act. Today it would be inappropriate, unthinkable. But at that time, it was appropriate to do this.[52]

From this perspective, being valid to the situation at that time, being appropriate to and consistent with an authoritarian regime, were the correct standards by which to evaluate the censorship.

Untrustworthy Press and Judiciary

A further argument made by some members of the regime to justify censorship focused upon the intrinsic character of the press and the judicial system. The animosity toward the press throughout the regime was revealed in the secret CIEx document and many other sources. For many in the regime, untrustworthiness was the defining quality of the press all across the political spectrum. Indeed, politics and ideology had little to do with the press's untrustworthiness. Rather, the press itself was deemed an untrustworthy profession interested only in self-promotion. Meira Mattos remarked: "I don't like the press. I don't talk to the press. They're incapable of reproducing what you say. The goal of the press is sensationalism, not truth. Official decrees should be sufficient [to inform the public]. Anything that needs to be divulged should be [officially] announced, and that's that."[53]

Given this kind of assessment of the untrustworthiness of the press, legal measures alone would never have been deemed sufficient by the regime to restrict the press. Even for those members of the regime with a somewhat higher opinion of the press, legal means were generally considered inadequate. This was in part because a Dirty War required dirty means, but also because many in the regime viewed the judiciary as compromised, incompetent, and inefficient. Although the regime readily employed the trappings of law—putting into the Constitution amendments that violated the Constitution, generating extensive legal instruments by way of several Institutional Acts, issuing backdated decrees to support repressive acts, even mimicking legal language in illegal *bilhetinhos*—the regime severely weakened the judiciary.[54]

When there was some question of relying upon the legal system, the complaints from the regime sounded pathetic. Coelho, as chief of the Federal Police, complained that his hands were tied when it came to using legal means to control the press. Where legal systems are inadequate, Coelho explained, vigilantism always fills the vacuum:

[The press was] offending authority gratuitously. This was demoralizing. We couldn't permit it. They would invent things against us, and there was no legal remedy.

Why do death squads exist? Because the justice system does not judge. Someone is imprisoned, freed by the judge, and the next day they're back committing crimes. And finally, the police cannot put up with this anymore, and they start killing too. This is so in every country of the world.

So there was no juridical mechanism to protect us. There was no legal remedy. Events had to be responded to. It was a war, and these were terrorists. We had to avoid allowing the press to help the terrorists. . . . [Press] responsibility is required. And here there isn't any. The press publishes everything without proof or source. And what could we do about it? *Nothing!*[55]

Coming from the head of a police force that issued news prohibitions and confiscated newspapers for a regime that had created such measures as AI-5 and the National Security Law, and had put in place an elaborate array of security forces, such an appeal for sympathy does not carry much weight. Yet it is interesting that this was how Coelho viewed his position.

Popular Support

A final approach to rationalizing the censorship was not to attempt to justify it *per se*, but to refer instead to the general support among Brazilians for the regime. Thus, even if the censorship was coercive, illegal by the government's own legal standards, and something the regime was unwilling to admit—nonetheless, the regime certainly had popular support. In this view, support did not make the censorship right, but it did diminish the importance of its illegitimacy. Yet it is noteworthy that the regime did not test the depth of popular support in this area, but rather concealed its acts of censorship or acted indirectly whenever possible.

Senator Resende, in a congressional debate on censorship, related popular support to censorship this way: "The real national sentiment is on the side, loyally on the side, of this government that is responsible for the climate of peace and for the tranquility of the Brazilian family, achieved via the readily observed portentous economic development; and, more than this, for the respect of the nations whose political civilization and economic development are the most advanced in the world."[56] Against the real national sentiment, loyally on the side of the government, press restrictions were a petty issue for Resende.

Coelho also frequently referred to the regime's popular support, although he did not try to collapse this with legitimacy. He cited the enormous popularity of the regime, such that, in his estimation, there was absolutely nothing that could have threatened the government: "There was nothing, *nothing,* that could counter our will. That's the truth. We were really strong; we had popular support." But this did not stop him from asserting the need for protection.

PRACTICE WITHOUT LEGITIMACY

There were many attempts by members of the regime to justify censorship, and many attempts to deny and conceal it. But censorship was illegitimate and coercive, and the regime members knew it. In what terms, then, did they nonetheless practice it? Some simply were never bothered by the issue of legitimacy and were comfortable with the idea that they were merely following orders. Others may have been driven by paranoia, by an enormous miscalculation of the power of the press; this, at least, was the view of some journalists who tried to look at the situation from the military's perspective. And then there were others who deflected the issue by formulating new labels and categories that pretended to reconcile both the coercion and the cooperation at once, and with no dilemma.

"It Wasn't Our Job to Ask."

Helio Romão, the man who was most in the position to say, "I was just following orders," indeed says just that. Romão headed the central censorship office in Brasília, which channeled the prohibitions issued by the Ministry of Justice and the security forces to newspapers all around the country. He was the central figure in the censorship's operation for many years. For the most part, Romão's attitude is that all this was just his job:

> We carried out orders. We received the order from the Ministry of Justice, to comply with, to execute. That's it. It wasn't our job to ask, "But why can't it be published?" . . . We didn't know why, and it wasn't appropriate for us to ask why. We simply carried out this determination. . . . It wasn't for us to be analyzing, thinking about whether this was taking away the liberty of the press. None of that. We weren't emotionally involved. This wasn't our thing. We functioned. It was very distinct.

Following orders was sufficient for Romão, and presumably for those working with him. In reflecting on this issue, his only other statement was this awkward comparison: "If you as a journalist are given a story to cover, say an assault, it may not be a pleasant thing for you to cover, but you're going to do it, you're paid to do that, that's your work, even if you would prefer to be doing another kind of reporting."[57] Covering an assault may be unpleasant, but it is legal, does not violate anyone's rights, and is not an exercise in domination. The comparison is awkward indeed. But for Romão, it was sufficient that censorship was identified as a professional task, a duty to be fulfilled. In Romão's eyes, censorship was consistent with the other practices of the authoritarian regime that employed him, and so required no further reflection. In the same way that press actors became accustomed to the routines of censorship, the censors accepted what became their professional duties.

Paranoia, Miscalculations, and Mistakes

Another view of how the censorship was practiced despite its illegitimacy comes from a few press actors who tried to see these events from the regime's perspective. The conclusion each arrived at was that the censorship was the result of paranoia, of a gross but not unique miscalculation on the part of the military regime with respect to the press's power.

Carlos Alberto Sardemburg, of both the mainstream *Estado de São Paulo* and the alternative *Movimento*, speculated on why the regime thought it worthwhile to incur the expense of subjecting *Movimento* to prior censorship: "*Movimento* thought it was going to make the revolution. And the state believed it too. Both were mistaken! . . . *Movimento*'s readers were the already engaged. But the government was convinced that if they let *Movimento* go, it would convince others. This was paranoia. *Movimento* would never have succeeded anyway, wouldn't have reached or convinced a large number, even if it had been free to speak and circulate as it wanted."

Sardemburg pointed to other examples of this attitude on the part of the regime, such as the regime's assessments of the guerrillas and direct elections. In these cases the regime committed similar errors:

The whole Araguaia episode—imagine! A bunch of guerrillas going off to the Amazon, as though you could start the revolution there, reach São Paulo from there. It was a joke, an obvious mistake. All you had to do was encircle them, and let them fade—just leave them be. But instead, the government got all wrapped up, engulfed, and committed such incredible atrocities. There was such misplaced energy—on both sides. Such paranoia. The state thought that if presidential elections were ever open and direct, this would deliver the country to the communists. And look, what do the people do: they still vote for Janio Quadros! They vote for Collor![58]

Carlos Eduardo Lins da Silva came to a similar conclusion when considering the regime's attitude toward both the mainstream and the alternative press. In his estimation, the regime greatly overestimated the press's power and underestimated its own strength: "I think that the leaders never knew exactly how powerful they were. They didn't need censorship. They could perfectly well have afforded freedom of the press, and they would not have lost control of the situation. That's how powerful they were, in every way [militarily, politically, and economically]."[59] For Lins da Silva, then, there was no doubt that the censorship revealed more about the paranoia of the regime than about the power of the press. Censorship was practiced without legitimacy, out of the exigency of paranoia.[60]

A Forced Agreement

A final way to account for the practice of censorship, despite its illegitimacy, was simply to assert the reconciliation of its coercive and cooperative aspects. Coelho did not imply that censorship, in any of its guises, was accepted by the press; to the contrary, he complained about press efforts to circumvent the Federal Police. Clearly, the press was not thoroughly cooperative. Nor would Coelho countence a characterization of censorship as the result of coercion, force, or intimidation. It was nothing of the kind. Rather, for Coelho, it was usually a gentleman's agreement. How to reconcile these two contradictory characterizations? Coelho united them to his own satisfaction with the phrase "a forced agreement." This, for Coelho, best captured the nature of the self-censorship. Pleased with the phrase, he used it several times in our discussion and ended the interview by repeating it, confirming it, qualifying it—although then adding a final coda of doubt, and of his own lack of choice:

> It was a forced agreement. A forced agreement. It was a very polite but forced agreement. I have not lived as I would have liked to live, but in order to survive I had to do this.[61]

9

ROUTINE REPRESSION, ROUTINE COMPLIANCE

A PATTERN OF QUIESCENCE in the face of domination is established in very specific ways—perhaps by terror, indoctrination, or cooptation. In the Brazilian press's case, acquiescence to the illegal system of state censorship was generated above all by the particular way censorship was practiced by the military regime. Banal routinization of "self-censorship" was paramount in shaping the press's behavior.

Other factors were relevant: the internal vertical organization of the press, the competitive and class divisions within the press, the difficulty of using the judicial system, and the possibility of violent retaliation from the military regime. These factors, however, were present also for the few publications subject to the distinct system of "prior censorship." Yet these publications responded very differently, by engaging in creative and persistent, although ultimately unsuccessful, resistance. The vast majority of publications, however, were subject to state-imposed self-censorship, and acquiesced.

PRIOR CENSORSHIP AND SELF-CENSORSHIP

Both types of censorship conducted by the Brazilian military regime from 1968 to 1978 were illegal, concealed, and denied. Prior censorship was imposed upon about seven very diverse publications, including a major daily newspaper of national distribution, a humor magazine, journals of political opposition, and a diocesan newspaper. A censor would directly mark all the material prepared for publication, liberating or vetoing each piece and often interacting with the journalists and editors involved.

Self-censorship was applied against every other publication in the country. In this system, unsigned news prohibitions on plain paper would be delivered by a uniformed police agent. These had to be transcribed and were then taken away by the police agent. These illegal prohibitions were issued and received on a regular basis for years. The contents of these verbose, formulaic prohibitions would be shared only among top editorial staff. The prohibitions often concerned events of which the press was ignorant, and preempted investigation.

This examination of prior censorship has been a means to sharpen the focus upon self-censorship. Prior censorship involved an agent who followed orders but also made decisions. When the agent worked in the publication's offices, there were opportunities to persuade, cajole, or exhaust that individual. Even when the censorship was conducted at a distant police headquarters, members of the press could still try to persuade or fool the censors, or at least oblige them to read the same material repeatedly. While this whole operation also had its regular schedules and strict rules, the process of prior censorship was distinguished from self-censorship by its use of more visible external agents, who would invade a publication's space, deface its articles with red markers and black stamps, and clearly exercise some degree of judgment in their decision making.

The counterpart to this external enemy was an internal sharing. Those who labored under prior censorship constructed rituals of solidarity and release that confirmed their experiences and efforts. Because prior censorship was imposed upon a wide variety of publications, such a response did not come from a shared identity among the publications; indeed, there was little solidarity. Each publication acted against prior censorship in its own way, from sending furious telegrams to politicians to launching carefully crafted lawsuits, while making every effort to alert its readers to the situation. Almost all of these endeavors failed, but the resistance was determined, imaginative, and continual.

By contrast, compliance and quiescence were the norm for publications subject to self-censorship. Although self-censorship involved authorities whose use of coercion in other areas of was unpredictable, in dealing with the press the authorities engaged in repression at its most routine. All over the country, for every type of publication, and for a period of many years, identical measures were followed for the distribution and delivery of illegal news prohibitions. The very language of the prohibitions was highly formulaic and elaborately patterned. Press contact with any agent of censorship was minimal. The press's vertical organization meant that only top editorial staff handled the prohibitions, which further narrowed the opportunity for direct confrontation. The system seemed to function automatically, virtually without agency of authority. It was all-encompassing; no topic or publication was exempt from its application. It was mundane in its reliance upon petty, repetitive routines and in its avoidance of stark confrontations. Against this routine repression, the press felt powerless and responded by acquiescing, even though it never considered the censorship legitimate. This pattern of acquiescence was established because of the routinization of repression, rather than the two other most likely sources of this outcome.

SUPPORT

Many members of the press did support the authoritarian regime. At no point, however, did the Brazilian press manifestly endorse the denial of its freedom. Those who accepted the censorship did so for other reasons, not because of their support for the regime.

In the vertical organization that characterized the press, the three relevant levels were owners, editors, and journalists. Support for the regime was greatest among the elite owners of the mainstream press.[1] For most of these owners, a newspaper was a business enterprise, one business holding among many. Compliance with self-censorship was a sound business decision that allowed one to avoid the more costly process of prior censorship, to maintain good relations with the state (an essential source of advertising revenue), and to protect one's other business ventures from state retaliation. And though in some cases owners had the final say with respect to the overall orientation of their publications, many played no role in daily management, including decisions about censorship.

Staff journalists were at the bottom of the press hierarchy. At mainstream publications they saw themselves as peons who did the bidding of those in power, and they often resented this. Indeed, because of the way self-censorship was organized, most journalists never heard about news blackouts, or if they did, were never sure whether a blackout had been ordered by an editor or was the result of a prohibition issued by the regime. Regardless of journalists' support for or opposition to the regime, they did not exercise significant power at their publications, and therefore had no voice in determining how prohibitions were handled.

Most of the responsibility for dealing with censorship fell to the editors, who were caught between conflicting commitments. As members of the middle class, many probably supported the regime and its antisubversive mission. With careers in the press, they also had an institutional and professional identity to defend, a stake in the freedom and integrity of the press. With their daily work, they saw that there were good reasons to court the regime (a source of revenue and inside information) and good reasons to oppose it (for the sake of professional freedom). Although the editors exercised significant control over the daily conduct of their publications, including how censorship was responded to, they were, of course, employed by the owners, and could be fired. The owners, however, could not protect them from the wrath of the state.

The editors were a crucial group, yet their choices were subject to conflicting demands. Because of their conflicting identities, commitments, and concerns, their political support of the regime did not necessarily translate into endorsement or acceptance of press restrictions. These factors were independent. One could support the regime politically and still fight for one's professional and institutional autonomy. The argument that support would lead to acceptance of the restrictions therefore requires independent corroboration, and it is lacking. To the contrary, those editors who most strongly identified with the regime also expressed their disgust at the censorship. As was mentioned earlier, Evandro Carlos de Andrade, the editor of *O Globo,* the newspaper most closely identified with the regime, disdained the "farce" of censorship and insisted that he had never "personally" accepted the delivery of a prohibition. Walter Fontoura, editor of the *Jornal do Brasil,* often readily accommodated the regime, but nonetheless recalled the censorship as being "morally intolerable." Another member of *O Globo's* editorial staff, Luis Alberto Bettancourt, was an active opponent of the regime who nonetheless worked within the illegal state restrictions and encouraged others to do so. He saw this as a way of maintaining at least some circumscribed autonomy, and not being completely silenced.

The political orientation of the editors was thus complex. Class and institutional interests were often in conflict and might not coincide with commitments to the rule of law. Support for the regime did not directly translate into endorsement of press restrictions. Conversely, in some cases opponents of the regime accepted the restrictions. Thus for editors, the most relevant group of press actors, as well as for owners and journalists in the vertically organized Brazilian press, support itself was an insufficient explanation for acquiescence. That the press tolerated and complied with the restrictions does not mean that they did so because they supported the regime.

THE CULTURE OF FEAR

A second interpretation of the quiescence is based upon a "culture of fear" approach put forward in an emerging body of literature, both testimonial and analytical. This approach addresses the experiences of populations ruled by authoritarian military regimes in Latin America.[2] These works explore from many angles what Norbert Lechner calls the "political potential of fear."[3]

According the culture of fear interpretation, the authoritarian Latin

American states exercised terror deliberately, brutally and arbitrarily. They maximized the intimidation caused by this terror via public displays of their coercive power and by the manipulation of formerly independent institutions. The impact of these practices extended well beyond the immediate victims or the precise moment of terror's perpetration. The result was a collective and paralyzing pattern of silence, isolation, and hopelessness on the part of the population, a self-perpetuating culture of fear. As one writer, Juan Rial, has characterized this phenomenon,

> For a majority, the authoritarian years were a period of nonexistence as citizens. ... Adaptation to extreme repression required people to show a complete lack of will. ... The citizenry learned to live on probation. Simulation and dissimulation were rampant. Through the pedagogy of terror people learned to classify themselves according to various gradations of shame for past beliefs and actions. ... [The culture of fear] involved the feeling of being trapped in time, with no possibility for action, a feeling that there was room for only inadequate individual solutions to collective problems, a feeling that not even those who belonged to the in-group could be safe. ... In general, hopelessness was not so much a function of violence as a consequence of the loss of a clear perception of the limits of fear.[4]

Some form of a culture of fear is what I expected to find when I began the research on the acquiesence of the Brazilian press to censorship. It is a reasonable expectation, but it is not what I found.

Given the repressive measures directed against the Brazilian press and the generally repressive nature of the regime, the notion that a culture of fear lay at the root of Brazilian self-censorship is a plausible one. Nonetheless, a culture of fear, with its own specific characteristics and momentum, does not seem to have arisen in Brazil. Although silence, anomie, and a profound sense of powerlessness were characteristics of the period, they may have had causes other than fear. With respect to the press, fear does not appear to have been of paramount importance in determining people's behavior or commitments, although it was a factor.

The 1964–1985 regime was a bureaucratic-authoritarian phenomenon underpinned by an ideology of national security, by a plethora of security agencies and repressive forces, and by the routine yet arbitrary practice of torture. However, by certain measures it did not compare in its severity to other bureaucratic-authoritarian regimes in Latin America. It "disappeared" about three hundred people, whereas the Argentine regime's victims numbered about fifteen thousand; it did not kill as many people in the immediate aftermath of its coup as did the Chilean regime; and it did not interrogate nearly as many people, or as large a percentage of its population, as did the Uruguayan regime.[5] The military regime in Brazil did murder Vladimir

Herzog, but, as the Nunca Mais project documents, the press was much less of a target than the clandestine political organizations, and was targeted less severely than student groups and organized labor.[6] Overall, the Brazilian military regime treated the press less harshly than other groups in Brazilain Society and was less coercive than other bureaucratic-authoritarian regimes in Latin America. Thus the objective basis for press terror was not as solid as for other sectors in Brazil, or for other countries.

Numbers, of course, do not tell the whole story. The regime's terror, even if it was not as widespread as terror elsewhere, was still terror to its victims. Furthermore, the figures that exist cannot be comprehensive, although they are useful. No one has quantified the beatings in the streets, the seizures of notebooks and tape recorders, the numbers of journalists placed in temporary detention. The comparisons with other sectors in Brazil and with other regimes do not tell the whole story, but they must also be incorporated. The data do not suggest the overwhelming presence that state terror may have had elsewhere.

Certainly, there was fear of the regime within the press, but there were many other dynamics as well that challenged the predominance of paralyzing terror. These were expressed in the actions and commitments of members of the press.

The alternative press, for example, flourished under the authoritarian regime. Many people who had successful careers in the self-censoring mainstream press contributed regularly to alternative newspapers, even those publications subject to onerous prior censorship. This was not a gadfly minority, but many who continued to pursue successful mainstream careers. Hundreds of alternative publications were begun and new kinds of press associations, such as collectives and cooperatives, were established. Efforts were made, particularly toward the end of the period, to gain increased control of the journalists' unions.

Individuals in the press were acting. They were not so fearful that they did not act. Indeed, they were quite creative. They did not frontally challenge the authoritarian regime, nor did they resist the system of self-censorship, but they were not paralyzed in all areas. They went on acting in interstices and creating alternative forms of association and new outlets for their work. These were not actions that fearful people who had retreated into a private realm of silence, isolation, dissociation, and hopelessness would have been inspired to create or would have risked.

But not all members of the press spoke up or organized. There was also silence and isolation, although these phenomena were not necessarily evidence of fear. In Brazil there were many other reasons for silence, isolation, and hopelessness, including poverty, racism, and the persistence of an authoritarian culture that predated the regime.[7] These would have contributed to a sense of powerlessness regardless of the regime. Many people were economically and politically disenfranchised by this regime in ways that did not involve the exercise of terror and the creation of fear. That important aspects of their lives were out of their control, were far beyond the scope of effective action, was a reasonable conclusion for them to make even without the effects of state terror.

The press in particular had other internal sources of silence and powerlessness, unrelated to the regime's actions. Vertical hierarchies reinforced the sense of powerlessness. Private ownership, business competition, job insecurity, and retaliation for political divisions also contributed to silence and withdrawal. When such withdrawl or a sense of futility occured, this was not solely a response to the coercive power of the state or a result of fear.

A final challenge to the culture of fear interpretation is that people who worked for the press at the time of the military regime do not cite fear or its permutations as a factor in their own experiences. Their accounts, of course, cannot be accepted at face value. Time has passed. There was fear then, and memory of it may become distorted. Furthermore, there are many reasons why informants might misunderstand or misrepresent their experiences. But it is still worth noting that few in the press cite fear as the dominant experience of the period.

This is not to say that members of the press assert that they experienced feelings of safety and confidence. No one implies that this was a comfortable period. They mention telephones being tapped, telexes being intercepted, and the presence of informers in newsrooms. They were and are aware that surveillance occurred. But even when discussing those burdens, they do not frame their accounts primarily in terms of fear.

Some aspects of this are well captured by Carlos Lins da Silva's explanation of why he chose to become a journalist during the era of censorship, even with all the attacks the press faced from the regime. "Well," recalled Lins da Silva, "I knew the regime would not last forever." Similar sentiments were echoed by several others in the press, and provide a notable contrast to the inescapable sense of unpredictability and vulnerability in the account provided by the culture of fear approach. This not uncommon perspective conveys some basic resilience, the maintenance of a sense of proportion, and an evaluation of the regime as limited, at least in time. Such statements were not assertions of power or confidence, not "I knew we would win; I knew we would topple the regime." Nor do they express taking on the challenge out of heroism or bravado, joining the press despite enormous fear.[8] Rather, Lins da Silva's perpective was one possible rational assessment (borne out, indeed, by his generation and career—an assessment that would have been quite improbable within the terror and distortion of a culture of fear.

Fear was not irrelevant to press behavior. It seems to have been most relevant, however, for those members of the press who were also active in clandestine organizations or militant groups. It is these individuals who pursued other dangerous commitments in addition to their position in the press, who today say that fear was a constant presence in their lives under the regime. Other members of the press say that they experienced profound fear only in particular crises, in situations of unusually intense exposure or surveillance.

For most of the press most of the time, fear was not the primary daily experience—as expressed in their recollections now, or their willingness to embark on journalistic careers, create alternative publications and associations, and write for targeted publications then. A diminished role for fear is also suggested by comparative data on the victims of state terror in Brazil. While there certainly was fear among the press, this did not constitute a "culture of fear," nor did it form the basis for press acquiesence.[9]

ROUTINIZATION

The most striking feature of the illegal restrictions imposed by the state upon the press was their routinization. This extended to their distribution, presentation, concealment, and even language of the prohibitions. Definite rules, procedures, and patterns existed for every aspect of the handling of prohibitions. They were never found on stamped paper, rarely bore an authorizing signature, could not be photocopied, and were never left behind. The police officer delivering them, however, always demanded a signed receipt. The rules were never significantly departed from, no matter what the circumstances or who the target was.

The language of the prohibitions exhibited notable patterns. Arriving frequently—sometimes several in one day—the prohibitions nevertheless always repeated the same elaborate formulas, as in the following prohibition delivered to the *Jornal do Brasil* on June 20, 1974:

> By superior order, it is definitively prohibited to disseminate via the written, spoken, or televised means of social communication any news, commentaries, transcription, reference, and other materials about the declaration of Representative Mario Teles attributing to Minister Golbery do Couto e Silva information regarding the suspension of censorship and the *abertura*.

Such language invoked authority by mimicking traditional legal formulas. The language that conveyed authority in this instance was masking exactly its absence, for this was an entirely illegal process articulated in the most legalistic style.

Amid all these routines were very few direct confrontations. No publication ever received an announcement that it was about to be censored; instead, a prohibition would simply arrive at a publication's offices, and be followed by another, and then another. The "superior order" referred to in most of the prohibitions avoided identifying anyone who could be held accountable or challenged. The face of censorship was that of impersonal, automatic routine. The prohibitions' language and the procedures for distribution and receipt were not consistently coercive, brutal, or outrageous, but consistently officious, bureaucratic, and formulaic. The way the censorship was conducted presented authority not at its most repressive and arbitrary, but rather at its most banal, conventional, and routine.

Routinization was the predominant felt experience of the press under censorship. Censorship was seen as an automatic, impersonal, smoothly functioning system. It seemed to be propelled by its own momentum, with no one openly in charge. The awareness of surveillance and potential violence was never lost, but the daily experience of censorship was that of mundane and all-encompassing routines. Censorship was also routine for those who exercised it. Key members of the Federal Police responsible for censorship saw it as just another in a series of bureaucratic police procedures, functioning for the most part smoothly and properly.

The press felt powerless against the automatic routines of censorship. Rejection and resistance were considered futile. In their accounts of the time, all members of the press, from editors-in-chief to junior reporters, mention the feelings of powerlessness and futility they experienced, no matter what publication they worked for and no matter what their political outlook. The common refrains are, "What could one do?" and "There was no point in trying; it would get one nowhere."

This was a very particular kind of powerlessness. It was the result of routinization and banality, not the result of terror. Because of the way censorship was practiced by the regime, it came to be perceived by the press as beyond specific agency or political responsibility. It was against these mundane, all-encompassing, automatic routines—and not against guns, police invasions, or kidnappings—that the press felt powerless.

Of course, the press could not openly and directly resist the state, given the regime's coercive and repressive capacities. But there nonetheless remains a vast difference between the silent and full compliance of those under self-censorship and the carefully crafted lawsuits and furious telegrams of those under prior censorship. The self-censored press did not equip itself with the resources to reject or challenge censorship.

Divisions and stratification within the press hampered the formation of solidarity that might have led to the growth of a united front against the regime. Vertical organization limited direct shared exposure to censorship and permitted responsibility to be deflected up or down the hierarchy. Perceived class, cultural, political, and business divisions also separated press actors from each other. Although solidarity alone would not have equipped the press to challenge the regime, its absence undoubtedly impeded the formation of a collective identity and shared strategies, or even confidence that one's own antagonism toward the regime would not be taken advantage of by a competitor.

The lack of a secure legacy of press freedom also may have made it difficult to articulate a rejection of censorship. Since the colonial period there had never been a time when the press was entirely free of state interference in the form of censorship, bribes, or propaganda. Although the ideal of press freedom was widely held, there was no institutional memory to refer to in justifying or encouraging challenges to the regime's censorship.[10]

Fear of the regime may have been another factor making it difficult to overcome the sense of powerlessness. While fear was not the predominant press experience, neither was it absent. Fear became most relevant precisely for those contemplating some overt challenge. Without necessarily generating the collective paralysis characteristic of a culture of fear, regime intimidation would have contributed to dissuading those at the margin. Not fear, but the routine, mundane, all-encompassing nature of the censorship was the root cause of the feeling of powerlessness. Nonetheless, fear, in the words of *Movimento* editor Raimundo Pereira, "helped you to concretize your justification [for inaction]."[11]

The sense of powerlessness that followed from the routinization of censorship could have been countered by some other press experience of empowerment, but there was nothing to counteract it. The press was internally divided along various lines, lacked a secure historical legacy of institutional freedom, and furthermore might be subject to fear.

Such factors were heavy baggage, difficult to set aside in formulating a response to regime repression. Yet other groups in Brazil, which also carried burdens of institutional weakness or historical rigidity, managed to develop innovative strategies and find the tools needed to confront regime restrictions. The new union movement, for instance, arose out of the legacy of corporatist labor organizations, and Christian based communities emerged out of the hierarchical structures of the Catholic Church. The press, by contrast, lost its opportunities or failed to pursue possibilities. Confronted by the automatic and impersonal routines of censorship, the press could feel only its own powerlessness, and so acquiesced.

THE PURSUIT OF LEGITIMACY

The regime could have exercised censorship with much greater coercion or with much greater openness. It pursued instead a course of routinization in both the operation and the concealment of censorship, always trying to keep open a claim to the legitimacy of its actions.

One factor in this pattern of routinization was simply bureaucratic momentum. Some have argued that the regime was distinctively bureaucratic, more so than other authoritarian regimes in Latin America. Others interpret the regime's bureaucratization as the continuation of a long state tradition, which was left intact. Either way, the regime was notable for maintaining a highly bureaucratized system.[12] As a result, anything it undertook was likely to be routinized.[13]

A second factor in the routinization of censorship was the sheer volume of material involved. News prohibitions were issued for years to all of Brazil's thousands of publications. The prohibitions received by all publications, large and small, in provincial cities and major metropolitan areas were remarkably consistent. The Federal Police maintained only a small staff to handle both self-censorship and prior censorship, even though the latter form of censorship involved the review of vast quantities of material. To organize the censorship operation and produce these results would require consistent routines and systematization.

The most distinctive factor in the routinization of censorship was the regime's pursuit of political legitimacy and its consequent mimicry of traditional legal forms. As was discussed in chapter 3, the regime was distinctive in its desire for legitimacy. That desire was not straightforward, for the regime exhibited a simultaneous and contradictory demand for authoritarian control. There were also multiple strategies toward legitimacy, coming from the different factions within the regime and directed toward different constituencies within the population at different times. Possible bases of legitimacy included economic growth, repression of terrorists, populist patriotism, constitutionality, and the continuation of traditional institutions.

The constitutionality strategy sought to maintain or mimic legal and traditional forms and to perpetuate existing symbols and rules, even if their substantive content was overridden. To the extent that these proper constitutional forms and legal procedures bore connotations of political legitimacy and appropriate authority, this was meant to carry over to the regime as well. An effort was therefore made to maintain the appearance of constitutionality and legality or at least to avoid direct evidence to the contrary. The regime retained all the symbols of traditional constitutional rule, even if it put them to its own use or reduced them to symbolic smokescreens for its illegal activities. This approach characterized many of the regime's practices, not just those related to the press. The regime passed laws that violated the Constitution, yet never abolished the Constitution; it purged and greatly reduced the power of Congress, but did not do away with that body; it placed severe restrictions upon elections, but continued to hold them. In like manner, even while issuing news prohibitions to every media outlet in the country, the regime always insisted that the press was entitled to freedom and was in fact free.

Understanding that the regime mimicked legality in its pursuit of political legitimacy helps to explain many of the peculiar but consistent aspects of the censorship. The prohibitions themselves mimicked the elaborately formulaic, almost ritualistic, language of law. The prohibitions were clearly meant to look like proper legal constructions, and thus to convey legitimacy. The fully addressed and properly signed receipt for each prohibition was part of the charade. A concern for the appearance of legality also helps to explain the careful removal of physical evidence and the absence of authorizing signatures on prohibitions. These egregiously illegal practices were very hard to trace. Where direct communication from the regime to the press was routinely necessary, it was couched in the most proper legal formulas possible.

The efforts made by the regime to conceal those aspects of censorship that could not be disguised by the paraphernalia of legality or bureaucracy indicate that the gradually built-up design of the censorship system was due in part to the regime's desire for legitimacy and was a piece of that endeavor. Although bureaucratic momentum and the sheer volume of the material that required scrutiny account to some extent for censorship's routinization, the underlying imperative derived from the pursuit of political legitimacy via mimicry of legal and constitutional forms.

QUIESCENCE WITHOUT LEGITIMACY

Although the press complied with the regime's news prohibitions, it did not find the censorship legitimate. Even those who supported the regime politically expressed their disgust at the use of extralegal and concealed restrictions. The regime's legalistic routines were central in generating a sense of powerlessness and futility, and therefore acquiescence, but did not succeed in the further step of gaining legitimacy for censorship among the press.

In part this was because the regime was simultaneously vitiating the very basis of legitimation. As discussed with reference to the work of Lúcia Klein, the regime destroyed any autonomy that Congress might have had, and thus destroyed Congress's potential to legitimate the regime. Likewise, it so weakened other traditional pillars of governance—such as elections and the Constitution—that these, too, could not successfully perform a legitimating function. In dealing with the press, neat bureaucratic routines could not outweigh the fact that there was no legal basis for the violation of press freedom. The regime did not provide the due process or rule of law that were the implied referents of the symbols it deployed. The regime's often empty mimicry of traditional legal forms and institutions, then, could not achieve the project of legitimation.

Characteristics of the press itself also obstructed that project. Although the press lacked the institutional resources to challenge censorship or counterbalance the sense of powerlessness that led to quiescence, it nonetheless did have the wherewithal to distance itself from the censorship and label that practice illegitimate. This was not sufficient for members of the press to fully comprehend and critique the censorship or their own response to it. But it was sufficient to forestall an endorsement of the censorship as correct and proper.

Many in the press considered the censorship illegal, unethical, or temporary. These were some of the grounds upon which they dismissed its legitimacy. Both mainstream and alternative publications cited illegality as the basis for their disapproval of the restrictions. To be aware of the illegality did not necessarily enable one to challenge it (a point best exemplified by the fact that the verdict in *Opinião*'s successful lawsuit was immediately nullified by presidential decree). Under a regime that had devertebrated the judiciary and rewritten many legal rules, it was not necessarily possible to know upon what grounds censorship was illegal, and such knowledge was insufficient for a successful legal challenge. But it was sufficient to form the basis for disgust with the restrictions. For the press, as for other elites, a commitment to legality was one central tenet of legitimate behavior. That which was illegal might be fully complied with because of the imbalance of power in the regime's favor, but could never be legitimate.

Others in the press considered the regime's treatment of the press to be unethical, and this also prevented its legitimation. Although the press as an institution had no secure and glorious legacy of independence to appeal to, those who chose the press as a career often had some sense of journalistic integrity, some commitment to investigating and telling the truth. Thus for some press actors the worst experience of all was to know that they were dealing with lies and not to be able to do anything about it. Under an authoritarian regime, to recognize something as a lie was not necessarily enough to be able to expose and condemn it, but it was grounds for finding the distortions and denials morally wrong. This provided another confirmation of the illegitimacy of censorship.

Some who acquiesced could not articulate the illegitimacy of the censorship upon legal or moral grounds, but nonetheless communicated a sense of its illegitimacy. They tolerated the censorship, but little more than that. Like Antonio Carlos Pereira, they "waited for it to end," and refused to recognize a legitimate place for censorship in the state's treatment of the press.

That censorship was an unavoidable part of their situation did not mean that it was a correct, just, or enduring practice. These journalists would not have considered themselves to be waiting for the end of something they considered legitimate.

Although the routinization of censorship did not succeed in bestowing legitimacy upon that practice, it does appear to have generated quiescence—an unintended but still, for the regime, highly functional outcome. The established routines of censorship, more than terror or panic, generated a sense of powerlessness among members of the press, who resented the censorship but also complied with its mundane and all-encompassing routines.

Thus the Brazilian press is left with a peculiar legacy. There is no doubt that the news prohibitions and other restrictions constituted an elaborate state-administered system, yet both press and state actors continue to refer to it as self-censorship. The press knows that it was not the source of the restrictions, yet also recognizes that its compliance was one factor in the successful functioning of the censorship system. Everyday forms of quiescence are not necessarily transparent, even to those who practice them.

Because the press never succeeded in publicly condemning or rejecting the system of illegal prohibitions, the last word remains with the regime, once again in the voice of Federal Police chief Coelho. Like press actors of the time, Coelho provides ambivalent accounts of his actions and of his responsibility for those actions. Press actors describe their compliance while noting the illegality of a system that they themselves confusedly called self-censorship. And Coelho, searching for a phrase to capture the facts of coercion and cooperation, settled upon the evasive formulation of "a forced agreement." Yet it was Coelho himself, and not a member of the press, who most comprehensively and accurately discounted any ambivalence in the character of this system:

"Legitimate? No, it wasn't legitimate. Where are you going to find a censorship that's legitimate, eh?"

NOTES

All interviews referred to in the notes were conducted by the author.

1. EVERYDAY FORMS OF QUIESCENCE

1. See Scott 1985, 1990.
2. Gaventa 1980 provides one of the best discussions of this issue.

2. HISTORY OF PRESS-STATE RELATIONS

1. See Evans 1979.
2. On labor relations in Brazil, see Cohen 1989; Erickson 1977; Keck 1992; and Mericle 1977. The experience of the National Council of Women, created—and destroyed—by the state in the 1980s, is a more recent case of corporatism in Brazil.
3. On the transformation of Carnaval through the intervention of the state, see Raphael 1980. On the transformation of Umbanda as a case study in Afro-Brazilian religions, see Brown 1986.
4. As in the "new unionism" of the 1970s; see Keck 1992.
5. An essay by Helio Bicudo on this topic is included in Talarico 1977.
6. The granting of radio and television licenses was at the discretion of the president rather than through open competition. The 1985 Constitution transferred this power to the minister of communications but did not create formal procedures or standards.
7. This account draws primarily upon Costella 1970; Nobre 1950; and Sodre 1977.
8. Quoted in Sodre 1977, 29.
9. Dines 1975, 21.
10. See Hahner 1986 and Huggins 1985.
11. For example, in 1903 the *Jornal do Brasil* installed electric lights in its offices, obtained electric energy for its presses, and adopted the international style of putting news shorts on the front page and continuing the stories inside (a style associated with the *New York Herald*, *The Times*, *La Prensa*, and *La Nación*). In 1910 the *Jornal do Brasil* moved into a new headquarters building, reputed to be the tallest in South America. In 1912 it adopted typewriters and in 1916 had the largest graphics park in Brazil. See Sodre 1977, 273, 326, 397. The newspapers embraced the tools of "progress" in this era, and themselves became symbols of industrial progress.

12. Sodre 1977, 419. Sodre does not say why the government halted circulation. It is interesting that the newspaper chose to move through the courts.

13. Costella 1970, 102–03.

14. Costella 1970, 112. Note that "propaganda" can signify "announcement" in Portuguese and does not necessarily carry overtones of instrumental falsehood.

15. Morel 1975, 4.

16. Morel 1975, 4.

17. Decree 1949, art. 2, December 30, 1939. See Costella 1970, 114.

18. General Otavio Costa interview. Costa was chief of the Assessoria Especial de Relações Públicas (Special Advisory Council on Public Relations) from 1969 to 1974.

19. Costella 1970, 112.

20. Dines 1975, 12; Costella 1970, 114; Sodre 1977, 439. At the time of the DIP takeover, the newspaper's owner, Julio de Mesquita Filho, was already in exile in Buenos Aires; his brother Francisco Mesquita and twenty others on the newspaper's staff were arrested.

21. Dines 1975, 11; Sodre 1977, 439.

22. Costella 1970, 115; Nobre 1950, 96.

23. *Unidade*, the bulletin of the São Paulo journalists' union, published several articles on the occasion of the union's fortieth anniversary which suggest that the Rio de Janeiro and São Paulo journalists' unions responded differently toward Vargas's "favors." In 1937 Vargas proposed that the two cities' journalists' unions be combined and placed under the Ministry of Labor in return for badly needed funds. The São Paulo union refused, irritating Vargas. When Vargas implemented Decree Law 7037, which set minimum salaries for professional journalists, the Rio de Janeiro union wanted to hold a ceremony for Vargas to show its appreciation, but the São Paulo union declined. See *Unidade* 20:20, April 1977, 10–12.

24. Sodre 1977, 354.

25. See Johnson 1989.

26. Morel 1975, 4.

27. Castello Branco interview; Dines 1975, 11.

28. Skidmore 1967, 125–26.

29. Sodre 1977, 460. An example of widespread and dubious press indebtedness to the state is the case of *O Globo* and the loans it secured for the purchase of imported equipment. Between October 1950 (with Vargas elected but not yet in office) and August 1952, *O Globo* obtained a total of more than one million dollars in five separate loans from the Bank of Brazil. For each loan *O Globo* offered as collateral the printing equipment to be imported as well as its ancient Goss printing machine. Although some of these loans were granted only a month apart, there seems to have been no trouble with the bank's repeated acceptance of the already committed (and perhaps valueless) Goss as collateral. According to Sodre 1977, 460ff., all the major newspapers were in the same situation, yet all participated in the 1953 outcry "against the 'favoritism of the Bank of Brazil.'"

30. The photograph is of Kubitschek apparently beseeching U.S. Secretary of State John Foster Dulles, who is seated with his wallet open.

31. Sodre 1977, 471.

32. See Dreiffus 1981. Mesquita recalled colonels consulting the *Estado de São Paulo* on the coup. See Moises and Benevides 1984.
33. See appendix 1, "Selections from *Correio da Manhã*," in Smith 1994.
34. See Andrade and Silveira 1991.
35. See, for example, Hagopian 1986 on continuities in civil administration.

3. THE MILITARY REGIME: AUTHORITARIANISM AND LEGITIMACY

1. See O'Donnell 1973 and Collier 1979. For the political history of this period, see Skidmore 1988. On the military, see Stepan 1988, and on the ideology and structure of the regime and changes in response to opposition, see Alves 1985. For nuanced contemporary analyses of the regime, see Klein and Figueiredo 1978; Sorj and Tavares de Almeida 1983. For the spirit of the period, see Ventura 1988; Gabeira 1988.

Although the original work on this regime type was very insightful, the notion of bureaucratic authoritarianism became reified. Subsequent work paid much attention to polemics on functionalist methodology and economic determinism, rather than to the Southern Cone regimes themselves. Rereading contemporary material, one glimpses historical contingencies that were buried in the debates upon the merits of the concept of bureaucratic authoritarianism as a regime type.

2. The majority of the 707 legal proceedings studied in the Nunca Mais project concern participation in banned political organizations. See *Torture in Brazil* 1986, chap. 10.
3. See, among others, Stepan 1989, pt. 3; Alves 1985.
4. Velasco e Cruz and Martins 1983, 22.
5. Quoted in Velasco e Cruz and Martins 1983, 30.
6. Probably the best telling of the story of AI-5 is Ventura 1988, who nicely captures the personalities and immediate disputes, the satiric insults of the key speech, and the overreaction of the military when the speech was generally ignored. On the events of 1968, see also Aarão 1988.
7. AI-5 also had tremendous cultural importance as the emblem of an era. The "AI-5 Generation" refers to a generation shaped and silenced by fear. See Martins 1979.
8. Alves 1985, 95.
9. Velasco e Cruz and Martins 1983, 38. See also Figueiredo 1978.
10. The laws affecting the press in particular are reviewed in Dupret, Gonzales, and Costa 1980.
11. Klein and Figueiredo 1978, 150; Velasco e Cruz and Martins 1983, 17.
12. See Stepan 1988, chap. 2. According to Stepan, Brazil was noteworthy for the institutionalization of its repressive apparatus, Argentina for the number of individuals "disappeared," Chile for the number of deaths in the immediate aftermath of its coup, and Uruguay for the percentage of the population detained and interrogated.
13. *Torture in Brazil* 1986, 65. See also Stepan 1988, chap. 2; Alves 1985, 120–32.
14. See *Torture in Brazil* 1986 and the reports of Amnesty International.

15. Such brutality preceded the regime and continues today, in the streets, in common prisons, and in army barracks. See Skidmore 1988 on this as a historical phenomenon, and Pinheiro 1991 on its continuation.

16. In a 1992 interview for *IstoÉ*, the police officer who interrogated Vladimir Herzog in 1975 stuck to the story, which in 1975 had immediately been discredited, that Herzog committed suicide. The officer simultaneously insisted that he himself had done nothing and that he was proud of what he had done. See *IstoÉ*, March 25, 1992, 20–26.

17. Figueiredo 1978, chap. 4, "O uso da coerção política e a burocracia do estado." Figueiredo's data are entirely numerical; he does not discuss the content of the disputes.

18. See, for example, Stepan 1988.

19. The passing of Institutional Acts by executive decree conflicted with the Constitution, which was never formally rejected. In trying to deal with this, the junta that ruled between the regimes of Costa e Silva and Medici in 1969 promulgated an amendment attaching AI-5 to the Constitution. Klein 1978, 33, remarks that "The basic contradiction inherent in the coexistence of the so-called constitutional and institutional orders is linked to the fact that the recourse by the Executive to the powers conferred by AI-5 constitute the absence of a legal observance of the Constitution itself; in other words, the Constitutional Amendment institutionalized disobedience of the Constitution."

20. In questioning a variety of Brazilian elites, McDonough found that they were most likely to agree upon the need for restoring the writ of habeas corpus, "one of the fundamental bourgeois decencies." He observed that "On this rule-of-law issue there exists virtual consensus." McDonough 1981, 178, 185.

21. Klein 1978, 99.

22. Effectiveness as the argued basis for legitimacy of a system of domination is not unique to Brazilian politics, nor even tied to authoritarianism. Veteran politician Adhemar de Barros sought the vote in São Paulo with the campaign slogan, "I steal, but I get things done."

23. See Klein 1978, 35.

24. McDonough 1981, 44, 201; Stepan 1985, 332, 335.

25. See Skidmore 1988, 110–12.

26. In Brazil, as in other bureaucratic authoritarian countries in Latin America, the military identified mobilization with leftist movements and never embraced the fascist pattern, entailing base-level mobilization.

McDonough argues that crosscutting cleavages among elites made a mass party unnecessary, and that the military was more concerned with incompetent elites than with the potential for a genuine mass uprising. "[T]he major step that remained to be taken in the direction of the total control was mass mobilization under the aegis of a single party. But the logic of Brazilian authoritarianism does not require such mobilization, and the regime settled for a public relations promotion of a stern yet populist image for its presidents." McDonough 1981, 232.

27. The hard-liners "never had illusions about the viability of representative democracy in Brazil," yet avoided repudiating the political elite's faith in it, because of U.S. support and international opinion. Skidmore 1988, 157–58.

28. The outrage of some officers at not being permitted to participate in the military selection of President Medici seems quite genuine, if incredibly one-sided. After a stroke incapacitated President Costa e Silva in 1969, a junta temporarily exercised presidential powers. The most senior officers then voted Medici into power. Certain hard-line junior officers, irate at being excluded, risked punishment to express their fury in terms of the "right" to elect the president. Despite having denied this right to the populace, they nonetheless phrased their anger in terms of this perduring norm. See Chagas 1970, 160.

29. Figueiredo 1978.

4. THE PRESS: MAINSTREAM AND ALTERNATIVE

1. When several organizations wanted to do a study on reports of the assassinations of street children, for example, they had to turn to the tabloid *O Dia* for data. Such events do not receive coverage in the sober *Jornal do Brasil* or *Estado de São Paulo*. See Movimento Nacional de Meninos e Meninas de Rua, Instituto Brasileiro de Análises Sociasi e Econômicas, and Núcleo de Estudos da Violência 1991.

2. The *Folha de São Paulo* was not a major actor in the early period of the military regime. It gained national prominence only in the 1980s, particularly through its coverage of the popular mobilization for direct presidential elections. It then self-consciously pursued new international trends in press format and content. See Lins da Silva 1988.

3. Japan printed 519 papers per 1000 inhabitants in 1972, the U.S. 297, Spain 98, and Venezuela 93. See United Nations 1972. Estimates for the 1990s suggest that the four major daily newspapers in Brazil have a combined circulation of less than 5 million in a population of 150 million.

4. The Brazilian figure is more comparable to the 33 percent illiteracy rate of the Dominican Republic. See Wilkie et al. 1990. Throughout Latin America, newspaper readership has been declining since the 1950s, despite decreasing illiteracy, as the following table shows:

	Illiteracy Rate (%)	Circulation per 1,000 Inhabitants
1940	48.5	78.4
1950	43.3	82.2
1960	32.7	76.4
1970	26.3	74.3
1980	19.2	70.2

Source: Wilkie et al. 1990.

5. A large television audience, however, does not necessarily mean competition and lower newspaper circulation. It could indicate a large potential audience of interested people. The two could be complementary.

6. National figures provided at a 1978 conference on the press indicated that

radio reached eighty-five million people, television forty-five million people, and newspapers twenty million people. See Nitrini et al., 34. The predominance of television as a medium for both news and entertainment has increased since then. See the essays in Skidmore 1993.

7. See Castro 1988.

8. *Visão*, August 1976.

9. Boris Casoy interview.

10. José Neumanne Pinto notes that the InterAmerican Press Association praised the design quality of the Brazilian press. Neumanne Pinto 1976, 6. Lins da Silva, considering the U.S. influence on Brazil's press, recalled the remark of a Mexican journalist: "Would that we were so influenced!" (Lins da Silva interview).

11. Editor Claudio Abramo of the *Estado de São Paulo* remarked of its owner, Julio Mesquita, that "Dr Julinho did not want national news on the first page, only international. It was his recondite colonialism, which considered Europe and the world to be more important than Brazil, even to Brazilians. Thus *Estado* put Vargas's suicide on the front page only by a major concession on the part of Dr Julinho after great and vehement insistence on the part of myself and his sons." Abramo considered the Mesquita family's editorial line "medieval." Abramo 1988, 35, 37.

12. Boris Casoy interview.

13. Quoted in *Visão*, August 1976.

14. Walter Fontoura interview.

15. Quoted in *Visao*, August 1976. Note his choice of the word "perfection" with respect to democracy. This echoed the authoritarian regime's description of its own project.

16. *Unidade* 1:8, March 1976, 9.

17. For example, Carlos Chagas was with the *Estado de São Paulo* for a very long time, and then became a news commentator for the Manchete television network, while also writing editorials for the *Tribuna da Imprensa*. Boris Casoy, who filled many posts at the *Folha de São Paulo*, including editor-in-chief, has become the newsanchor for the SBT television network. Marcos Sá was an editor at *Veja*, then editor-in-chief of the *Jornal do Brasil* and later of *O Dia*.

18. On this situation, see *Boletim ABI* and the union newspapers, especially *Unidade*, published by the São Paulo journalists' union.

19. An article in *Movimento* about the fate of the bankrupt Diários chain pointed out that its newspaper, the *Estado da Minas*, was one of the most lucrative publications in the country and also paid particularly low wages. The director asserted that this was justified because a newspaper job could lead to other sources of income. The economics reporter, for example, although responsible for business reporting, was also press agent for Fiat. *Movimento*, no. 127, December 5, 1977.

Opinião, no. 24, April 1973, stated that 50 of the 330 journalists working for the *Estado de São Paulo* in Pernambuco also worked for the state or local government.

20. This varied from newspaper to newspaper. The *Folha de São Paulo* had a reputation for barring unions, while the *Jornal do Brasil* had a more open atmosphere. *O Globo* had a reputation for police informers, and everyone readily praised Evandro Carlos de Andrade, even those who disagreed with him politically, for removing them.

21. See, for example, *I Congresso Nacional de Jornalistas Pela Liberdade de Imprensa* 1980.
22. *Unidade* 1:8, March 1976, 9.
23. *Visão*, August 1976.
24. *Visão*, August 1976.
25. Caparelli 1986, 64. See also Abramo 1988, 116.
26. The state was even more key for television stations, which operated on concession. If a company held a television concession and published a newspaper, it faced even greater jeopardy. See Marconi 1980, 130-34, and *Unidade* 1:3, October 1975, 8-9.
27. State pressure took advantage of many financial channels in which to operate. According to an article published in *Movimento* in December 1977, the major communications network Diários e Emissoras Associados, owner of nine television stations, fifteen radio stations, and thirty newspapers, was in major financial difficulty and filing for bankruptcy. The options were either a direct state takeover or permitting the government to appoint a new director and have a say in the running of the business while also granting it financial favors, so that the network's "political fidelity would be secured in exchange for the financial favors necessary for the recuperation of the business." The latter, according to *Movimento*, is what happened. The state appointed Mauro Salles director and provided loans for paying debts to the government and advertisers. Salles listed his three goals for the company: to pay its debts, compete with the *Globo* network, and support the government. "The mission of the leadership of social communication is to support the words of those who govern." *Movimento*, no. 127, December 5, 1977.
28. This was the *Catologo de imprensa alternativa*, a catalog of the holdings of the Centro de Imprensa e Cultura Popular of the Rio de Janeiro's Municipal Secretariat of Culture.
29. They no longer do. Very few alternative publications exist today, and none with the circulation and reputation that the earlier publications had. See Pereira 1986 on different interpretations of the demise of the alternative press.
30. Caparelli 1986, 66; Kenski 1990, 76. Teodomiro Braga asserted that *Opinião*'s sales in Belo Horizonte sometimes exceeded the sales of the mainstream newsweekly *Veja* (interview).
31. See Kenski 1990, 86.
32. Caparelli 1986, 47, 65.
33. Indeed, this was in part the intent of at least Fernando Gasparian, owner of *Opinião*. "Gasparian's idea was to produce a journal that would directly influence the ruling class of the Brazilian economy, a journal to influence the leadership 'of the intellectual and financial elites' as Gasparian declared, 'to influence the union leadership, the military . . .' The critical positions, the opinions and analyses presented, therefore, were meant 'to awaken,' according to Gasparian, 'these people who weren't believing in anything any more, who had been victims of terrorism, and who came to believe in something.'" Kenski 1990, 85.
34. Luis Alberto Bettancourt interview.
35. "We are a generation of journalists formed by AI-5, by paranoia. We are fear. It flows through every line we write. It stains the paper with shame. Our manner

of writing was shaped by the mainstream press—by self-censorship. Our work has rarely had a social purpose. It has had a practical purpose: to survive fear. We should not accuse anyone for what we did not say: with rare exception, we should accuse ourselves.

"This preliminary issue of *Repórter* could have been much better. Much more truthful. But it was not possible: we were afraid. And exactly because of this we understand those who refuse to join us. Or even to speak. They are our companions in the fear which suffocates this country." *Repórter*, no. 0, November 1977.

36. Carlos Alberto Sardemburg interview.
37. These quotations are from the *Catalogo de imprensa alternativa*.
38. *Movimento*, no. 0, July 1, 1975.
39. Carlos Alberto Sardemburg interview.
40. Teodomiro Braga interview.
41. *Unidade* 1:1, August 1975, 13.
42. These figures are presented in Caparelli 1986, 65; he does not identify his sources.
43. Interviews with Carlos Alberto Sardemburg and Luis Alberto Bettancourt, among others.
44. Talarico 1977. This source is unpaginated.
45. Moacyr Coelho interview.
46. *Unidade* 1:8, March 1976.

5. THE MANY FORMS OF PRESS CONTROL

1. Quoted in Marconi 1980, 24. This is one of over fifty such statements that Marconi culled from the mainstream press for his chapter entitled "The Psychosis of National Security."
2. *Jornal do Brasil*, February 26, 1977, 4.
3. *Jornal do Brasil*, August 3, 1974, 4.
4. *O Globo*, June 21, 1977, 8.
5. *Estado de São Paulo*, June 10, 1977, 5.
6. Meira Mattos interview.
7. Jarbas Passarinho interview.
8. This story was prepared for the police page of the *Estado de São Paulo*, April 10, 1974, 17, but vetoed by the authorities.
9. In addition to its self-consciousness, another intriguing aspect of the document was its appearance in 1978 during the *abertura*. The *abertura* was a program for "limited" democracy, for a "gradual, controlled" transition to freedom. What was given with one hand could be taken away with the other. Another issue is the position of CIEx toward any political openness at all. It is possible that CIEx was preparing this strategy without the Geisel's knowledge.
10. My source is an unpaginated document produced by the Conselho Parlamentar de Defesa dos Direitos da Pessoa Humana of the State Legislative Assembly of São Paulo, entitled "As pressões do governo Brasileiro contra a imprensa independente," which was prepared by Deputy Fernando Morais and appeared in June 1979. It includes lengthy quotations from and a discussion of the CIEx document, appendixes containing accounts of the experiences of several journals, and

copies of orders and correspondence from the Ministry of Justice and Federal Police.

11. This and the following examples come from Conselho Parlamentar de Defesa dos Direitos da Pessoa Humana 1979.

12. Waldir de Góes interview. Conselho Parlamentar de Defesa dos Direitos da Pessoa Humana 1979.

13. See chap. 4. The international pattern for newspaper revenue is 50 percent from sales and 50 percent from advertising. The Brazilian pattern was 30 percent from sales and 70 percent from advertising.

14. Governor Garcia Neto of Mato Grosso refused to place any public announcements with the *Correio da Imprensa* after it published articles on irregularities at the state bank: Talarico 1977. Governor Prates of the Federal District withdrew official advertising from the *Jornal do Brasília* after its coverage of a real estate scandal in which he and his staff were involved (story vetoed from the *Estado de São Paulo*, December 13, 1973, 5). *O Municipio*, a newspaper in the interior of São Paulo state, had its headquarters expropriated by the mayor (owner of a rival paper) following its reporting on irregularities in the local administration (story censored from the *Estado de São Paulo*, October 17, 1973, 5).

The *Estado de São Paulo* engaged in a well-known feud with the governor of São Paulo state, Laudo Natel. When Natel removed all state advertising from the *Estado de São Paulo*, the newspaper responded by asserting that those most deeply hurt would be the public, and it therefore insisted upon carrying all public service announcements free of charge. (Story censored from the *Estado de São Paulo*, October 17, 1973, 5.)

In the state of Bahia, the powerful governor Antônio Carlos Magalhães boycotted the *Jornal da Bahia*, which had been critical of his administration. To survive the boycott, the *Jornal da Bahia* mounted a campaign with the slogan, "Don't Let this Flame be Extinguished." The newspaper held a subscription drive in the early 1970s that reportedly netted thousands of new subscriptions (in a state where only eighty thousand people bought newspapers). Had it not been for these new subscriptions, the newspaper would have folded. In 1970 state advertising brought in four times as much revenue as sales; in 1973 it brought in only two-thirds as much. This is the only case I found of readers coming to the support of a targeted newspaper. The source is an article censored from *Movimento*, no. 67, October 11, 1976.

15. *Correio da Manhã*, September 11, 1969. See also Andrade and Silveira 1991.

16. The most important source here is the Waldir de Góes interview. See also Soares 1989. The *Jornal do Brasil* was perhaps particularly vulnerable at this time because it was also trying very hard to obtain a license for a television station. See Marconi 1980, 131–34.

17. Why was this so? Perhaps Geisel was truly determined to control the *Jornal do Brasil*'s editorial line. On the other hand, perhaps Geisel was sacrificing the *Jornal do Brasil* and press freedom as a bargaining chip, conceding to the hard-liner Abreu in this matter in order to gain advantage elsewhere.

18. According to Góes, none of the offices or companies expressed any disagreement with the order. They simply shifted the *Jornal do Brasil*'s usual share of their advertising to the other three national newspapers.

19. Góes concluded this part of the story: "And then came Figueiredo and the Figueiredo government was simply a big mess. It just didn't have the capacity [to do anything of the kind]."

20. This was by no means surprising, given that most of the alternative papers opposed the regime. Nonetheless, with state funds going to so many businesses, the regime's selectivity was considered worthy of note: "In 200 issues already published, the journal [*Movimento*] has not received a single announcement from any public enterprises administered directly or indirectly by federal, state, or municipal government. The publication of such announcements in newspapers of much smaller circulation indicates a deliberate boycott." *Movimento* statement quoted in Conselho Parlamentar de Defesa dos Direitos da Pessoa Humana 1979.

21. Pinheiro Machado 1978, 121–23.

22. Pinheiro Machado 1978, 121–23. The government's decision to let foreign companies buy risk contracts and explore for oil in Brazil was extremely controversial. An entire issue of *Movimento* devoted to this topic was first censored and then prohibited entirely (no. 15, October 13, 1975). *Opinião* was prohibited not only from publishing anything on risk contracts, but even from submitting any articles on this topic to the censor.

23. Conselho Parlamentar de Defesa dos Direitos de Pessoa Humana 1979.

24. Talarico 1977.

25. Conselho Parlamentar de Defesa dos Direitos da Pessoa Humana 1979.

26. Moacyr Coelho interview.

27. *Unidade* 2:18, January 1977, 10; 2:23, July 1977, 14.

28. Luis Alberto Bittencourt interview.

29. Walter Fontoura interview. Attesting to the readiness of this concern are the precautions that the *Jornal do Brasil* took in 1976 when it published what Marcos Sá had discovered in the Lyndon Johnson Library regarding CIA surveillance of Brazil in 1963–1964 (Marcos Sá interview). The newspaper worked night and day to publish all the material as swiftly as possible, even haphazardly, because the staff expected it to be apprehended at any moment. Each day the newspaper would reveal highlights of the next day's installment, so that if shut down its readers would at least know that more material had been coming.

Although the *Jornal do Brasil* was allowed to publish this series, and a small book publisher (L&PM Editores) later printed it as a separate volume, this already published material was censored from *Movimento*.

30. In 1977 the ABI recorded the seizure of the *Jornal do Povo* (the only daily in Macapá, Amapá) on May 8, apparently as a reprisal for denouncing arbitrary acts by the Macapá police; of *Posição* (Vitória, Espirito Santo) in July by the military police, reportedly on the orders of Governor Elcio Alvares; and of *A Notícia* (Julio de Castilhos, Rio Grande do Sul) by police commissioner Paulo Roberto Power Araujo after it had published statements by politicians accusing the commissioner of negligence. Talarico 1977.

31. President Figueiredo famously remarked that he preferred the smell of his horse to that of the people. That the people were not "ready" to vote was a common assessment not only of the government but of the elite generally. Colonel Moacyr Coelho was among many to lament the low cultural level of the masses, which rendered them vulnerable to manipulation, whether by communists or the Catholic Church (Moacyr Coelho interview).

32. Moacyr Coelho interview.

33. This was a frequent complaint. In Rio de Janeiro the Department of Transportation played press releases over a tape recorder ("Assessoria de Comunicação Social,' a barriera dos repórteres," *Boletim ABI,* May/June 1975, 10). The Ministry of Health in Brasília prohibited reporters covering the ministry from moving freely about its premises. It issued an order limiting them to attending readings of press releases. Talarico 1977.

34. See, for example, "'Assessoria de comunicação social,' a barreira dos repórteres," *Boletim ABI,* May/June 1975, 10.

Even at key moments, such as the heart attack of President Costa e Silva, the press advisor would be the only official available to the press. Even very well-placed journalists had little access. Marcos Sá, the *Veja* correspondent in Brasília, recalls being permitted to meet with Cabinet ministers only two or three times during his five years in Brasília (Marcos Sá interview).

35. Talarico 1977.
36. Marconi 1980, 101.
37. Marconi 1980, 110.
38. Marconi 1980, 111–12. The censorship referred to here was the moral censorship of music, theater, film, and television. The Luftalla case was a financial corruption scandal involving then Governor of Sao Paulo, Paulo Maluf.

The Portuguese phrase "nada a declarar" inspired the title of Falcao's memoir *Tudo a declarar* (Rio de Janeiro: Editora Nova Fronteira, 1989)—which, needless to say, by no means declares everything.

39. This commentary by the journalist Clovis Rossi was prohibited by the authorities from appearing in the *Estado de São Paulo,* July 26, 1974, 16. Rossi's essay is entitled "Epidemic of Silence" and addresses the unavailability of any kind of official data or statements during an outbreak of meningitis in São Paulo. The essay continues: "The reporter today in Brazil is invariably treated by whatever authority—or by anyone pretending to be an authority, even when they're not—as an enemy to be avoided, a dangerous subversive . . . or maybe an expert Russian or American spy."

40. See, among other sources, *Unidade* 1:2, September 1975, 7.
41. Luis Alberto Bittencourt interview.
42. The first legal proceeding was to pressure Chagas not to publish a book chronicling the succession crisis following Costa e Silva's heart attack. Chagas adamantly refused to withdraw the book. It was confiscated upon publication, but the legal proceedings against it were dropped. A second action, concerning the publication of news of a kidnapping, was dropped when the military judge declared the indictment "nonsense." The third was seen as a provocation by the Army Minister Sylvio Frota, and was dismissed by Geisel himself. For further details, see Smith 1994, 189–92.

43. While still press advisor to the incapacitated president, he was told by an ally in the military to get himself out of town, for the animosities of the different military factions meant that his physical protection could not be guaranteed. Chagas 1970, 196–97.

44. Jaime Sautchuk interview.

45. This story has now attained folkloric proportions. The impetus for the imprisonment was a cartoon of Dom Pedro I in classic pose, but this time declar-

ing his desire for bone marrow jelly ("O que eu quero é mocotó") rather than independence. Bone marrow jelly is reputedly good for the health of growing children, and "Eu quero é mocotó" was an advertising jingle of one of its producers. The line was as innocuous as "I want my Maypo," or "Eat your Wheaties," and carried no other connotations. At worst, it made Dom Pedro seem infantile.

During the two months that the *Pasquim* staff were in jail, other journalists in Rio de Janeiro kept the magazine in production. As *Pasquim* was under censorship, they could not openly discuss the imprisonments. (This raises another puzzle: how did the initial offending remark get through if the journal was under censorship? This is a further indication that the line was not necessarily offensive.) Millôr Fernandes's signature cartoon rat lamented the "flu" that had incapacitated the entire staff, and readers turned to the rat for hints of any news regarding their fate. Circulation fell and *Pasquim* lost all paid advertising, but it did keep printing until the return of the staff.

Sources relating to the imprisonment of the *Pasquim* staff include Chagas's testimony in the National Congress's "Simpósio sobre censura," *Diário do Congresso Nacional*, supplement to no. 154, December 3, 1980, 9, and Millôr Fernandes's editorial reprinted in Pinheiro Machado 1978, 86–89.

46. Marconi 1980, 103. This was true not only for journalists, but for many government functionaries, university employees, and so on. Oliveiros Ferreira interview; Marconi 1980, 31; Alves 1985, 128–29. Although this might look to some like a sinister grand scheme, it may simply have been a by-product of an overgrown bureaucracy.

47. The editor-in-chief of the *Estado de São Paulo*, Oliveiros Ferreira, had good personal relations with several members of the military hierarchy. One of them once took the rare step of reading aloud to Ferreira from the editor's personal file. Ferreira was astonished at the detail. At the end of the recitation, he ventured a correction: "Yes, but that organization, you know, the one you list as communist, that wasn't communist." To which the officer retorted: "Yes, it was." There was no debate on these matters. The military regime held power; you were what they said you were. (Oliveiros Ferreira interview.)

In 1975 Leda Floro, a journalist with the *Estado de São Paulo*, was covering the president's office on provisional credentials while her application was being processed. The application was rejected, as she eventually learned "off the record" from an official in the Ministry of Justice, because the SNI suspected that she was a KGB agent planted to seduce President Geisel's press secretary. Marconi 1980, 105.

48. Interviews with Teodomiro Braga, Carlos Chagas, and Antonio Carlos Pereira. See also Marconi 1980, 103–04.

49. Marconi 1980, 104. Marconi does not indicate where he found these figures, nor does he give the total size of the bureau. Antonio Carlos Pereira of the *Estado de São Paulo* estimated forty journalists. Note that this was *after* the period of prior censorship.

50. Carlos Chagas interview. According to a footnote in Marconi, Chagas himself was denied press credentials to cover the president's office after 1972. Marconi 1980, 104.

51. Antonio Carlos Pereira interview.

52. Ferreira 1985b, 106.

53. *Boletim ABI* is full of stories of harassment, as is *Unidade,* the newspaper of the São Paulo journalists' union. See, for example, 1:8, March 1976, 12.
54. Pinheiro Machado 1978, 29–30.
55. Pinheiro Machado 1978, 70.
56. Oliveiros Ferreira interview.
57. Evandro Carlos de Andrade interview.
58. From a censored article in the *Estado de São Paulo,* March 15, 1974, 3. See also Chagas's testimony to the "Simpósio sobre censura," 11.
59. Skidmore 1988, 176–77; Alves 1985, 156–58. *Unidade* provides numerous articles covering many aspects of the case. See 1:4–6, November 1975–January 1976. See also *Boletim ABI,* November/December 1975, 9–16. *IstoÉ,* March 25, 1992, has an interview with Herzog's interrogator.
60. Gasparian interview
61. See *Torture in Brazil* 1986, chaps. 10–11.

6. PRIOR CENSORSHIP

1. For example, *A Notícia* in Manaus and *Inéditos* in Belo Horizonte are mentioned in the first uncensored issue of *Movimento* (no. 154, June 12, 1978, 13) as still being under prior censorship. Argemiro Ferreira lists the usual seven but also refers to "lesser-known publications from other states." Ferreira 1985b, 95.
2. Dassin counted fourteen hundred newspapers (dailies and others) in 1982. With the efflorescence of the alternative press in the 1970s, the number was probably much larger during that decade. Dassin 1984, 386.
3. Each had a rich story. The *Estado de São Paulo* may have been seen as a potential locus for independent elite action, if disaffected sectors were to leave the coalition that supported the regime. The oppositional content of *Opinião* and *Movimento* would have provided the obvious justification for their control, although material that was approved for other publications was vetoed in these. *O São Paulo* had a unique readership of working-class Catholics "conscienticized" by their church and labor involvement. They were poor, barely literate, and probably reading no other publication. These readers were potential opposition leaders in São Paulo's working class districts. Censorship of the other publications, *Veja,* the *Tribuna da Imprensa,* and *Pasquim,* seems to have come about from distrust, dislike, and even personal vendettas. The *Tribuna da Imprensa*'s owner had many enemies; *Pasquim*'s lampoons of authority endeared it to few in the military regime. See Smith 1994, 208–27.
4. The difference between prior censorship and self-censorship was thus not so sharp. The *Estado de São Paulo,* for example, had been accepting state news prohibitions under self-censorship before being placed under prior censorship in 1972.
5. See Rabello Duarte 1983.
6. Quoted in Moreira 1985, 23.
7. Oliveiros Ferreira interview. Talarico 1977.
8. *Movimento*'s editor Pereira took the proofs to the Federal Police in São Paulo for final approval. On these visits he always experienced two kinds of anxiety: that by heading so frequently to police headquarters he would be viewed as a police informer, or that the Federal Police headquarters would be blown up while he was inside.
9. Determination of location seems to have been based upon two factors. The

first was whether the transfer was technically feasible. For an enormous daily such as the *Estado de São Paulo* it was not, but for smaller weekly publications such as *Movimento* and *Opinião* it was. The second factor was tied to punitiveness. In some cases prior censorship initially conducted on the premises was transferred to police offices as punishment for a specific challenge to the regime. Thus *Opinião*'s deliberately provocative coverage of the death of a student under torture immediately resulted in the censorship being transferred from the publication's offices to the distant Federal Police headquarters. See Smith 1994, 227–34.

10. The censored portions of the *Estado de São Paulo* are in the newspaper's archives at its São Paulo headquarters. The originals are bound together and there is just one copy. They have not been the subject of a thorough study, and access is difficult. Photocopying them was not permitted at the time of this research. *Movimento*'s censored articles are in the municipal archives of RioArte in Rio de Janeiro. They are in very poor condition but are open to the public. *Opinião*'s censored material was given to the library of the University of São Paulo at Campinas. *O São Paulo* keeps its censored materials in its offices in São Paulo.

11. The newspaper began to save these pages only in March 1973, six months after censorship began. As time went on the record began to include the smallest details, such as the sums stolen in petty thefts. It is possible that such minuscule cuts were not made early on. It is also possible that they were made but that the newspaper did not deem them worth preserving. In October 1973, owner Julio Mesquita observed that some 240 articles and editorials had been vetoed, but he emphasized that the newspaper was preserving only the most important pieces. Article censored from the *Estado de São Paulo*, October 17, 1973, 5. The *Estado de São Paulo* has no figures of its own on the patterns of censorship, or on how much was cut. For further discussion of the quality of the record and other examples of censored articles, see Smith 1994.

12. During Geisel's inauguration ceremony in March 1974, Pinto condemned Pinochet for the human rights violations occurring in Chile. The regime considered this an insult to a foreign dignitary, which contravened the National Security Law.

13. Censorship covered every aspect of reporting on this public health crisis, including stories dealing with fatality figures, preventive measures, vaccine quality, and hospital conditions. Every source of information was subject to censorship, including interviews with doctors, official hospital statements, and even Ministry of Health news releases. Whenever material was partially liberated, every mention of the numbers of ill or dead was vetoed. The nature of some of the cuts is notable (vetoed portions in square brackets): "[for his part, Governor Laudo Natel has also discovered a way to diminish the number of cases in São Paulo: he has prohibited the entire network of state hospitals from giving information about the epidemic to the press. Nonetheless, the position of the director of the Emilio Ribas Hospital,] Carlos de Oliveira Bastos [is just the opposite. He] thinks that journalists should have access to information." Censored article in the *Estado de São Paulo*, July 28, 1974, 1. Reading what was left—"Bastos thinks that journalists should have access to information"—one would reasonably believe that what followed was a full account.

14. Article censored from the *Estado de São Paulo*, July 4, 1974, 16.

15. Article censored from the *Estado de São Paulo*, July 6, 1974, 4.

16. Article censored from the *Estado de São Paulo*, March 3, 1974, 3. Perhaps the *Estado de São Paulo* expected the incoming administration to repudiate the actions of the previous. Asked about the submission of this editorial, Oliveiros Ferreira asserted that all that was censored there was facts.

17. Articles censored from the *Estado de São Paulo*, July 18, 1974, 19, and July 19, 1974, 10.

18. Article censored from the *Estado de São Paulo*, November 5, 1974, 5. Similarly, there are references to Governor Paulo Egydio's "criticisms of [censorship and] INPS." (square brackets indicate vetoed phrase; INPS was part of the state health care system). Censored from the *Estado de São Paulo*, November 12, 1974, 6. Representative Edson Khair delivered a speech in which he listed respect for human rights, [freedom of the press,] freedom of association. Censored article from the *Estado de São Paulo*, July 30, 1974, 4.

19. Censored from the *Estado de São Paulo*, September 6, 1973, 6.

20. Censored from the *Estado de São Paulo*, August 17, 1974, 4.

21. Censored from the *Estado de São Paulo*, November 20, 1974, 7, and November 14, 1974, 1.

22. Censored from the *Estado de São Paulo*, January 3, 1975, 4.

23. An archive of this material is held by RioArte in Rio de Janeiro. The record includes material from every issue but is not complete. This was a living archive. *Movimento* staff were continually consulting it as a library and selecting pieces for resubmission to the censors. Notable lacunae include the editorials of Francisco Pinto and works of fiction, which were, perhaps, returned to their authors. Based upon comparisons with what was published during and after the censorship and information from interviews, what is there does seem representative of what was being produced.

24. These reports provided a careful review of the censorship, with a listing of how many articles were cut entirely or partially, a statement of the number of pages, and an accounting of censored illustrations, cartoons, and photographs. The reports also included quick summaries of the content of censored material. Although these reports could not be located, they were evidently the source used by *Movimento* in producing periodic evaluations of the censorship, and thus their cumulative content remains in the general historical record. I examined the few weekly reports found in the RioArte archives. Another was reproduced in issue no. 155, June 17, 1978.

25. The issues of June 1978 review the experience of censorship. The issues of July and August 1980 include all the self-evaluation of the fifth anniversary meetings. The final issues, of November 1981, recount the history of *Movimento* as a "journalistic and political project." Other issues, such as that of November 7, 1977, mention elections to the board of directors, the structure of the publishing enterprise, and so on.

26. *Movimento*, no. 154, June 12, 1978, 13–14.

27. *Movimento*, no. 154, June 12, 1978, 18. Over the next several months, a number of articles prepared for this issue were resubmitted, approved, and published one at a time. Appearing in this fashion, the material lost its critical mass and its status as a collection of special reports capable of concentrating attention and raising issues through their comprehensive treatment.

28. See *Movimento*, no. 154, June 12, 1978, 18.

29. *Movimento*, no. 154, June 12, 1978, 14.

30. For example, an article censored from the August 1, 1977, issue (no. 109) reported on government subsidies to farmers in the south of Brazil for the purchase of fertilizers and pesticides, which were then resold at enormous profit. Although this situation had come to the attention of the federal authorities a year earlier, nothing had been done about it because of the powerful people involved. Another article, censored in December 1976, covered the congressional hearings in which it was revealed that Volkswagen was putting required safety features only into vehicles meant for export and not into those destined for the domestic market, and that pharmaceutical companies in Brazil were selling drugs that had been banned elsewhere.

31. Censored from *Movimento*, no. 32, February 9, 1976.

32. Censored from *Movimento*, no. 101, June 6, 1976.

33. Censored from *Movimento*, no. 153, July 5, 1976.

34. Censored from *Movimento*, no. 100, May 30, 1977.

35. A short from *O Globo*, for example, briefly told of a poor black youth gaining entrance to an exclusive hotel in Bahia for eight hours by pretending to be the son of soccer star Pelé. In *O Globo* this is told as an odd little story, which ends with the youth being taken away to juvenile court. *Movimento* recounted the story, but also noted the grandeur of the hotel, the government assistance given to its construction, and its inaccessibility for most citizens. Censored from *Movimento*, no. 116, September 19, 1977.

36. Another instance of an odd source, indicative of *Movimento*'s connections, probably came from an employee of the *Jornal do Brasil*. Preparations for *Movimento* issue no. 67, October 11, 1976, included a brief report on Rede Globo's broadcast of the U.S. presidential debates between Gerald Ford and Jimmy Carter, and viewer reactions to this. The reactions were contained in letters addressed to but evidently not published in the *Jornal do Brasil*, with readers expressing wonder at the exorbitant cost of the broadcast and the inundation of the airwaves by imported material: "Upon turning on the television, I was surprised to see the images of two elegantly dressed blue-eyed white men, debating economic and social topics in English. . . . Do you suppose that if the indigenous spoke in English they would be able to discuss national problems without constraint?"

How did *Movimento* get these letters? Perhaps a journalist working at the *Jornal do Brasil*, knowing that this self-censoring newspaper would not be publishing the letters, lifted them from the newspaper's offices, transcribed them for *Movimento*, and submitted them there. There are no marks to indicate whether the prepared article was liberated or vetoed, but it was not published.

37. Fontoura had been chief of the SNI under Medici. He was appointed ambassador to Portugal just days before the 1974 revolution. Exiled Brazilians and Portuguese citizens protested his presence and wondered whether his appointment was part of preparations for another Chile, for helping to set up a Portuguese Pinochet to destroy the revolution.

An article on Fontoura prepared for *Movimento*, no. 32, February 9, 1976, had several parts vetoed (and what remained was not published). The following portion is for the most part *Movimento*'s quotation of an *Estado de São Paulo* article;

the censored material is in square brackets: "'The Geisel government has kept him in Lisbon [because, with the ample activity of Brazilian exiles in Portugal, his presence became even more than opportune, it became necessary,' explained the *Estado de São Paulo* on August 24, 1975, concluding, 'Reasons of Brazilian national security have made the presence of General Carlos Alberto Fontoura in Portugal practically indispensable].'" Another part of the same article, also censored, recorded intense popular animosity in Lisbon toward Fontoura, such that he had to bring a mechanic from Brazil, for local mechanics refused to repair his car.

38. The note was annotated with the date and issue of *Movimento* for which it would have been submitted (no. 150, May 15, 1978), but there were no censor's marks on it to indicate that it had been either liberated or vetoed, or even read, and it was not published in no. 150. Its presence in these files of censored materials would suggest that it was submitted.

39. Censored from *Movimento*, no. 4, July 28, 1975.

40. Censored from *Movimento*, no. 16, October 20, 1975.

41. Censored from *Movimento*, no. 138, February 20, 1978.

42. In Amazonia they had found no infrastructure, no services, no medical care, no unions, no churches. They were miserable, their complaints were loud, and their—censored—challenges were direct. In a deposition many pages long, they wanted to know: "Where is the minister of justice, for us? Where is the President of the Republic, to take a look at these things?"

43. Disputes between politicians also appeared in the pages of *Movimento*. Elsewhere one read of the two parties, ARENA and MDB. Here one would have read, were it not for the censor, of the Renovadores within ARENA, or the Autênticos or the Youth Wing (Jovem Alla) of the MDB. *Movimento* was by no means broadly supportive of the MDB. It had much greater interest in the popular movement generally, and this also relativized its coverage of formal politics.

Movimento even managed to provide some coverage of disputes within the military, including a piece censored in May 1978 (just a month before the end of prior censorship), which contained statements from Colonel Tarcision Ferreira, including his criticisms of Geisel's hypocrisy, the bogus nature of the liberalization, and the inadequacy of the process for selecting Geisel's successor. Censored article in *Movimento*, no. 151, May 22, 1978. Under what circumstances these statements were made is not clear; they were not from an interview granted to *Movimento*.

44. Marcos Sá interview.

45. Kenski 1990, 70.

46. Censored from *Estado de São Paulo*, April 5, 1974, 8.

47. "Don't be pained by my silence / I am tired of words. / Don't you know I love you? / Place your hand on my forehead / And capture there in the ineffable palpitation / the meaning of the only essential word / —Love." (Manoel Bandeira.) This was on the editorial page for *Estado de São Paulo*, September 25, 1973, 3. That day two long editorials on the inability of the MDB to broadcast its convention on television were submitted. Both were vetoed. The television stations had prepared to broadcast the convention but were waiting for official approval. An official note was distributed: transmission of the broadcast would be the exclusive responsibility of the stations. This was utterly ambiguous. It was not a prohibition, but it was not an approval. Rede Globo began to transmit the convention,

then decided not to, and went off the air. When the monitors in the control rooms of the other networks showed Rede Globo's blank screen, they went off the air as well. News and commentary was thus replaced by "ineffable palpitations."

48. See Smith 1994, 327–29.
49. *Estado de São Paulo,* April 4, 1974, 22.
50. *Estado de São Paulo,* April 5, 1974, 4.
51. *Veja* also tried using repetition of a familiar image to indicate censorship. It created a series of images of devils and inserted these into the text (see, for example, March 13, 1974, 27, 29). Sá subsequently lamented this stratagem also, as taking up so much time and energy, and achieving so little (interview).
52. See Kenski 1990, especially the "Os leitores" chapter, 84–98.
53. Teodomiro Braga interview.
54. See the examples reproduced in Smith 1994, appendix 5.
55. Argemiro Ferreira interview.
56. *Movimento,* no. 154, June 12, 1978, 15.
57. Raimundo Pereira interview.
58. Argemiro Ferreira interview; Raimundo Pereira interview; *Movimento,* no. 154, June 12, 1978, 14.
59. In one 1978 letter, a reader praised "this pearl of a publication" and asked to receive copies of censored articles: "Personally, I don't accept that these jackasses can come and tell me what I can or ought to read. Forgive the expression, but since I was born my father taught me to call a dog a dog, a snake a snake, and a pig a pig." The writer then suggested replacing the phrase "Read and Publicize *O São Paulo*" with "Pray and Publicize *O São Paulo.*"
60. Ricardo Kotscho interview. He continued: "After prior censorship, however, there was in-house censorship, an explicit list of prohibited persons, a blacklist of individuals who couldn't appear in the newspaper. These included Dom Helder and Cardinal Arns. . . . During the censorship there was great solidarity within the *Estado de São Paulo.* We were facing a common enemy. During the censorship the owners didn't worry much about what we wrote, because they knew the censors would cut it. Afterwards, when it was lifted, came the great crisis, and control."
61. Carlos Alberto Sardemburg interview; Oliveiros Ferreira interview.
62. Ricardo Kotscho interview.
63. Ricardo Kotscho interview.
64. Oliveiros Ferreira interview.
65. Raimundo Pereira interview.
66. Argemiro Ferreira interview.
67. Argemiro Ferreira interview.
68. It disturbed Ferreira that *Opinião* was therefore seen as having a greater interest in international news than in domestic news. "The least onerous manner [of ensuring some bulk despite the censorship] was by increasing the translations of material available in *Le Monde, Le Nouvel Observateur,* the *Washington Post,* the *Guardian,* and the *New York Review of Books,* with which we had republication contracts. The censorship had greater toleration for foreign materials, apparently considering them drier. The aim was to maintain the number of pages of *Opinião,* but it wound up giving the publication an undeserved reputation for being preoccupied with international matters." Ferreira 1985b, 104.

69. Jaime Sautchuk interview.
70. Marcos Sá interview.
71. Marcos Sá interview.
72. Censored submission to *O São Paulo*, August 22, 1977.
73. National Congress 1980, 9. When the *Correio do Povo* of Porto Alegre tried to publish this telegram, the newspaper was confiscated.
74. Material censored from the *Estado de São Paulo* also included a report of a discussion in Congress of a telegram sent to Buzaid by Mesquita, who was angry about news prohibitions regarding Sergeant Fleury (a member of the São Paulo death squads). The tone was the same: "For the first time in the history of Brazil the government has taken sides in a criminal process—in favor of the indicted criminal. . . . None of this, however, surprises us. We never expected, in a regime of prior censorship of the press and other media, that the government would keep itself within the limits of good sense and of respect for minimal ethical principles that any regime, no matter how revolutionary, must respect. . . . We merely feel ashamed, as Brazilians mindful of the image our country projects to the civilized world." Also vetoed was a report on the Senate having prevented Senator Montoro from reading Mesquita's telegram into the record. According to Senator Ruy Santos, the Senate did this because the telegram contained "expressions discourteous and insulting to the authorities." Censored from the *Estado de São Paulo*, October 26, 1973, 5, and October 27, 1973, 6.
75. Ferreira 1991, 26.
76. The case brought by *Opinião* was unique in many respects, but it was not the only case brought by the censored press. On the case brought by *O São Paulo*, see Dias and Malheiros Filho 1977. Whether because of *Opinião*'s resources, connections, and commitment, or the timing and particulars of the case, this one got much farther than any of the others.
77. See Pinheiro Machado 1978, 45, and National Congress 1980, 148.
78. Decree Law 1077 required magazines to register with the Federal Police and permitted prior censorship upon moral grounds. This decree was seen by many as a possible basis for political censorship of the press. It stated that violations of good morals "obey a subversive plan and put national security at risk," a statement that left the door open to the reverse argument that that which is politically subversive is also morally wrong.

The MDB brought suit charging that the law was unconstitutional. The Supreme Court refused to rule upon the case, arguing that the MDB did not itself publish a newspaper and was thus not directly affected by the law. Cardoso, reportedly, was disgusted, threw off his robe, and stalked out, declaring that he would return only when there was an opportunity to challenge censorship.

According to Pinheiro Machado, Cardoso was originally contacted by *Opinião* in January 1973, when the journal was first on the lookout for an opportunity to bring suit. Pinheiro Machado 1978, 38.
79. Sources include Pinheiro Machado 1978; interviews with Gasparian and Chagas; and Gasparian's testimony to Congress in National Congress 1980.
80. The quoted phrase is Carlos Chagas's. They were as disinclined to have anything to do with *O Globo*'s Roberto Marinho—"that mulatto"—as with "that leftist" Gasparian. Chagas interview. Gasparian also recalled Mesquita's surprise

upon seeing him at IAPA meetings: "What are *you* doing here?" Gasparian interview.

81. *Mandato de segurança* does not translate precisely because of differences in the U.S. and Brazilian legal systems. In the United States one seeks an immediate injunction and then files a further suit. In Brazil the two are combined. In the United States the standards for issuing an injunction are fairly strict and require irreparable damage. In Brazil the standards are considerably more lax, with judges having substantial discretion to grant an injunction.

The suit was brought against the director of the Federal Police. The text of the brief prepared by Cardoso is found in Pinheiro Machado 1978, 40–56.

82. Pinheiro Machado 1978, 53–54.

83. Pinheiro Machado 1978, 49.

84. And even on that day, as they began to prepare what they thought would be their first postcensorship issue, they received a telephone call from the police warning them not to publish it because a confiscation order had been issued (Pinheiro Machado 1978, 59).

7. SELF-CENSORSHIP

1. The censorship discussed here is political censorship, and excludes the moral censorship of cultural productions, which was and had long been legal and socially acceptable in Brazil. Furthermore, this chapter examines only the censorship conducted by the state and responded to as "self-censorship" by the press, not the economic censorship practiced by or in deference to press owners.

2. Raimundo Pereira interview; Sergio Buarque interview.

3. Censored from the *Estado de São Paulo,* October 26, 1973, 5.

4. Walter Fontoura interview.

5. Moacyr Coelho interview. The scholar Glaucio Soares asserts that there were jurisdictional disputes over the censorship, especially between CIEx and the SNI for primary control. Soares 1989, 35. This is not an implausible assertion, but it is not sufficiently documented. Throughout the regime's history, a more prevalent route than direct dispute or confrontation was to multiply the actors. With respect to repression, the array of security forces seems to have overlapped and duplicated rather than competed for targets. See Skidmore 1988, 128–29.

6. See also Soares 1989, 35; Dassin 1982, 171.

7. See Dassin 1982, 168–70, and Dassin 1984, 391, on the fragmentation of censorial power. With *bilhetinhos* passing through every regional police office, there would seem to have been many possible footholds for local powerholders, many opportunities for local initiative. It is notable that abuse did not happen more often.

8. Moacyr Coelho interview.

9. Carlos Chagas interview.

10. For example, on March 31, 1977, a supposed *bilhetinho* concerning coverage of the Senate was delivered to Radio JB by telephone by a woman who refused to identify herself and stated that she was following the orders of a Mr. Mario of the Federal Police. She gave his office room number but refused to provide a telephone number. Radio JB then contacted the office and was informed that no one by the name of Mario worked there. According to Radio JB, efforts to verify the

genuineness of *bilhetinhos* arriving by telephone were met with rebuffs. The official response was, "no one else is complaining" and *bilhetinhos* can be confirmed "only by superior order." Talarico 1977.

11. Among the best sources on this point are Ferreira 1985b and Ferreira interview.

12. This paralleled the practice in Argentina. See Graham-Yooll 1981.

13. There are different accounts of this. Censor Romão says that the police agent would deliver the order only to the head of the office *(chefe da redação)*, but Romão was in Brasília and did not actually act as a messenger. Evandro Carlos de Andrade, editor of *O Globo*, insisted that the agents delivered the *bilhetinhos* to whomever they came across first, even employees of the "third rank." It is evidently a matter of pride for de Andrade that he never besmirched himself by personally accepting delivery of a *bilhetinho* (see chap. 8). Argemiro Ferreira's reference to "a person of responsibility" as the usual recipient makes the most sense, and is confirmed by other accounts.

14. This receipt was photocopied at the offices of *Opinião*, which, despite being under prior censorship, received *bilhetinhos*. Argemiro Ferreira's comment: "It was raining on the already drenched" (interview). The document repeated prohibitions against the publication of "any material whatever relative to Dom Heder [sic] Camara."

15. Walter Fontoura interview; Waldir de Góes interview.

16. Nuinio Spinola interview.

17. Most say the *bilhetinhos* were known about although not discussed. At the largest publications, however, the lack of discussion could conceivably result in ignorance. Spinola raised the issue of increasing compartmentalization and specialization, which he said resulted in his business reporters—whose topics were infrequently censored—sometimes not learning of the censorship of political topics.

18. José Neumanne Pinto interview.

19. Jaime Sautchuk interview. Sautchuk himself was turned over to the police by his editor. See Smith 1994, 191.

20. Many of the people interviewed for this book confirmed the presence of police and other security agents in the newsrooms. Oliveiros Ferreira was aware of police informers even among the most senior editorial staff at the *Estado de São Paulo*. Evandro Carlos de Andrade of *O Globo* today commands great respect among journalists, regardless of what they think of *O Globo*'s politics, because he got the police out of the newsrooms.

21. Unions provided little refuge, Lins da Silva noted, "The union wasn't a place to discuss. It was complacent until the presidency of Audalio Dantas. Then it became much more, an important shift, real movement among the journalists" (interview).

22. Carlos Lins da Silva interview.

23. Denis de Morães interview.

24. These unreported stories remained unknown, except for the content of the *bilhetinhos* themselves, and then only among the relevant staff of the newspapers. The elite also shared information through their own channels. Fontoura would occasionally receive telephone calls asking whether the *Jornal do Brasil* had

received any prohibitions regarding a particular incident, in response to which he would check the black book.

25. José Neumanne Pinto interview; Waldir de Góes interview; Walter Fontoura interview.

26. Denis de Morães interview.

27. Combing the public records does not help, because those records are incomplete and censored. Gathering evidence from the historical record about the centralized activity of the Federal Police is further complicated by the fact that power became dispersed and local. One cannot tell, looking at an instance of confiscation, whether it flowed from a regime decision or local initiative. For example, in May 1977 the *Jornal do Povo,* the only daily in Macapá, Amapá, was invaded by armed men saying they were Federal Police and confiscated in reprisal for denouncing arbitrary acts by the Macapá police (Talarico 1977). Was that done by order of the Federal Police following the issuance of a *bilhetinho,* or was it an example of local initiative?

28. Waldir de Góes interview.

29. Walter Fontoura interview.

30. The public (that is, organized civil society) became an important resource for winning debates internal to the regime. In May 1978, for example, the Brazilian Bar Association was pursuing an aggressive public campaign for return of the rule of law, a new constitution, and reform of labor legislation. According to Skidmore 1988, 200, citing an interview with Brazilian Bar Association president Raymond Faoro, "The pro-liberalization leaders within the government wanted more public pressure to show why change 'had' to come. Minister of Justice Petronio Portella asked Faoro if he could increase the pro-amnesty publicity."

In 1969 this same Portella, then an ARENA senator, had declared that all Brazil's woes were due to politicians who meddled in disputes "that benefit only the radicals, those destroyers of the constitutional order. There was no choice but the heroic remedy of the Fifth Institutional Act." Quoted in Skidmore 1988, 346.

31. Rabello Duarte 1983, 181, 192. Stepan argues that Geisel believed that the existence of censorship allowed extremists to level unanswered charges against the government. Stepan 1988, 38.

32. The *Jornal do Brasil* published its black book on June 18, 1978, including any names from authorizing signatures. The newspaper announced this as complete with 256 *bilhetinhos,* however two content analyses by *Jornal do Brasil* staff members cite a total of 288 and 270 bilhetinhos, respectively (cited in Soares 1989, 26). The *Folha de São Paulo* published a selection on March 5, 1978, but excluded names that appeared in authorizing signatures, on the grounds that that was "not the objective." For the ABI conference materials, see *I Congresso Nacional de Jornalistas Pela Liberdade de Imprensa* 1980. Marconi's compilation is intended to be complete and includes an additional 257 *bilhetinhos* from Rio de Janeiro and São Paulo, for a total of 565 (although this figure includes duplicates and orders for the withdrawal of *bilhetinhos*). He also provides helpful footnotes on the events and people mentioned in the prohibitions. Marconi 1980, 225–303.

33. Soares 1989, 27.

34. "The period from 1975 to 1978 was typical of Geisel's mandate: moderate use of dictatorial recourse, without a commitment to their extinction. In the

moment of truth, Geisel preferred to govern with the instruments of dictatorship and not with those of democracy." Soares 1989, 27. See also Soares 1989, 41, for a graph showing the frequency of *bilhetinhos* and disappearances.

35. Marconi 1980, 49.

36. Unfortunately, there are no comparable content analyses of newspapers during the period just before the beginning of censorship, and thus it is difficult to know whether a topic is absent from the *bilhetinhos* because it was not a concern of the regime or because it was not a concern of the press. Nonetheless, the *bilhetinhos* are generally taken to denote the chief concerns of the regime.

37. Soares 1989, 30. Soares classifies the prohibitions into four categories: protection of the state, social problems, economic problems, and other issues. He finds that protection of the state was the largest category every year, ranging from 82 percent to 100 percent of all *bilhetinhos*. For further discussion of Soares's analysis see Smith 1994, 410–12.

38. General Albuquerque Lima was known for his nationalist and populist positions. He opposed the policies of economics minister Delfim Neto. While minister of the interior under Costa e Silva, he announced his candidacy for the presidency after the president suffered a stroke in 1969. Because of these acts of dissent along with his call for the military to support his campaign, his actual campaigning, and his willingness to go public, Albuquerque Lima became a prime target for those worried about military discipline, dissent, and hierarchical order.

For several decades the journalist Carlos Castello Branco wrote a political column for the *Jornal do Brasil*. Although the reference here makes it sound as if he was sometimes granted an exemption from censorship, I have found no evidence of this. Branco was very prestigious, and perhaps the reference to him was a way of reiterating the seriousness of the *bilhetinho*, of making the point that the prohibition applied to absolutely everybody.

39. August 29 through October 9, 1970, for example.

40. I have the impression that the strength of the regime's hatred of the Church has been underestimated. The *bilhetinhos* and the documents relating to prior censorship may contribute to a reassessment of this subject. Coelho had this to say: "I'm not Catholic. I was, but I'm not anymore—because I couldn't separate the priests from the Church. We had priests here who were subversives, really. From Holland, from France, Padre Jentel, the Dominicans. They came to Brazil precisely to cause enormous trouble for the regime. . . . Tupumaros and Montoneros were funded by the Catholic Church and by international organizations, German money. I documented the Church paying money to families of Tupumaros, these extremely violent groups" (interview). Nonetheless, the Church is still a paradigmatic institution for Coelho. He justified the torture practiced by the regime by pointing to the Inquisition and saying that every institution has this sort of thing in its past.

41. Cubatão was a city in São Paulo state notorious for its industrial pollution, synonymous with environmental health hazards.

42. The source of the telex was not identified.

43. Did readers nonetheless know that there was censorship? One could only have learned about it from other sources, as there were no clues in the newspapers themselves. The consensus in the press was that readers did not know. Perhaps, as

one reader said, a few "had antennas" and were alert to the censorship, but for the most part readers were unaware of it. The journalist Ricardo Kotscho's view is that people were censoring themselves, preferring not to know, not to question, not to be aware (Luiza Fernandes interview; Ricardo Kotscho interview).
44. Denis de Morães interview.
45. Evandro Carlos de Andrade interview.
46. Helio Romão interview.
47. Boris Casoy interview; Walter Fontoura interview.
48. Evandro Carlos de Andrade interview.
49. João Sant'anna interview.
50. Waldir de Góes interview.

8. REPRESENTATIONS AND REFLECTIONS

1. See chap. 6.
2. See chap. 5.
3. The regime treated all publications essentially the same. Both alternative and mainstream publications were subject to prior censorship; all publications under self-censorship received the same prohibitions; the same topics were prohibited under prior censorship and self-censorship; all publications were placed under surveillance and harassed. Some publications did have better access to state elites, but that did not necessarily mean favorable treatment, for it left them more vulnerable to pressure.
4. The predominance of a class analysis is notable in other areas of Brazilian society as well. With respect to racism, for instance, the position of much of the Brazilian left has been to assert the primary importance of economic class, with race as a secondary variable.
5. Despite the rhetoric of class analysis, educated journalists did not unite with labor beyond abstract expressions of solidarity. *Movimento* tried the hardest, yet it often lamented that its language was inaccessible, its links with unions not yet realized.
6. See, for example, Laurindo Leal Filho, "O direito social a informação"; João Alves dos Santos, "O jornalista, a sociedade e a liberdade de imprensa"; Carlos Pompe, "O papel do jornalista na sociedade"; Célio Nunes, "O controle da informação: uma alternativa para Romper o Cerco," all in *I Congresso Nacional de Jornalistas Pela Liberdade de Imprensa* 1978.
7. Miguel et al. 1978, 8. This essay was not included in the ABI collection of documents from the conference (note 6 above), which suggests that there may have been other unpublished contributions, and confirms that the consistency of the ABI collection is not the result of the selectivity of its compiler.
8. Interview in *IstoÉ*, August 14, 1991.
9. Carlos Chagas interview.
10. This phenomenon requires further examination. Alves 1985 begins by assuming that there was a popular commitment to democracy. Cohen 1989 argues that support for authoritarianism was the result of the state's manipulation of previous generations of Brazilians. Pinheiro 1991 discusses support for authoritarianism generally, but does not present empirical research. Geddes and Zaller 1989 examine why some people are susceptible to manipulation, rather than why they support authoritarianism.

Since the end of the military regime in Brazil, many people have claimed that their support was merely pragmatic. But there was popular support for the regime at the time, and there is nostalgia for it now. On the similar experience of Argentina, see O'Donnell 1986.

11. All of the Boris Casoy quotations below come from the Casoy interview.

12. Illustrating this stance is an anecdote Casoy related while simply recounting the early part of his career. In November 1973 he served as director of the Brazilian pavilion at the world trade fair in Brussels, during which there were enormous, unprecedented public demonstrations against the military regime and its human rights abuses. Casoy was caught off balance by these demonstrations and asked his friend, General Otavio Costa of Assessoria Especial de Relaçoes Publicas, for guidance. Costa replied, in Casoy's recollection, "Aiee, a regime that practices torture cannot participate in world fairs." (Casoy interview).

13. On one level, Casoy was well aware of how this provided the regime with an excuse for holding on to power. Asked whether a democratic government could not also have fought the guerrillas, his answer was qualified and addressed the contingencies and perceptions of the time, not the qualities of different regimes: "Yes, but nobody believed at that time that there would be an *abertura*, a transition during this period when the very institutions were under threat. And they were. It was a good pretext for the military to stay put. People supported the military regime because they were the only ones around to combat the guerrillas."

14. In juxtaposition to Casoy's remarks is very different statement of João Sant'anna, a journalist and militant imprisoned by the regime, regarding the veracity of the terrorist threat: "There was no terrorism of the left. There was terrorism of the right—the dictatorship. AERP set up these shows: the tortured saying there is no torture, or stories of a militant sleeping with the lover of one who'd been imprisoned, et cetera. *Veja,* Elio Gaspari, treated us all like terrorists. He's a terrorist. There is all the difference between the armed struggle and substantive terrorism—blowing up bus stations. We never did anything terroristic. The kidnapping of the U.S. ambassador is arguable, but that was at a time when the U.S. was sending people down to teach torture." João Sant'anna interview.

15. Carlos Chagas interview.

16. João Sant'anna interview.

17. This paralleled what Stepan finds regarding the support of the private sector for the regime, despite the state's extensive involvement in the economy. Stepan 1985, 332–35.

18. Carlos Castello Branco interview.

19. Luis Alberto Bettancourt interview.

20. Often the only way to judge the wisdom of such a decision was after the fact, and here it bears repeating that Marcos Sá of *Veja* had to turn to the files of *O Globo* to write a retrospective series on the 1970s (see chap. 6).

21. Both quotations are from Talarico 1977.

22. President Geisel and his moderate faction, including General Golbery, favored the candidacy of João Figueiredo. Hard-liners, including General Hugo Abreu, coalesced around the candidacy of General Sylvio Frota, then minister of the army. A confrontation between the factions almost led to a coup in October 1977, when Frota was successfully ousted.

23. The press had been definitively excluded from the succession disputes pre-

ceding Geisel's presidency (which were the catalyst for the prior censorship of the *Estado de São Paulo* as well as a very frequent *bilhetinho* topic). In this case, however, Geisel saw bringing the dispute into the public press as one way of helping to prevent behind-the-scenes manipulation by the hard-line military.

24. This was the period of General Abreu's careful monitoring of the *Jornal do Brasil*, during which two hundred telexes were issued to state companies instructing them to cease advertising in the newspaper, and Geisel insisted that the newspaper deal only with Abreu (thus perhaps sacrificing the newspaper to the hardliners). It was also the period when Carlos Chagas was the target of a legal proceeding that Geisel eventually rescinded on the gournds that it was a provocation by army minister Frota. (See chap. 5.) Frota had also decided, without Geisel's knowledge, to pursue legal action against the *Folha de São Paulo*, the *Jornal do Brasil*, and *O Globo*. When Geisel learned of Frota's move, he condemned it as impertinent and provocative, and reduced the scope of the proceedings to an indictment of just one of the *Folha de São Paulo*'s journalists, Lourenço Diaféria. The Diaféria case is discussed in the text below. See also the excellent discussion in Rabello Duarte 1983.

25. He had several run-ins with the regime and was held by the DOI in 1975. See Abramo 1988, 88.

26. Boris Casoy interview.

27. Boris Casoy interview; Abramo 1988, 90.

28. This was similar to the reception given to Márcio Moreira Alves's 1968 speech, which went unnoticed except by the military, which copied the text and mailed it to barracks around the country. See Ventura 1988.

29. Boris Casoy interview.

30. Boris Casoy interview. Abramo says the following: "With [Diaféria's] imprisonment, the newspaper decided to publish the column in white . . . [the decision was made] at a meeting in which Frias, his business associate Carlos Caldeira Filho, Ruy Lopes, and I participated. There was a vote, in which Frias, Caldeira, and Ruy voted in favor of the column in white. I opposed it, voted against it, saying that they had no resources to resist and would definitely be forced to fall. But at that point I was already as good as fired." Abramo 1988, 90. Diaféria was held for seventeen days, then charged under the National Security Law.

31. Boris Casoy interview. Casoy states that Abreu and Frias had dinner together, from time to time but were not really friends. By summoning Frias to his office, Abreu was not arranging a chat between old friends, but calling Frias to account.

32. Abramo claims that the episode was a pretext to get rid of him, that Diaféria was an agent provocateur planted to cause Abramo's ouster. See Abramo 1988, 87, 90. Casoy discounted this interpretation.

33. Boris Casoy interview.

34. Luis Alberto Bettancourt interview.

35. José Neumanne Pinto interview.

36. Antonio Carlos Pereira interview.

37. Denis de Morães interview.

38. Walter Fontoura interview.

39. McDonough 1981, 177–78. The professed commitment of the mainstream

press to the rule of law was evident in its dealings with other Brazilian governments. For example, the *Correio da Manhã*'s attack on Goulart was based not only upon the fact that he was mobilizing the masses, but that he was going about it in an unconstitutional way, that he was departing from his oath of office.

40. Evandro Carlos de Andrade interview. Decree Law 1077 provided for prior moral censorship of books and magazines.

41. Oliveiros Ferreira interview.

42. *Movimento*, no. 154, June 12, 1978, 18.

43. José Neumanne Pinto interview.

44. Moacyr Coelho interview.

45. *Diário do Congresso Nacional*, October 26, 1977, 4282. Resende's MDB counterpart, Senator Franco Montoro, retorted that the censorship was a sacrifice made not by the press, but by the nation, the people. Montoro further charged that exceptionality could hardly be invoked for years on end, which was what the regime had done.

46. See, for example, *Diário do Congresso Nacional*, April 6, 1973, 488–92; September 6, 1973, 3288–91; October 26, 1973, 4280–83; October 31, 1973, 4402–03.

47. Mesquita himself, in several of his speeches and telegrams, referred to the humiliation suffered by Brazil and the harm done to the country's image by the imposition of censorship. See *Diário do Congresso Nacional*, October 26, 1973, 4282; October 31, 1973, 4402.

48. According to Resende, the proposed law would "project throughout the world a harmful image of this country, which has already been the target of cowardice and betrayal by evil Brazilians, who direct injurious news to the foreign market or who seek there, in an underworld of malice, hatred, and anger, to compromise all institutions, attempting to characterize our country as a collection of African hovels or vengeful executioners." *Diário do Congresso Nacional*, September 6, 1973, 3289.

49. Moacyr Coelho interview.

50. Jarbas Passarinho interview.

51. Meira Mattos interview. And yet this was not sufficient for Meira Mattos, either. After the interview ended, he stopped me to add, "Look, if you take the regime on balance, the good outweighs the bad. When the military came in, the economy was ranked twenty-third [in the world]; when we left it was ranked eighth." To Meira Mattos, that was the final, irrefutable justification.

52. Helio Romão interview.

53. Meira Mattos interview.

54. Former members of the regime often cite legal details when it serves their purposes. Meira Mattos, who was in charge of closing Congress, had this to say: "The press is wrong to call that a closing. The Congress was in official recess; it was election time and the politicians were home campaigning. A group of [congressional] representatives decided, outside of the law, to reopen the Congress, use it for their own purposes. . . . [They] opened the radio, started giving speeches. It was in recess. These clandestine sessions were illegal. So the president declared a recess by executive order, and gave me the job of getting them out. So I encircled the Congress." Meira Mattos also mentioned how the (purged) Congress voted for the Institutional Acts, and thus endorsed their legality. He can be

quite precise when he wants to be. But on the unconstitutionality of censorship, or on the point that AI-5 required a declared state of emergency before censorship could be instituted, he hedged: "I'm not capable of addressing these."

55. Moacyr Coelho interview.
56. *Diário do Congresso Nacional*, September 6, 1973, 3289.
57. Helio Romão interview.
58. Carlos Alberto Sardemburg interview.
59. Carlos Eduardo Lins da Silva interview.
60. Trying to see things from the press's point of view, Coelho made the following remarks with respect to his characterization of self-censorship as a "gentleman's agreement": "I tell you, if I were a journalist, I would prefer a repressive censorship to a gentleman's agreement." Moacyr Coelho interview.
61. Moacyr Coelho interview.

9. ROUTINE REPRESSION, ROUTINE COMPLIANCE

1. Some owners who were opponents of the regime may also have submitted to the regime's dictates, to avoid harming the position of moderates in the government. See Rabello Duarte 1983, 187.
2. The culture of fear approach is found in testimonial writing and in works of history, sociology, political science, psychology, feminist theory, poetry, fiction, and literary criticism. See, for example, Corradi, Fagen, and Garreton, eds. 1992; Yudice, Franco, and Flores, eds. 1992; Lira and Castillo 1991; Politzer 1989; O'Donnell 1986; Timerman 1981; Smith 1987.
3. Norbert Lechner, "Some People Die of Fear: Fear as a Political Problem," in Corradi, Fagen, and Garreton, eds. 1992, 30.
4. Juan Rial, "Makers and Guardians of Fear: Controlled Terror in Uruguay," in Corradi, Fagen, and Garreton, eds. 1992, 101.
5. See Stepan 1988, chap. 6, for these and other comparisons.
6. See *Torture in Brazil* 1986, pt. 3.
7. See, for example, Pinheiro 1991; Debrun 1983; DaMatta 1979.
8. See Javier Martínez, "Fear of the State, Fear of Society: On the Opposition Protests in Chile," on the counterproductive hero syndrome, in Corradi, Fagen, and Garreton, eds. 1992, 142–60; Politzer 1989 provides examples from Chile of people joining organizations despite enormous fear.
9. For further discussion of the culture of fear approach, see Smith 1994, appendix 6.
10. Two interesting exceptions were the *Estado de São Paulo*, which had a uniquely long and impressive history of defending its own freedom, and *Opinião*, which in its lawsuit against the regime departed from its Brazilian context and referred primarily to similar journals around the world.
11. Raimundo Pereira interview.
12. For these two perspectives, see Stepan 1988 and Hagopian 1986, respectively.
13. Even repression was recorded with bureaucratic meticulousness. The Military Court archives were the major source of information for the authors of *Torture in Brazil* 1986.

BIBLIOGRAPHY

Aarão Reis Filho, Daniel, and Pedro de Morães. 1988. *1968: A paixão de uma utopia*. Rio de Janeiro: Espaço e Tempo.
Abramo, Claudio. 1988. *A regra do jogo*. São Paulo: Companhia das Letras.
Alves, Maria Helena Moreira. 1985. *State and Opposition in Military Brazil*. Austin, TX: University of Texas Press.
Andrade, Jeferson de, and Joel Silveira. 1991. *Um jornal assassinado: A última batalha do Correio da Manhã*. Rio de Janeiro: José Olympio Editora.
Aparecido Pereira, Antonio. 1982. "A igreja e a censura à imprensa no Brasil, 1968–78, com particular atenção à censura ao semanário arquidiocesano *O São Paulo*." Centro Internazionale per gli Studi sull Opinione Pubblica, Rome. June.
Brown, Diana DeGroat. 1986. *Umbanda: Religion and Politics in Urban Brazil*. Ann Arbor: UMI Research Press.
Caparelli, Sérgio. 1986. *Comunicação de massa sem massa*. São Paulo: Summus.
Castro, Maria Helena de Magalhães. 1988. "Television and the Elites in Post-Authoritarian Brazil." Unpublished paper.
Chagas, Carlos. 1970. *113 dias de angústia*. Guanabara: Agência Jornalistica Image.
Cohen, Youssef. 1989. *The Manipulation of Consent: The State and Working-Class Consciousness in Brazil*. Pittsburgh: University of Pittsburgh Press.
Collier, David, ed. 1979. *The New Authoritarianism in Latin America*. Princeton: Princeton University Press.
Conselho Parlamentar de Defesa dos Direitos da Pessoa Humana. 1979. "As pressões do governo Brasileiro contra a imprensa independente." State Legislative Assembly of São Paulo. June.
Corradi, Juan, Patricia Weiss Fagen, and Manuel Antonio Garreton, eds. 1992. *Fear at the Edge: State Terror and Resistance in Latin America*. Berkeley: University of California Press.
Costella, Antonio. 1970. *O contrôle da informação no Brasil*. Petropolis: Editora Vozes.
DaMatta, Roberto. 1979. *Carnavais, malandros e heróis*. Rio de Janeiro: Zahar Editores.
Dassin, Joan. 1982. "Press Censorship and the Military State in Brazil." In *Press Control Around the World*, ed. Jane Leftwich Curry and Joan Dassin. New York: Praeger Publishers.

———. 1984. "The Brazilian Press and the Politics of Abertura." *Journal of Interamerican and World Affairs* 26, no. 3: 385–414.

Debrun, Michel. 1983. *Brasil: A "conciliação" e outras estratégias*. São Paulo: Editora Brasiliense.

Dias, José Carlos, and Arnaldo Malheiros Filho. 1977. "Contra a censura prévia: Mandado de segurança no Supremo Tribunal Federal." São Paulo. Photocopy.

Dines, Alberto. 1975. "Censorship of the Press in Brazil." Unpublished manuscript, Columbia University.

Dreiffus, René Armand. 1981. *1964: A conquista do estado, ação política, poder e golpe de classe*. Rio de Janeiro: Editora Vozes.

Dupret, Allen Augusto, Luiz Gonzales, and Mirian Paglia Costa. 1980. "Legislação e Liberdade de Imprensa." In *I Congresso Nacional de Jornalistas Pela Liberdade de Imprensa* (São Paulo, October 26–28, 1978), Unpublished collection. Rio de Janeiro: Associação Barsileira de Imprensa, Biblioteca Bastos Tigre.

Erickson, Kenneth Paul. 1977. *The Brazilian Corporative State and Working Class Politics*. Berkeley: University of California Press.

Evans, Peter. 1979. *Dependent Development: The Alliance of Multinational, State, and Local Capital in Brazil*. Princeton: Princeton University Press.

Ferreira, Argemiro. 1985a. "Imprensa e resistência." *Unidade e ação* 13: 18–21.

———. 1985b. "Informação sob controle." *Revista arquivos* 165: 95–110.

Ferreira, Oliveiros. 1991. "Vivir con la censura." *Pulso*, September 1991, 26–29.

———. Undated. Untitled Memoir. Photocopy.

Figueiredo, Marcus. 1978. "A Politica de coação no Brasil pós-64." In Klein and Figueiredo, *Legitimidade e coação no Brasil pós-64*, 107–97. Rio de Janeiro: Forense-Universitária.

Gabeira, Fernando. 1988. *O que é isso, companheiros?* Rio de Janeiro: Editora Guanabara.

Gaventa, John. 1980. *Power and Powerlessness: Quiescence and Rebellion in an Appalachian Valley*. Urbana: University of Illinois Press.

Geddes, Barbara, and John Zaller. 1989. "Sources of Popular Support for Authoritarian Regimes." *American Journal of Political Science* 33, no. 2 (May): 319–47.

GenoGraham-Yooll, Andrew. 1981. *A Matter of Fear*. Westport, CT: Lawrence Hill.

Hagopian, Frances. 1986. "The Politics of Oligarchy: The Persistence of Traditional Elites in Contemporary Brazil." Ph.D. diss., Massachusetts Institute of Technology.

Hahner, June E. 1986. *Poverty and Politics: The Urban Poor in Brazil, 1870–1920*. Albuquerque: University of New Mexico Press.

Huggins, Martha. 1985. *From Slavery to Vagrancy in Brazil: Crime and Social Control in the Third World*. New Brunswick, N.J.: Rutgers University Press.

I Congresso Nacional de Jornalistas Pela Liberdade de Imprensa (São Paulo, October 26–28, 1978). 1980. Unpublished collection. Rio de Janeiro: Associação Brasileira da Imprensa, Biblioteca Bastos Tigre.

Johnson, Randal. 1989. "Literature, Culture, and Authoritarianism in Brazil, 1930–45." Wilson Center Working Paper no. 179.

Keck, Margaret E. 1992. *The Workers' Party and Democratization in Brazil*. New Haven: Yale University Press.

Kenski, Vani Moreira. 1990. "O fascinio do *Opinião*." Doctoral diss., Universidade Estadual de Campinas, Faculdade de Educação.
Klein, Lúcia. 1978. "Brasil pós-64: A nova ordem legal e a redefinição das bases de legitimidade." In Klein and Figueiredo, *Legitimidade e coação no Brasil pós-64*, 15–103. Rio de Janeiro: Forense-Universitária.
Klein, Lúcia, and Marcus Figueiredo. 1978. *Legitimidade e coação no Brasil pós-64*. Rio de Janeiro: Forense-Universitária.
Lins da Silva, Carlos Eduardo. 1985. *Muito além do jardim botânico*. São Paulo: Summus.
———. 1988. *Mil dias: Os bastidores da revolução em um grande jornal*. São Paulo: Trajetória Cultural.
Lira, Elizabeth, and María Isabel Castillo. 1991. *Psicologia de la amenaza politica y del miedo*. Santiago: CESOC.
Marconi, Paulo. 1980. *A censura política na imprensa Brasileira*. São Paulo: Global Editora.
Martins, Luciano. 1979. "A geração AI-5." In *Ensaios de Opinião*. Rio de Janeiro: Paz e Terra.
McDonough, Peter, 1981. *Power and Ideology in Brazil*. Princeton: Princeton University Press.
Mericle, Kenneth. 1977. "Corporatist Control of the Working Class: Authoritarian Brazil Since 1964." In *Authoritarianism and Corporatism in Latin America*, ed. James Malloy, 303–38. Pittsburgh: University of Pittsburgh Press.
Miguel, Edison, et al. 1978. "Direito social à informação." Prepared for the I Congresso Nacional de Jornalistas Pela Liberdade de Imprensa (São Paulo, October 26–28, 1978). Unpublished photocopy.
Moises, José Álvaro, and Maria Victória Benevides. 1984. "O *Estadão* e o golpe de 64: Entrevista de Ruy Mesquita." *Lua Nova* 1, no. 2: 26–40.
Montenegro, Julio Cesar. 1976. "Imprensa: Além da censura." *Revista de cultura vozes* 70, no. 4 (May): 5–16.
Moore, Barrington, Jr. 1987. *Injustice: The Social Bases of Obedience and Revolt*. White Plains, N.Y.: M.E. Sharpe.
Moreira, Sonia Virgínia. 1985. "Retratos Brasileiros: 20 anos de imprensa alternativa." In *Antologia prêmio Torquato Neto, ano 2*, 13–46. Rio de Janeiro: RioArte.
Morel, Edmar. 1975. "A egua farpa enfrenta a censura." *Boletim ABI* (January-February).
Movimento Nacional de Meninos e Meninas de Rua, Instituto Brasileiro de Análises Sociais e Econômicas, and Núcleo de Estudos da Violência. 1991. *Vidas em risco: Assassinatos de crianças e adolescentes no Brasil*. Rio de Janeiro: MNMMR, IBASE, NEV-USP.
National Congress. 1980. "Simpósio sobre censura" (May 16–August 30, 1979). Published in the *Diário do Congresso Nacional*, supplement to no. 154, December 3, 1980.
Neumanne Pinto, José. 1976. "Os impasses da imprensa Brasileira." *Revista de cultura vozes* 70, no. 1 (January): 5–14.
Nitrini, Dácuio, et al. "Censura a Radio e Televisão." In *I Congresso Nacional de Jornalistas Pela Liberdade de Imprensa* (São Paulo, October 26–28, 1978), Unpublished collection. Rio de Janeiro: Associação Barsileira de Imprensa, Biblioteca Bastos Tigre.

Nobre, Freitas. 1950. *História da imprensa de São Paulo*. São Paulo: Editôra Leia.
O'Donnell, Guillermo. 1973. *Modernization and Bureaucratic-Authoritarianism: Studies in South American Politics*. Berkeley: Institute of International Studies, University of California.
———. 1986. "On the Fruitful Convergence of Hirschman's *Exit, Voice, and Loyalty* and *Shifting Involvements:* Reflections from the Recent Argentine Experience." In *Development, Democracy, and the Art of Trespassing: Essays in Honor of Alberto O. Hirschman*, ed. Alejandro Foxley, Michael S. McPherson, and Guillermo O'Donnel, 249–67. Notre Dame: University of Notre Dame Press.
Pereira, Raimundo Rodrigues. 1986. "Viva a imprensa alternativa." In *Comunicação popular e alternativa do Brasil*, ed. Regina Festa and Carlos Eduardo Lins da Silva. São Paulo: Edições Paulinas.
Pinheiro, Paulo Sergio. 1991. "The Legacy of Authoritarianism: Violence and the Limits of Democratic Transitions." Unpublished paper prepared for the Sixteenth Congress of the Latin American Studies Association, April 4–6, 1991, Washington, D.C.
Pinheiro Machado, José Antonio. 1978. *Opinião x censura: Momentos da luta de um jornal pela liberdade*. Porto Alegre: L&PM Editores.
Politzer, Patricia. 1989. *Fear in Chile: Lives Under Pinochet*. New York: Pantheon.
Rabello Duarte, Celina. 1983. "Imprensa e redemocratização no Brasil." *Dados* 26, no. 2: 181–96.
Raphael, Alison. 1980. "Samba and Social Control: Popular Culture and Racial Democracy in Rio de Janeiro." Ph.D. diss., Columbia University.
Scott, James C. 1985. *Weapons of the Weak: Everyday Forms of Peasant Resistance*. New Haven: Yale University Press.
———. 1990. *Domination and the Arts of Resistance: Hidden Transcripts*. New Haven: Yale University Press.
Skidmore, Thomas. 1967. *Politics in Brazil, 1930–1964: An Experiment in Democracy*. New York: Oxford University Press.
———. 1988. *The Politics of Military Rule in Brazil, 1964–85*. New York: Oxford University Press.
Skidmore, Thomas, ed. 1993. *Television, Politics, and the Transition to Democracy in Latin America*. Washington, D.C.: Woodrow Wilson International Center for Scholars.
Smith, Anne-Marie. 1987. "State Terror in Argentina: A Frankfurt School Perspective." *Praxis International* 6, no. 4 (January): 477–87.
———. 1994. "Explaining Quiescence: Self-Censorship in Brazil, 1968–1978." Ph.D. diss., Massachusetts Institute of Technology.
Soares, Glaucio. 1989. "A censura durante o regime autoritário." *Revista Brasileira de ciências sociais* 4, no. 10 (June): 21–43.
Sodre, Nelson Werneck. 1977. *História da imprensa no Brasil*. Rio de Janeiro: Edições do Brasil.
Sorj, Bernardo, and Maria Hermínia Tavares de Almeida, eds. 1983. *Sociedade e política no Brasil pós-64*. São Paulo: Brasiliense.
Stepan, Alfred. 1985. "State Power and the Strength of Civil Society in the Southern Cone of Latin America." In *Bringing the State Back In*, ed. Peter Evans, Dietrich Reuschemeyer, and Theda Skocpol, 317–46. New York: Cambridge University Press.

———. 1988. *Rethinking Military Politics: Brazil and the Southern Cone*. Princeton: Princeton University Press.

Stepan, Alfred, ed. 1989. *Democratizing Brazil: Problems of Transition and Consolidation*. New York: Oxford University Press.

Talarico, José Gomes, ed. 1977. "O estado da imprensa no Brasil em 1977 e documentos da Associação Brasileira de Imprensa em torno da defesa da liberdade de imprensa e direitos humanos." Unpublished collection of documents. Rio de Janeiro: Associação Brasileira da Imprensa, Biblioteca Bastos Tigre.

Timerman, Jacobo. 1981. *Prisoner Without a Name, Cell Without a Number*. Trans. Toby Talbot. New York: Knopf.

Torture in Brazil: A Report by the Archdiocese of São Paulo. 1986. New York: Random House.

United Nations. *Anuario Estadístico*. 1972.

Velasco e Cruz, Sebastião, and Carlos Estevem Martins. 1983. "De castello a figueiredo: Uma incursão na pré-história da 'abertura.'" In *Sociedade e política no Brasil pós-64*, ed. Bernardo Sorj and Maria Hermínia Tavares de Almeida, 13–61. São Paulo: Brasiliense.

Ventura, Zuenir. 1988. *1968: O ano que não terminou*. Rio de Janeiro: Nova Fronteira.

Visão. 1976. "Nossos jornais e suas empresas." August 9, 36–48.

Wilkie, James W., et al. 1990. *Statistical Abstract on Latin America*. Vol. 28.

Yudice, George, Jean Franco, and Juan Flores, eds. 1992. *On Edge: The Crisis of Contemporary Latin American Culture*. Minneapolis: University of Minnesota Press.

INDEX

abertura (political opening), 67, 89, 215n; described, 26, 198n; and Geisel, 32, 66; and Golbery, 32; and press freedom, 64, 83, 129, 198n; reasons for, 26, 33
ABI (Associaçao Brasileira da Imprensa; Brazilian Press Association), 19–20, 56–58, 77, 129–30, 151, 156, 200n
Abramo, Claudio, 158–60, 196n, 216nn
Abreu, Hugo, 33, 67–68, 80, 150, 159, 199n, 215–16nn
Academia Brasileira de Letras, 92 AERP, 215n
Aguiar, Flavio, 97
AI-1 (Institutional Act), 27–29, 32
AI-2 (Institutional Act), 27–29, 34
AI-5 (Institutional Act), 34, 51, 173, 212n; cultural importance of, 193n; legal and institutional impact of, 28–29, 194n; origin of, 27–28; and press freedom, 31, 82, 115–16, 165–67, 169, 218n
AI-13 (Institutional Act), 29
AI-14 (Institutional Act), 29
AI-17 (Institutional Act), 29, 37
Albuquerque Lima, [General], 136, 213n
Almanaque Biotônico Vitalidade, 53
Althusser, Louis, 151
Alvares, Elcio, 200n
Alves, Márcio Moreira, 216n
Alves, Maria, 28
Amazonia, 98, 207n
Amnesty Law, 43, 145
Andrade, Evandro Carlos de: and the censorship of *O Globo,* 145, 165, 180, 211n; military regime harassment of, 78; on *O Globo*'s objectives, 44, 196n; and police informers at *O Globo,* 197n, 211n; and Roberto Marinho, 142
A Noticia, 200n, 203n
Araguaia episode, 175

Araujo, Paulo Roberto Power, 200n
ARENA (Aliança de Renovação Nacional; Alliance for National Renovation), 62, 91, 94, 119, 207n, 212n; creation of, 25; technocratic language of, 35
Arendt, Hannah, 161
Argentina, 40, 181, 193n, 211n
Army Ministry, 73
Arns, Paulo Evaristo, 78–79, 85, 208n
Assessoria Especial de Relações Públicas (Special Advisory Council on Public Relations), 192n, 215n
Assis, Machado de, 102
A Tarde, 130

Baer, Werner, 89
Banco do Brasil, 21, 155, 192n
Bandeira, Antonio, 62, 138
Bandeira, Manoel, 102, 207n
Barros, Adhemar de, 194n
Bastos, Carlos de Oliveira, 204n
Belo Horizonte, 197n
bilhetinhos, 149, 156, 173; etymology of the term, 120; issuance and delivery of, 120–24, 126–34, 142–46, 149–51, 161–62, 165, 174, 178, 180, 184–85, 187–88, 210–11nn, 214n; language and content of, 120–24, 127, 130–41, 146, 161, 165, 172, 178, 184–85, 187–88, 212–14nn, 216n; press reactions to, 120–21, 124–30, 140–46, 150–51, 162, 164–65, 167, 178–80, 188, 190, 211nn, 213n
Bittencourt, Luis Alberto, 49–50, 70, 75, 156, 160, 180
Bittencourt, Niomar Sodre, 66
Bloch, Ricardo, 109, 144
BNDES, 69
Boca de Inferno, 69
Boletim CIEC, 105–06

225

Bonifácio, José, 62, 80
Brasil Mulher, 48
Brazil: class analysis of, 214n; illiteracy in, 40, 195n; judiciary in, 27, 29, 172; newspaper readership in, 40–41, 195nn; role of the state in, 11–14, 191n; television and radio in, 14, 40–41, 191n, 195–97nn
Buarque, Sergio, 119
Buzaid, Alfredo, 82, 89–90, 112–13, 209n

Cabinet, 112, 201n. *See also* Civilian Cabinet; Military Cabinet
Caldeira Filho, Carlos, 216
Camara, Helder, 88, 90, 99–100, 110, 137–38, 208n
Camões, Luiz Vaz de, 91–92, 102–03, 107
Caparelli, Sérgio, 47, 49
Cardoso, Adauto Loecio, 113–15, 209n
Carnaval, 13
Carneiro, Nelson, 170
Carter, Jimmy, 206n
Casoy, Boris, 43, 144, 150, 153–54, 157–60, 196nn, 215nn
Castello Branco, Carlos, 20, 42, 136, 155–57, 213n
Castello Branco, Humberto, 28, 32, 78, 115
Catholic Church: and *Boletim CIEC,* 105; censorship of news about, 87, 135, 137–38; and Christian-based communities, 186; Coelho on, 170, 200n, 213n; military regime hatred of, 213n; opposition to Goulart of, 22
Cavalcanti, Rogerio Alberto, 63, 80, 198n
Caxias, Duque de, 158
"Cena Brasileira" (series), 51, 98
CENIMAR, 30
Cenoura, 53
censorship, 14; defined, 118; under the military regime, 4, 15, 26–27, 35, 37, 42, 48, 62, 71–72, 114–15, 119, 149–90, 201n, 210n, 212n, 214n, 217–18nn (*see also* under *der* military regime (1964–1985)); before 1964, 15–22, 186
Chagas, Carlos, 75–76, 121, 152, 154–57, 196n, 201nn, 216n
Chile, 88, 95, 181, 193n, 204n, 218n
CIA, 200n
CIEx, 30, 79, 121, 210n; press document (1978), 63–65, 67, 80, 172, 198n
CISA, 30
Civilian Cabinet, 67. *See also* Cabinet
Civita, Roberto, 45–46

CNBB (Conferência Nacional dos Bispos do Brasil; National Conference of Brazilian Bishops), 56–57, 137
Code of Civil Procedure, 114–15
Coelho, Moacyr: on the Brazilian masses, 200n; on the Catholic Church, 170, 200n, 213n; on censorship, 72, 121–22, 133, 170–71, 173–74, 176, 190, 218n; on confiscation of publications, 70, 128; on press restrictions generally, 168–69
Collor de Mello, Fernando, 175
Congress, 115, 209n; and censorship, 91–92, 103, 112–13, 119, 168–70, 173; military regime actions against, 25, 28, 34–35, 92, 134, 187–88, 217n. *See also* House of Representatives; Senate
Constituent Assembly, 17
Constitution, 34–35, 165, 172, 187–88; and the Institutional Acts, 80, 82, 115, 134, 194n; of 1985, 191n; of 1967, 29; of 1934, 17; of 1937, 115
Coojornal, 48, 55, 69, 77
Cordão, 53
Correio Brasiliense, 15, 40
Correio da Imprensa, 199n
Correio da Manhã: circulation of, 40; economics of, 66; government actions against, 16, 22–23, 70, 77, 155, 192n; views and journalism of, 22, 217n
Correio do Povo, 46, 209n
Costa, Otavio, 18, 192n, 215n
Costa e Silva, Artur da, 32, 36, 75, 195n, 201nn, 213n
Costella, Antonio, 19
Council of State, 15
Crítica, 48
Cubatão, 139, 213n

Dantas, Audalio, 57, 211n
Decree Law 477: 29, 91
Decree Law 1077: 82, 115, 209n, 217n
Decree Law 7037: 192
De Fato, 55
Delfim Neto, Antonio, 25, 213n
Department of Transportation, 201n
Diaféria, Lorenço, 75, 158–59, 216nn
Diário de Brasília, 126
Diário de Notícias, 130
Diário de Pernambuco, 40, 94
Diário Oficial, 66, 165
Diários e Emissoras Associados, 196–97nn
Dias, Gonçalvo, 102
Dias, José Carlos, 110–11, 161

Dines, Alberto, 16, 20, 125, 159
DIP (Department of Press and Propaganda), 17–20, 192nn
Dissidencia Comunista, 145
DOI (Destacamento de Operações Interna; Internal Operations Unit), 30–31, 77, 79, 216n
Dominican Republic, 195n
Duarte, Celina Rabello, 129
Dulles, John Foster, 192n

Editora Abril, 45
Egydio, Paulo, 114, 205n
Emilio Ribas Hospital, 204n
Em Tempo, 48, 54, 70, 77, 83
Estado da Minas, 40, 196n
Estado de São Paulo, 56, 95, 152, 154, 158, 175, 193n, 196n, 202nn, 204n; circulation of, 40, 43; economics of, 47, 114; elite status of, 108, 111–12, 114; government actions against (other than censorship), 18, 70, 75–79, 165–66, 192n, 199n, 201–02nn, 211n, 216n; and the Mesquita family, 18, 45, 79, 111–14, 192n, 196n, 209n; prior censorship of, 7, 33, 44, 82, 84–85, 87–93, 99–100, 102–03, 106–08, 111–14, 142, 144, 150, 161, 170, 201n, 203–05nn, 207–09nn, 216n, 218n; receipt of IAPA Golden Prize by, 91; self-censorship of, 203n; views and journalism of, 18, 43–44, 87–92, 195n, 199n, 204–05nn, 208n
Estado do Parana, 40, 46–47
Estado Novo, 12, 16–22, 115
EX, 48
Extra, 83

Falçao, Armando, 33, 73–74, 76, 145, 201n
Faoro, Raymond, 212n
Federal Police, 62, 130, 151, 168–74, 176, 185, 190; actions against the press by (other than censorship), 65, 69–70, 158–59, 166, 173, 210–12nn; and Decree Law 1077, 209n; and prior censorship, 81–82, 84–111, 113–16, 143, 170, 177, 187, 203nn, 210n; and self-censorship, 4, 66, 81, 117, 119–24, 126–28, 132–33, 135, 137, 140, 142–46, 149, 156, 165, 173–76, 178, 184, 187, 211n
Federal Revenues Office, 64–65, 69
Fernandes, Helio, 78
Fernandes, Millôr, 84, 202n
Fernando de Noronha, 78

Ferreira, Antonio Carlos, 75
Ferreira, Argemiro, 104–05, 108–09, 161, 208n, 211nn
Ferreira, Oliveiros, 112, 211n; and the censorship of the *Estado de São Paulo*, 85, 102–03, 107–08, 144; and the confiscation of the *Estado de São Paulo* (1968), 165–66; military regime detention of, 78; military regime on, 202n
Ferreira, Tarcision, 207n
Figueiredo, João, 96, 170, 200nn, 215n
Figueiredo, Marcus, 32, 37
Fleury, [Sergeant], 209n
Floro, Leda, 202n
Folha de São Paulo, 95, 150, 152, 196nn; circulation of, 40, 43; government actions against (other than censorship), 33, 43, 75, 157–60, 216nn; self-censorship of, 126–27, 130–31, 138, 144, 212n; unionism at, 196n; views and journalism of, 42–43, 153–54, 157–59, 195n
Fontoura, Carlos Alberto, 96, 206–07nn
Fontoura, Walter: on censorship, 119, 125, 127–28, 145, 163, 180, 211n; on confiscation of publications, 70, 163; and the return of political exiles in 1979, 43
Ford, Gerald, 206n
Franco, Francisco, 82, 95
Frente Ampla (Broad Front), 26, 28
Freud, Sigmund, 119
Frias, Otavio, 158–60, 216nn
Frota, Sylvio, 158, 201n, 215–16nn
Fundação Getúlio Vargas, 69

Garcia, Carlos, 78–79
Garcia Neto, [Governor], 199n
Gaspari, Elio, 215n
Gasparian, Fernando, 78–80, 113–14, 197n, 209n
Geisel, Ernesto, 73, 131, 198n, 202n, 204n; appointment of Coelho as Federal Police chief by, 170; and the *Estado de São Paulo*, 75, 84, 113–14, 216n; and the *Folha de São Paulo*, 216n; government of, 32–33, 66–68, 79, 129, 144, 156–57, 199n, 201n, 207n, 212nn, 215–16nn; and the *Jornal do Brasil*, 66–68, 216n
Góes, Waldir de, 66–68, 125, 127–28, 146, 200n
Golbery, [General], 32, 67, 215n
Golden Prize (IAPA), 91
Goulart, João, 14–15, 22, 26, 32, 36–37, 44, 217n
Guimarães, Ulysses, 89

INDEX

Herzog, Vladimir, 33, 57, 79–80, 181–82, 194n
Hora do Povo, 77
House of Representatives, 62. *See also* Congress
IAPA (InterAmerican Press Association), 196n, 210n; as an advocate of press freedom, 56, 58, 115; and the *Estado de São Paulo*, 56, 90–91, 102, 112, 170; and the mainstream press in Brazil, 55–56, 58

Ibiuna, 28
Inéditos, 203n
INPS, 205n
Institutional Acts, 77, 172; and the Constitution, 80, 134, 194n; and the legal system, 27, 38; Mattos on, 171, 217n; and the military, 32, 37. *See also specific Institutional Acts*
International Press Freedom Day, 156–57
IPEA, 103

Japan, 195n
Jornal da Bahia, 199n
Jornal do Brasil, 70, 95, 119, 163, 196nn; circulation of, 40–41, 43; economics of, 66, 68, 128, 155, 199–200nn; government actions against (other than censorship), 21, 66–68, 80, 150, 192n, 199nn, 216n; hierarchy of authority at, 125; and *O Globo*, 152; self-censorship of, 66, 122, 125, 127–28, 130–32, 135–38, 140–42, 144–45, 180, 184, 206n, 211–12nn; unionism at, 196n; views and journalism of, 16, 20, 42–43, 67, 152, 180, 191–92nn, 195n, 199–200nn, 213n
Jornal do Brasília, 199n
Jornal do Comércio, 94
Jornal do Povo, 200n, 212n
José Olympio Editora, 69
journalists' organizations: in the Estado Novo, 19; under the military regime, 55, 92, 129, 157, 182. *See also* journalists' unions; *specific organizations*
journalists' unions: in the Estado Novo, 19; under the military regime, 46, 55, 57–58, 92, 150, 157, 182, 211n. *See also specific unions*
Juan Carlos, King, 95

Kenski, Vani Moreira, 103
Khair, Edson, 205n
Klein, Lúcia, 35, 188

Kotscho, Ricardo, 78, 106–07, 214n
Kubitschek, Juscelino, 21, 26, 192n

L&PM Editores, 200n
Lacerda, Carlos, 26
Laconicus, 53
Lampião, 48
Latin America: authoritarian military regimes in, 180–81, 218n; illiteracy in, 195n; newspaper readership in, 195n
Lechner, Norbert, 180
Le Monde, 78
Lemos, Carlos, 125
Levy, Herbert, 94–95
Lima, Circe, 88
Lins da Silva, Carlos, 126, 175–76, 183–84, 211n
Lisbon, 207n
Lopes, Ruy, 216n
Luis, Edson, 28

Macapá (Amapá), 200n, 212n
Mackenzie University, 171
Magalhães, Antônio, 199n
Maluf, Paulo, 201n
Manchete television network, 196n
mandato de segurança, 114, 210n
Marconi, Paulo, 73, 129–33, 212n
Marinho, Roberto, 20, 44–45, 142, 145, 152, 209n
Marinho, Rogerio, 78
Marx, Karl, 151
Mattei, Enrico, 89
Mattos, Meira, 62, 71, 171–72, 217nn
McDonough, Peter, 36, 165, 194nn
MDB (Movimento Democrático Brasileiro; Brazilian Democratic Movement), 78, 89, 91, 207nn; creation of, 25; and the Frente Ampla, 26; and press freedom, 91, 170, 209n, 217n
Medici, Emílio Garrastazu, 18, 26, 68, 89, 131, 206n; assumption of presidential office by, 195n; and *Opinião*, 115–16, 169; political reputation of, 32; populism of, 36
Mesquita, Francisco, 192n
Mesquita, Ruy, 56, 112, 114, 209n
Mesquita family, 18, 45, 79, 111–14, 209n
Mesquita Filho, Julio de, 192n
Mesquita Neto, Julio de, 90, 102, 112–13, 196n, 204n, 209n, 217n
Military Cabinet, 67, 159. *See also* Cabinet
military police, the, 121

military regime (1964–1985): actions against individual journalists by, 7, 23, 33, 45–46, 57, 61, 66, 68, 74–80, 113,146, 155, 157–60, 183, 194n, 198n, 201–02nn, 215–16nn, 218n; bombing of press targets by, 23, 49, 66, 68, 77; closure of publications by, 22, 56; confiscation of publications by, 22–23, 55, 66, 68, 70–71, 80, 113, 128, 145–46, 155, 163, 165–66, 173, 200–01nn, 209–10nn, 212n; control of the news by, 45, 71–74, 80, 201nn; economic actions against the press by, 7, 23, 45, 47–48, 55, 61, 63–71, 80, 155, 199–200nn; general nature and views of, 5–6, 24–38, 71–72, 74, 79–80, 95, 131, 157, 168, 170, 172, 181, 187–89, 193–95nn, 200–02n, 210n, 212–13nn, 215nn, 218n; prior censorship under, 7, 33, 44, 80–116, 128, 135–36, 138–39, 141–44, 146, 150–51, 156, 161–63, 166, 169–70, 175, 177–79, 182, 185, 187, 201n, 203–11nn, 213–14nn, 216–18nn; public support for, 153, 214–15nn; self-censorship under, 4–7, 66, 80–81, 100, 109, 111, 116–46, 149–51, 156, 161–62, 164–65, 167, 172–74, 177–82, 184–85, 187–88, 190, 198n, 203n, 206n, 210–16nn, 218n. *See also under* censorship; press-state relations
Minas Gerais, 26
Ministry of Health, 201n, 204n
Ministry of Justice, 33, 67, 72–73, 79, 114; and prior censorship, 84; and self-censorship, 120–22, 132, 135, 137, 174
Ministry of Labor, 64–65, 192n
Montoro, Franco, 209n, 217n
Morães, Denis de, 127–28, 142, 163
Morel, Edmar, 17–18
Movimento, 48, 119, 186, 204n; circulation of, 49; dissension at, 54; economics of, 55, 92–93, 105, 200n; government actions against (other than censorship), 49, 75, 77, 166; origin of, 54; preliminary issue of, 53; prior censorship of, 7, 82, 84–85, 92–100, 103–05, 108–09, 151, 156, 166, 173, 200nn, 203–07nn; staff meetings at, 54; views and journalism of, 50–51, 53, 87, 92–99, 164, 175, 196n, 200n, 205–07nn, 214n
Muller, Filinto, 3, 138, 166
Myamoto, Minoro, 62

Nascimento Brito, M.F. de, 41, 43, 67, 125, 152
Natel, Laudo, 199, 204n

National Congress of Journalists for the Liberty of the Press, 150–52
National Council of Women, 191n
National Intelligence Service, 65
National Security Law, 173; and press freedom, 31, 64, 74–75,151, 158, 160, 167, 216n; provisions of, 29, 204n
Neumanne Pinto, José, 126–27, 161–62, 166–67
news prohibitions. *See bilhetinhos Nós Mulheres*, 48
Nunca Mais project, 30, 79–80, 157, 160, 182, 193n

OAB (Ordem dos Advogados do Brasil; Brazilian Bar Association), 22, 56–57, 212n
OBAN (Operação Bandeirantes; Operation Bandeirantes), 30, 77
O Dia, 40, 195–96nn
Official Department of Propaganda, 17
O Globo, 75, 95, 110, 156, 196n, 209n, 215n; circulation of, 40, 43; economics of, 192n; government actions against (other than censorship), 20, 78, 196n, 211n, 216n; and the *Jornal do Brasil*, 152; Roberto Marinho's influence on, 44–45, 142, 145; self-censorship of, 127, 142, 145, 163, 165, 180, 211n; views and journalism of, 44, 50, 152, 165, 180, 196n, 206n
Old Republic, 16
O Municipio, 199n
Opinião, 48, 79, 204n; beach ritual at, 101, 106, 142; circulation of, 49, 197n; closure of, 84; dissension at, 54; economics of, 54, 68–69, 86, 105; government actions against (other than censorship), 68–69, 77–78, 113, 210n; prior censorship of, 68, 82, 84–86, 101, 103–06, 108–09, 113–16, 142, 144, 150, 161, 169, 189, 200n, 203–04nn, 208–11nn,218n; self-censorship of, 211n; views and journalism of, 50–51, 68–69, 197n
o *press release*. *See* press releases
O São Paulo, 204n; prior censorship of, 82, 84–85, 103, 105–06, 110–11, 151, 156, 161, 203n, 208–09nn
Osasco, 28
Os Lusiades (Camões), 102–03

Paraná, 98
Pasquim, 48; circulation of, 49, 202n; economics of, 55, 202n; government ac-

tions against (other than censorship), 75, 201n; Passarinho on, 62; prior censorship of, 82, 84, 203n; views and journalism of, 39
pasquims, 15–16
Passarinho, Jarbas, 62, 170–71
Pedro I, 201n
Pereira, Antonio Carlos, 77, 162, 167, 189, 202n
Pereira, Raimundo Rodrigues: on censorship, 105, 108, 119, 186; detention of, 78; indictment of, 75; on the *Opinião* beach ritual, 101; visits to the Federal Police by, 203n
Petrobrás, 69, 89
Philip Morris (cigarette manufacturer), 97
Pinochet, Augusto, 88, 95, 204n
Pinto, Francisco, 78, 88, 90, 204–05nn
"Poem to the Censor" (Dias), 110–11, 161
Política, 83
Portella, Petronio, 212n
Portugal, 82, 96, 206n
Posição, 200n
Prates, [Governor], 199n
press, the: alternative, 7, 39–40, 48–56, 58, 63, 65, 68–70, 75,77, 83, 164–67, 175, 182, 189, 197–98nn, 200n, 203n, 214n; as an economic actor, 13–14; lack of solidarity within, 150–52, 163, 178, 185–86, 214n; mainstream, 7, 39–50, 53–56, 58, 65–70, 75, 77, 83, 164–65, 175, 179, 189, 195–99nn, 214n, 216n; modernization of, 16, 191n; as a sociopolitical actor, 13–15. *See also* censorship; journalists' organizations; journalists' unions; press-state relations; *specific publications; under* military regime (1964–1985)
press advisors, 72–74, 201n
press briefing rooms, 72–74
press law, legal proceedings under, 74–75
press releases, 72–74, 80, 95, 201n
press-state relations, 11–15, 23; under the military regime, 11, 15, 17–18, 20, 23, 26–27, 31–39, 42–49, 52–53, 55–58, 61–63, 80, 129, 149–76, 179–84, 188–89, 196–202nn, 215nn, 218n (*see also under* military regime (1964–1985)); before 1964, 15–23, 192nn. *See also* censorship

Quadros, Janio, 21–22, 175
Quercia, Orestes, 91

Radio JB, 130, 196n, 210n
Realidade, 45–46

Recife, 94
Rede Globo, 196–97nn, 206–07nn
Reis, Kondor, 62
Repórter, 48, 75, 156; government actions against, 55, 64, 70, 160; preliminary issue of, 51–52, 197n; views and journalism of, 49–52, 197n
repression, responses to, 3–4
Resende, Eurico, 91, 169–70, 173, 217nn
Resistência, 70
Rial, Juan, 181
Ribeiro, Nina, 119
Rio de Janeiro, 26, 28, 40
Rio de Janeiro journalists' union, 57, 192n
Rio Grande do Sul, 99
Romão, Helio: on censorship, 128, 133, 143, 171–72, 174–75, 211n; identified, 84, 120
Rossi, Clovis, 201n

Sá, Marcos, 100–01, 109–10, 196n, 200–01nn, 208n, 215n
Salazar, António de Oliveira, 82
Salles, Mauro, 197n
Salvador (Bahia), 130–32
Sant'anna, João, 145, 155, 215n
Santos, Ruy, 209n
Sardemburg, Carlos Alberto, 52, 107, 175
Sarney, José, 170
São Paulo (city), 40, 194n, 203n
São Paulo (state), 26, 88, 139, 201n, 204n
São Paulo governor's office, 74
São Paulo journalists' union, 54, 57, 129, 192n
Sautchuk, Jaime, 75, 109, 126, 161, 211n
SBT television network, 196n
Scott, James, 3
Second Army, 79, 112, 121
Secretariat of Health, 99
Senate, 209n. *See also* Congress
Simonsen, Mario Henrique, 67
SNI (Serviço Nacional de Informações; National Information Service), 202n; activities of, 30, 76–77, 96–97, 121, 145, 210n; Division of Security and Intelligence, 76; and Golbery, 32
Soares, Glaucio, 131, 135, 210n, 213n
Sobrinho, Barbosa Lima, 92
Sodre, Nelson Werneck, 19, 21
Souza, Tarik de, 78
Spain, 82, 95, 195n
Special Advisory Council on Public Relations, 36
Spinola, Nuinio, 125, 142, 211n
State Assembly of Pernambuco, 78

Stepan, Alfred, 36, 193n, 212n
Supreme Court, 113, 209n
Supreme Military Court, 79–80

Tribuna da Bahia, 130
Tribuna da Imprensa, 40, 196n; government actions against (other than censorship), 21, 70, 77–78, 192n; journalism of, 39, 192n; prior censorship of, 82, 84, 151, 156, 203n
Tribunal da Luta Operária, 77
Tudo a declarar (Falcão), 201n
TV Bandeirantes, 130

UDN (União Democratica Nacional; Democratic National Union), 43
ufanismo, 36
Ultima Hora, 21
Unidade, 54, 57, 192n
unions. *See* journalists' unions

United Press International, 16
United States, 67, 194–96nn, 215n
Uruguay, 88, 139, 181, 193n

Vargas, Getúlio, 14, 16–21, 95, 115, 192nn, 196n
Vasconcelos, Jarbas, 78–79
Veja, 45, 196n, 201n, 215nn; circulation of, 197n; prior censorship of, 82, 84, 100–01, 106, 109–10, 142, 161, 203n, 208n; tea ritual at, 100–01, 106, 142
Venezuela, 195n
Versus, 48, 55, 65, 69
Visão, 46
Volkswagen, 206n
Voz da Unidade, 77

Wainer, Samuel, 21

Zero Hora, 98–99, 164